JANE AUSTEN:
HER LIFE AND LETTERS;
A FAMILY RECORD

By

Austen-Leigh And Austen-Leigh

PREFACE

SINCE 1870-1, when J. E. Austen Leigh published his *Memoir of Jane Austen*, considerable additions have been made to the stock of information available for her biographers. Of these fresh sources of knowledge the set of letters from Jane to Cassandra, edited by Lord Brabourne, has been by far the most important. These letters are invaluable as *mémoires pour servir;* although they cover only the comparatively rare periods when the two sisters were separated, and although Cassandra purposely destroyed many of the letters likely to prove the most interesting, from a distaste for publicity.

Some further correspondence, and many incidents in the careers of two of her brothers, may be read in *Jane Austen's Sailor Brothers*, by J. H. Hubback and Edith C. Hubback; while Miss Constance Hill has been able to add several family traditions to the interesting topographical information embodied in her *Jane Austen: Her Homes and Her Friends*. Nor ought we to forget the careful research shown in other biographies of the author, especially that by Mr. Oscar Fay Adams.

During the last few years, we have been fortunate enough to be able to add to this store; and every existing MS. or tradition preserved by the family, of which we have any knowledge, has been placed at our disposal.

It seemed, therefore, to us that the time had come when a more complete chronological account of the novelist's life might be laid before the public, whose interest in Jane Austen (as we readily acknowledge) has shown no signs of diminishing, either in England or in America.

The *Memoir* must always remain the one firsthand account of her, resting on the authority of a nephew who knew her intimately and that of his two sisters. We could not compete with its vivid personal recollections; and the last thing we should wish to do, even were it possible, would be to supersede it. We believe, however, that it needs to be supplemented, not only because so much additional material has been brought to light since its publication, but also because the account given of their aunt by her nephew and nieces could be given only from their own point of view, while the incidents and characters fall into a somewhat different perspective if the whole is seen from a greater distance. Their knowledge of their aunt was during the last portion of her life, and they knew her best of all in her last year, when her health was failing and she was living in much seclusion; and they were not likely to be the recipients of her inmost confidences on the events and sentiments of her youth.

Hence the emotional and romantic side of her nature—a very real one—has not been dwelt upon. No doubt the Austens were, as a family, unwilling to show their deeper feelings, and the sad end of Jane's one romance would naturally tend to intensify this dislike of expression; but the feeling was there, and it finally found utterance in her latest work, when, through Anne Elliot, she claimed for women the right of 'loving longest when existence or when hope is gone.'

Then, again, her nephew and nieces hardly knew how much she had gone into society, or how much, with a certain characteristic aloofness, she had enjoyed it. Bath, either when she was the guest of her uncle and aunt or when she was a resident; London, with her brother Henry and his wife, and the rather miscellaneous society which they enjoyed; Godmersham, with her brother Edward and his county neighbours in East Kent;—these had all given her many opportunities of studying the particular types which she blended into her own creations.

A third point is the uneventful nature of the author's life, which, as we think, has been a good deal exaggerated. Quiet it certainly was; but the quiet life of a member of a large family in the England of that date was compatible with a good deal of stirring incident, happening, if not to herself, at all events to those who were nearest to her, and who commanded her deepest sympathies.

We hope therefore that our narrative, with all its imperfections and its inevitable repetition of much that has already been published, will at least be of use in removing misconceptions, in laying some new facts before the reader, and in placing others in a fresh light. It is intended as a narrative, and not as a piece of literary criticism; for we should not care to embark upon the latter in competition with biographers and essayists who have a better claim to be heard.

Both in the plan and in the execution of our work we have received much valuable help from another member of the family, Mary A. Austen Leigh.

An arrangement courteously made by the owners of the copyright has procured for us a free and ample use of the Letters as edited by Lord Brabourne; while the kindness of Mr. J. G. Nicholson of Castlefield House, Sturton-by-Scawby, Lincolnshire, has opened a completely new source of information in the letters which passed between the Austens and their kinsmen of the half-blood—Walters of Kent and afterwards of Lincolnshire. Miss Jane Austen, granddaughter of Admiral Charles Austen, and Miss Margaret Bellas, great-granddaughter of James Austen, are so good as to allow us to make a fuller use of their family documents than was found possible by the author of the *Memoir;* while Mr. J. H. Hubback permits us to draw freely upon the *Sailor Brothers*, and Captain E. L. Austen, R.N., upon his MSS. Finally, we owe to Admiral Ernest Rice kind permission to have the photograph taken, from which the reproduction of his Zoffany portrait is made into a frontispiece for this volume. We hope that any other friends who have helped us will accept this general expression of our gratitude.

W. A. L.
R. A. A. L.

April 1913.

IN the notes to the text, the following works are referred to under the shortened forms here given:—

Memoir of Jane Austen, by her nephew, J. E. Austen-Leigh: quoted from second edition, 1871. As *Memoir*.

Letters of Jane Austen, edited by Edward Lord Brabourne, 1884. As *Brabourne*.

Jane Austen's Sailor Brothers, by J. H. Hubback and Edith C. Hubback, 1906. As *Sailor Brothers*.

Jane Austen: Her Homes and her Friends Constance Hill, 1902. As *Miss Hill*.

CONTENTS

CHAPTER I.
 AUSTENS AND LEIGHS 1600-1764 8

CHAPTER II.
 STEVENTON 1764-1785 16

CHAPTER III.
 WARREN HASTINGS AND THE HANCOCKS 1752-1794 . 31

CHAPTER IV.
 FAMILY LIFE 1779-1792 43

CHAPTER V.
 GROWTH AND CHANGE 1792-1796 60

CHAPTER VI.
 ROMANCE 1795-1802 74

CHAPTER VII.
 AUTHORSHIP AND CORRESPONDENCE 1796-1798 83

CHAPTER VIII.
 GODMERSHAM AND STEVENTON 1798-1799 95

CHAPTER IX.
 THE LEIGH PERROTS AND BATH 1799-1800 110

CHAPTER X.
 CHANGE OF HOME 1800-1801 123

CHAPTER XI.
 BATH AGAIN 1801-1805 143

CHAPTER XII.
 FROM BATH TO SOUTHAMPTON 1805-1808 163

CHAPTER XIII.

FROM SOUTHAMPTON TO CHAWTON 1808-1809 179
CHAPTER XIV.
SENSE AND SENSIBILITY 1809-1811 200
CHAPTER XV.
PRIDE AND PREJUDICE 1812-1814 216
CHAPTER XVI.
MANSFIELD PARK 1812-1814 231
CHAPTER XVII.
EMMA 1814-1815 252
CHAPTER XVIII.
PERSUASION 1815-1816 273
CHAPTER XIX.
AUNT JANE 1814-1817 285
CHAPTER XX.
FAILING HEALTH 1816-1817 309
CHAPTER XXI.
WINCHESTER 1817 324
CHRONOLOGY OF JANE AUSTEN'S LIFE 339
LITERARY ANALYSIS 345
ABOUT THE AUTHOR 350

JANE AUSTEN

CHAPTER I.

AUSTENS AND LEIGHS 1600-1764

AT the end of the sixteenth century there was living at Horsmonden—a small village in the Weald of Kent—a certain John Austen. From his will it is evident that he was a man of considerable means, owning property in Kent and Sussex and elsewhere; he also held a lease of certain lands from Sir Henry Whetenhall, including in all probability the manor house of Broadford in Horsmonden. What wealth he had was doubtless derived from the clothing trade; for Hasted instances the Austens, together with the Bathursts, Courthopes, and others, as some of the ancient families of that part 'now of large estate and genteel rank in life,' but sprung from ancestors who had used the great staple manufacture of clothing. He adds that these clothiers 'were usually called the Gray Coats of Kent, and were a body so numerous that at County Elections whoever had their vote and interest was almost certain of being elected.'

John Austen died in 1620, leaving a large family. Of these, the fifth son, Francis, who died in 1687, describes himself in his will as a clothier, of Grovehurst; this place being, like Broadford, a pretty timbered house of moderate size near the picturesque old village of Horsmonden. Both houses still belong to the Austen family. Francis left a son, John, whose son was another John. This last John settled at Broadford (while his father remained at Grovehurst), and, when quite young, married Elizabeth Weller. He seems to have been a careless, easy-going man, who thought frugality unnecessary, as he would succeed to the estate on his father's death; but he died of consumption in 1704, a year before that event took place. One of his sisters married into the family of the Stringers (neighbours engaged in the same trade as the Austens), and numbered among her descendants the Knights of Godmersham—a circumstance which exercised an important influence over the subsequent fortunes of the Austen family.

Elizabeth Weller, a woman happily cast in a different mould from her husband, was an ancestress of Jane Austen who deserves commemoration. Thrifty, energetic, a careful mother, and a prudent housewife, she managed, though receiving only grudging assistance from the Austen family, to pay off her husband's debts, and to give to all her younger children a decent education at a school at Sevenoaks; the eldest boy (the future squire) being taken off her hands by his grandfather. Elizabeth left behind her not only elaborately kept accounts but also a minute description of her actions through many years and of the motives which governed them. It may be interesting to quote one sentence relating to her move from Horsmonden to Sevenoaks for the sake of her children's education. 'These considerations with ye tho'ts of having my own boys in ye house, with a good master (as all represented him to be) were ye inducements that brought me to Sen'nock, for it seemed to me as if I cou'd not do a better thing for my children's good, their education being my great care, and indeed all I think I was capable of doing for 'em, for I always tho't if they had learning, they might get better shift in ye world, with w^t small fortune was alloted 'em.'

When the good mother died in 1721, her work was done. Schooldays were over, the daughter married, and the boys already making their way in the world.

The young squire and his son held gentle sway at Broadford through the eighteenth century; but much more stirring and able was the next brother, Francis. He became a solicitor. Setting up at Sevenoaks 'with eight hundred pounds and a bundle of pens,' he contrived to amass a very large fortune, living most hospitably, and yet buying up all the valuable land round the town which he could secure, and enlarging his means by marrying two wealthy wives. But his first marriage did not take place till he was nearer fifty than forty; and he had as a bachelor been a most generous benefactor to the sons of his two next brothers, Thomas and William.

His second wife, who became in due course of time godmother to her great-niece, Jane Austen, was the widow of Samuel Lennard, of West Wickham, who left her his estate. Legal proceedings ensued over the will, and Mrs. Lennard took counsel of Francis Austen, who ended by winning both the case and her hand. Francis's son by his first wife (known as Motley Austen) rounded off the family estate at Sevenoaks by purchasing the Kippington property. Motley's third son, John, eventually inherited the Broadford estate. Francis's two most distinguished descendants were Colonel Thomas Austen of Kippington, well known as M.P. for Kent, and the Rev. John Thomas Austen, senior wrangler in 1817.

Both the two next brothers of Francis Austen adopted the medical profession. Thomas, an apothecary at Tonbridge, had an only son, Henry, who graduated at Cambridge, and, through his uncle's interest, held the living of West Wickham for twenty years. His descendants on the female side are still flourishing.

William, the surgeon, Jane Austen's grandfather, is more immediately interesting to us. He married Rebecca, daughter of Sir George Hampson, a physician of Gloucester, and widow of another medical man, James Walter. By her first husband she had a son, William Hampson Walter, born in 1721; by her second she had three daughters, and one son, George, born in 1731. Philadelphia—the only daughter who grew up and married—we shall meet with later. Rebecca Austen died in 1733, and three years later William married Susanna Holk, of whom nothing is known except that she died at an advanced age, and did not mention any of the Austens in her will; neither is there any trace of her in any of the family records with which we are acquainted; so it is hardly probable that little George Austen (Jane's father), who had lost both his parents when he was six years old, continued under the care of his stepmother. However, all that we know of his childhood is that his uncle Francis befriended him, and sent him to Tonbridge School, and that from Tonbridge he obtained a Scholarship (and subsequently a Fellowship) at St. John's College, Oxford—the

College at which, later on, through George's own marriage, his descendants were to be 'founder's kin.' He returned to teach at his old school, occupying the post of second master there in 1758, and in the next year he was again in residence at Oxford, where his good looks gained for him the name of 'the handsome proctor.' In 1760 he took Orders, and in 1761 was presented by Mr. Knight of Godmersham—who had married a descendant of his great-aunt, Jane Stringer—to the living of Steventon, near Overton in Hampshire. It was a time of laxity in the Church, and George Austen (though he afterwards became an excellent parish-priest) does not seem to have resided or done duty at Steventon before the year 1764, when his marriage to Cassandra Leigh must have made the rectory appear a desirable home to which to bring his bride.

Before we say anything of the Leighs, a few sentences must be devoted to George Austen's relations of the half-blood—the Walters. With his mother's son by her first husband, William Hampson Walter, he remained on intimate terms. A good many letters are extant which passed between the Austens and the Walters during the early married life of the former, the last of them containing the news of the birth of Jane. Besides this, William Walter's daughter, 'Phila,' was a constant correspondent of George Austen's niece Eliza.

The Walter family settled in Lincolnshire, where they have held Church preferment, and have also been well known in the world of sport. Phila's brother James seems to have been at the same time an exemplary parson, beloved by his flock, and also a sort of 'Jack Russell,' and is said to have met his death in the hunting-field, by falling into a snow-drift, at the age of eighty-four. His son Henry distinguished himself in a more academical manner. He was second wrangler in 1806, and a Fellow of St. John's. Nor was he only a mathematician; for in June 1813 Jane Austen met a young man named Wilkes, an undergraduate of St. John's, who spoke very highly of Walter as a scholar; he said he was considered the best classic at Cambridge. She adds: 'How such a report would have interested my father!' Henry Walter was at one time tutor at Haileybury, and was also a beneficed clergyman. He was known at Court; indeed, it is said that, while he declined higher preferment for himself, he was consulted by George IV and William IV on the selection of bishops.

The wife that George Austen chose belonged to the somewhat large clan of the Leighs of Adlestrop in Gloucestershire, of which family the Leighs of Stoneleigh were a younger branch. Her father was the Rev. Thomas Leigh, elected Fellow of All Souls at so early an age that he was ever after called 'Chick Leigh,' and afterwards Rector of Harpsden, near Henley.

Both these branches of the Leigh family descended from Sir Thomas Leigh, Lord Mayor of London, behind whom Queen Elizabeth rode to be proclaimed at Paul's Cross. He was rich enough and great enough to endow more than one son with estates; but while the elder line at Adlestrop remained simple squires, the younger at Stoneleigh rose to a peerage. The latter branch, however, were now rapidly approaching extinction, while the former had many vigorous scions. The family records have much to say of one of the squires—Theophilus (who died in 1724), the husband of Mary Brydges and the father of twelve children, a strong character, and one who lived up to fixed, if rather narrow, ideas of duty. We hear of his old-fashioned dress and elaborate bows and postures, of his affability to his neighbours, and his just, though somewhat strict, government of his sons. It is difficult to picture to oneself a set of modern Oxford men standing patiently after dinner, in the dining-parlour, as Theophilus's sons did, 'till desired to sit down and drink Church and King.' Meanwhile, his brother-in-law, the Duke of Chandos (the patron of Handel), used to send for the daughters to be educated in the splendour of Canons (his place in Middlesex), and to make such matches as he chose for them with dowries of £3000 a-piece.

Cassandra's father, Thomas, was the fourth son of Theophilus Leigh. An older and better known brother was another Theophilus, Master of Balliol for more than half a century.

The story of his election, in 1727, is remarkable. The Fellows of Balliol could not agree in the choice of any one of their own body; and one set, thinking it would be no disadvantage to have a duke's brother as master, invited their visitor, Dr. Brydges, to stand. On his declining, they brought forward his nephew, Theophilus Leigh, then a young Fellow of Corpus. The election resulted in a tie, and the visitor had no qualms of conscience in giving his casting vote to his nephew. Theophilus proved to be a man 'more famous for his sayings than his doings, overflowing with puns and witticisms and sharp retorts; but his most serious joke was his practical one of living much longer than had been expected or intended.' He no doubt became a most dignified Head, and inspired the young men with fear and respect; but he must have sometimes remembered the awful day when he first preached before his father, who immediately turned his back on the divine, saying afterwards: 'I thank you, Theo, for your discourse; let us hereafter have less rhetoric and more divinity; I turned my back lest my presence might daunt you.' When Theo in turn was an old man, and when Jane Austen's eldest brother went to Oxford, he was asked to dine with this dignified kinsman. Being a raw freshman, he was about to take off his gown, when the old man of eighty said with a grim smile: 'Young man, you need not strip; we are not going to fight.'

Cassandra Leigh's youth was spent in the quiet rectory of Harpsden, for her father was one of the more conscientious of the gently born clergy of that day, living entirely on his benefice, and greatly beloved in his neighbourhood as an exemplary parish-priest. 'He was one of the most contented, quiet, sweet-tempered, generous, cheerful men I ever knew,' so says the chronicler of the Leigh family, 'and his wife was his counterpart. The spirit of the pugnacious Theophilus dwelt not in him; nor that eternal love of company which distinguished the other brothers, yet he was by no means unsocial.' Towards the end of his life he removed to Bath, being severely afflicted with the gout, and here he died in 1763. His peaceful wife, Jane Walker, was descended on her mother's side from a sufficiently warlike family; she was the daughter of an Oxford physician, who had married a Miss Perrot, one of the last of a very old stock, long settled in Oxfordshire, but also known in Pembrokeshire at least as early as the fourteenth century. They were probably among the settlers planted there to overawe the Welsh, and it is recorded of one of them that he slew 'twenty-six men of Kemaes and one wolf.' A contrast to these uncompromising ancestors was found in Mrs. Leigh's aunt, Ann Perrot, one of the family circle at Harpsden, whom tradition states to have been a very pious, good woman. Unselfish she certainly was, for she earnestly begged her brother, Mr. Thomas Perrot, to alter his will by which he had bequeathed to her his estates at Northleigh in Oxfordshire, and to leave her instead an annuity of one hundred pounds. Her brother complied with her request, and by a codicil devised the estates to his great-nephew, James, son of the Rev. Thomas Leigh, on condition that he took the surname and arms of Perrot. Accordingly, on the death of Mr. Thomas Perrot at the beginning of 1751, James Leigh became James Leigh Perrot of Northleigh. His two sisters, Jane and Cassandra, also profited by the kindness of their great-aunt, who left two hundred pounds to each. Another legacy which filtered through the Walkers from the Perrots to the Austens was the advantage of being 'kin' to the Founder of St. John's College, Oxford—Sir Thomas White—an advantage of which several members of the family availed themselves.

Northleigh, for some reason or other, did not suit its new owner. He pulled down the mansion and sold the estate to the Duke of Marlborough, buying for himself a property at Hare Hatch on the Bath Road, midway between Maidenhead and Reading. We shall meet him again, and his devoted wife, Jane Cholmeley; and we shall see a remarkable instance of his steadfast love for her.

George Austen perhaps met his future wife at the house of her uncle, the Master of Balliol, but no particulars of the courtship have survived. The marriage took place at Walcot Church, Bath, on April 26, 1764, the bride's father having died at Bath only a short time before. Two circumstances connected with their brief honeymoon—which consisted only of a journey from Bath to Steventon, broken by one day's halt at Andover—may be mentioned. The bride's 'going-away' dress seems to have been a scarlet riding-habit, whose future adventures were not uninteresting; and the pair are believed to have had an unusual companion for such an occasion—namely, a small boy, six years old, the only son of Warren Hastings by his first wife. We are told that he was committed to the charge of Mr. Austen when he was sent over to England in 1761, and we shall see later that there was

14

a reason for this connexion; but a three-year-old boy is a curious charge for a bachelor, and poor little George must have wanted a nurse rather than a tutor. In any case, he came under Mrs. Austen's maternal care, who afterwards mourned for his early death 'as if he had been a child of her own.'

CHAPTER II.

STEVENTON 1764-1785

STEVENTON is a small village tucked away among the Hampshire Downs, about seven miles south of Basingstoke. It is now looked down upon at close quarters by the South-Western Railway, but, at the time of which we are writing, it was almost equidistant from two main roads: one running from Basingstoke to Andover, which would be joined at Deane Gate, the other from Basingstoke to Winchester, joined at Popham Lane. Communication with London was maintained—at any rate, in 1800—by two coaches that ran each night through Deane Gate. It does not appear, however, to have been by any means certain that an unexpected traveller would get a place in either of them.

The surrounding country is certainly not picturesque; it presents no grand or extensive views: the features, however, being small rather than plain. It is, in fact, an undulating district whose hills have no marked character, and the poverty of whose soil prevents the timber from attaining a great size. We need not therefore be surprised to hear that when Cassandra Leigh saw the place for the first time, just before her marriage, she should think it very inferior to the valley of the Thames at Henley. Yet the neighbourhood had its beauties of rustic lanes and hidden nooks; and Steventon, from the fall of the ground and the abundance of its timber, was one of the prettiest spots in it. The Rectory had been of the most miserable description, but George Austen improved it until it became a tolerably roomy and convenient habitation. It stood 'in a shallow valley, surrounded by sloping meadows, well sprinkled with elm-trees, at the end of a small village of cottages, each well provided with a garden, scattered about prettily on either side of the road. . . . North of the house, the road from Deane to Popham Lane ran at a sufficient distance from the front to allow a carriage drive, through turf and trees. On the south side, the ground rose gently and was occupied by one of those old-fashioned gardens in which vegetables and flowers are combined, flanked and protected on the east by one of the thatched mud walls common in that country, and overshadowed by fine elms. Along the upper or southern side of the garden ran a terrace of the finest turf, which must have been in the writer's thoughts when she described Catherine Morland's childish delight in "rolling down the green slope at the back of the house."

'But the chief beauty of Steventon consisted in its hedgerows. A hedgerow in that country does not mean a thin formal line of quickset, but an irregular border of copse-wood and timber, often wide enough to contain within it a winding footpath, or a rough cart-track. Under its shelter the earliest primroses, anemones, and wild hyacinths were to be found; sometimes the first bird's nest; and, now and then, the unwelcome adder. Two such hedgerows radiated, as it were, from the parsonage garden. One, a continuation of the turf terrace, proceeded westward, forming the southern boundary of the home meadows; and was formed into a rustic shrubbery, with occasional seats, entitled "The Wood Walk."

The other ran straight up the hill, under the name of "The Church Walk," because it led to the parish church, as well as to a fine old manor-house of Henry VIII's time, occupied by a family named Digweed, who for more than a century rented it, together with the chief farm in the parish.'

The usefulness of a hedgerow as a place where a heroine might remain unseen and overhear what was not intended to reach her ears must have impressed itself early on the mind of our author; and readers of *Persuasion* will remember the scene in the fields near Uppercross where Anne hears a conversation about herself carried on by Captain Wentworth and Louisa Musgrove. The writer had possibly intended to introduce a similar scene into *Mansfield Park*, for, in a letter to her sister, of January 29, 1813, when turning from *Pride and Prejudice* to a new subject, she says: 'If you could discover whether Northamptonshire is a country of hedgerows I should be glad again.' Presumably, her question was answered in the negative, and her scrupulous desire for accuracy did not allow of her making use of the intended device.

Steventon Church 'might have appeared mean and uninteresting to an ordinary observer; but the adept in church architecture would have known that it must have stood there some seven centuries, and would have found beauty in the very narrow Early English windows, as well as in the general proportions of its little chancel; while its solitary position, far from the hum of the village, and within sight of no habitation, except a glimpse of the grey manor-house through its circling green of sycamores, has in it something solemn and appropriate to the last resting-place of the silent dead. Sweet violets, both purple and white, grow in abundance beneath its south wall. One may imagine for how many centuries the ancestors of those little flowers have occupied that undisturbed sunny nook, and may think how few living families can boast of as ancient a tenure of their land. Large elms protrude their rough branches; old hawthorns shed their annual blossoms over the graves; and the hollow yew-tree must be at least coeval with the church. But whatever may be the beauties or defects of the surrounding scenery, this was the residence of Jane Austen for twenty-four years. This was the cradle of her genius. These were the first objects which inspired her young heart with a sense of the beauties of nature. In strolls along these wood-walks, thick-coming fancies rose to her mind, and gradually assumed the forms in which they came forth to the world. In that simple church she brought them all into subjection to the piety which ruled her in life and supported her in death.'

To this description of the surroundings of the home, given by the author of the *Memoir*, whose own home it was through childhood and boyhood, we may add a few sentences respecting its interior as it appeared to his sister, Mrs. Lefroy. She speaks of her grandfather's study looking cheerfully into the sunny garden, 'his own exclusive property, safe from the bustle of all household cares,' and adds:

'The dining- or common sitting-room looked to the front and was lighted by two casement windows. On the same side the front door opened into a smaller parlour, and visitors, who were few and rare, were not a bit the less welcome to my grandmother because they found her sitting there busily engaged with her needle, making and mending. In later times—but not probably until my two aunts had completed their short course at Mrs. Latournelle's at Reading Abbey, and were living at home—a sitting-room was made upstairs: "the dressing-room," as they were pleased to call it, perhaps because it opened into a smaller chamber in which my two aunts slept. I remember the common-looking carpet with its chocolate ground, and painted press with shelves above for books, and Jane's piano, and an oval looking-glass that hung between the windows; but the charm of the room with its scanty furniture and cheaply painted walls must have been, for those old enough to understand it, the flow of native wit, with all the fun and nonsense of a large and clever family.' Such was the room in which the first versions of *Sense and Sensibility* and *Pride and Prejudice* were composed.

We have anticipated somewhat in describing the Rectory as it appeared after George Austen's reforms, and when his children were growing up in it. As it appeared to him and his wife on their arrival, it must have left much to be desired.

The young couple who now entered upon a home which was to be theirs for thirty-seven years had many excellent and attractive qualities. George Austen's handsome, placid, dignified features were an index to his mind. Serene in temper, devoted to his religion and his family, a good father and a good scholar, he deserved the love and respect which every evidence that we have shows him to have gained from his family and his neighbours. His wife's was a somewhat more positive nature: shrewd and acute, high-minded and determined, with a strong sense of humour, and with an energy capable of triumphing over years of indifferent health, she was ardently attached to her children, and perhaps somewhat proud of her ancestors. We are told that she was very particular about the shape of people's noses, having a very aristocratic one herself; but we ought perhaps to add that she admitted she had never been a beauty, at all events in comparison with her own elder sister.

If one may divide qualities which often overlap, one would be inclined to surmise that Jane Austen inherited from her father her serenity of mind, the refinement of her intellect, and her delicate appreciation of style, while her mother supplied the acute observation of character, and the wit and humour, for which she was equally distinguished.

Steventon was not the only preferment in the neighbourhood that George Austen was to hold. His kind uncle Francis, who had helped him in his schooling, was anxious to do something more for him. He would have liked, it is said, to have put him into the comfortable living of West Wickham in Kent, which was in the gift of his wife; but he considered that another nephew, the son of a brother older than George's father, had a prior claim. Francis, however, did the best thing he could by buying the next presentations of two parishes near Steventon—namely, Ashe and Deane—that his nephew might have whichever fell vacant first.

The chances of an early vacancy at Ashe, where Dr. Russell—the grandfather of Mary Russell Mitford—had been established since 1729, must have seemed the greater; but fate decided otherwise. Dr. Russell lived till 1783, and it was Deane that first fell vacant, in 1773.

The writer of the *Memoir*, who was under the impression that George Austen became Rector of both Steventon and Deane in 1764, states that the Austens began their married life in the parsonage at Deane, and did not move to Steventon till 1771, seven years later. This cannot be quite correct, because we have letters of George Austen dated from Steventon in 1770; nor is it quite easy to understand why Mr. Austen should have lived in some one else's Rectory in preference to his own, unless we conceive that the Rector of Deane was non-resident, and that George Austen did duty at Deane and rented the parsonage while his own was under repair. It seems impossible now to unravel this skein. The story of the move to Steventon, in 1771, is connected with a statement that the road was then a mere cart-track, so cut up by deep ruts as to be impassable for a light carriage, and that Mrs. Austen (who was not then in good health) performed the short journey on a feather-bed, placed upon some soft articles of furniture in the waggon which held their household goods. This story is too circumstantial to be without foundation, nor is there any reason to doubt the badness of a country lane; but the particular family-flitting referred to must be left uncertain.

George Austen was thirty-three years old when he settled down at his Hampshire living. His wife was some eight years younger. Their means were not large, but George was able to supplement his income both by farming and by taking pupils. Life too was simpler in those days; and we read of Mrs. Austen being without a new gown for two years, and spending much of the time in a red riding-habit, which even then had not finished its usefulness, for it was cut up some years later into a suit for one of her boys. Her time, indeed, was soon busily employed; her eldest boy, James, was born on February 13, 1765; the second, George, on August 26, 1766; and the third, Edward, on October 7, 1767. The Austens followed what was a common custom in those days—namely, that of putting out their children to nurse. An honest woman in Deane had charge of them all in turn, and we are told that one or both of their parents visited them every day.

The only excitements to vary the tranquil life at Steventon were occasional visits to or from their near relations. Cassandra's brother was now living on his property called Scarlets, at Hare Hatch, in the parish of Wargrave, and was thus within a day's journey from Steventon. He had married a Miss Cholmeley, of Easton in Lincolnshire, but they had no children. Cassandra's only sister, Jane (the beauty of the family), was married at the end of 1768 to Dr. Cooper, Rector of Whaddon, near Bath. Edward Cooper was the son of Gislingham Cooper, a banker in the Strand, by Ann Whitelock, heiress of Phyllis Court and Henley Manor. Dr. and Mrs. Cooper divided their time between his house at Southcote, near Reading, and Bath—from which latter place no doubt he could keep an eye on his neighbouring parish. The Coopers had two children, Edward and Jane. They and the Austens were on very intimate terms, and it is probable that Jane Austen's early knowledge of Bath was to a great extent owing to the visits paid to them in that place. Another family with whom the Austens were on cousinly terms were the Cookes. Samuel Cooke, Rector of Little Bookham in Surrey and godfather to Jane, had married a daughter of the Master of Balliol (Theophilus Leigh), and their three children, Theophilus, Mary, and George, belonged, like the Coopers, to an inner circle of relations on both sides (Leigh Perrots, Coopers, Cookes, Walters, and Hancocks), who made up—in addition to the outer-circle of country neighbours—the world in which the Austens moved.

A few letters addressed to Mr. and Mrs. Walter (extracts from which we shall venture to quote) will give the best idea of the happy, peaceful life passed at Steventon Rectory during these early years. On July 8, 1770, George writes from Steventon of his wife's journey to London to be present at the birth of her sister's child, and adds:—

. . . My James . . . and his brother are both well, and what will surprise you, bear their mother's absence with great philosophy, as I doubt not they would mine, and turn all their little affections towards those who were about them and good to them; this may not be a pleasing reflection to a fond parent, but is certainly wisely designed by Providence for the happiness of the child.

A month or so later Cassandra is back again, and writing:—

I was not so happy as to see my nephew Weaver—suppose he was hurried in time, as I think everyone is in town; 'tis a sad place, I would not live in it on any account, one has not time to do one's duty either to God or man. . . . What luck we shall have with those sort of cows I can't say. My little Alderney one turns out tolerably well, and makes more butter than we use, and I have just bought another of the same sort, but as her calf is but just gone, cannot say what she will be good for yet.

December 9, 1770.—My poor little George is come to see me to-day, he seems pretty well, tho' he had a fit lately; it was near a twelve-month since he had one before, so was in hopes they had left him, but must not flatter myself so now.

In June 1771, the Austens' fourth child, Henry, was born, and Mrs. Austen writes on November 8, 1772:—

My little boy is come home from nurse, and a fine, stout little fellow he is, and can run anywhere, so now I have all four at home, and some time in January I expect a fifth, so you see it will not be in my power to take any journeys for one while. . . . I believe my sister Hancock will be so good as to come and nurse me again.

Unfortunately, poor little George never recovered sufficiently to take his place in the family, and we hear no more of him, though he lived on as late as 1827.

The fifth child, Cassandra, was born in January 1773, and on June 6, 1773, Mrs. Austen writes:—

We will not give up the hopes of seeing you both (and as many of your young people as you can conveniently bring) at Steventon before the summer is over. Mr. Austen wants to show his brother his lands and his cattle and many other matters; and I want to show you my Henry and my Cassy, who are both reckoned fine children. Jemmy and Neddy are very happy in a new playfellow, Lord Lymington, whom Mr. Austen has lately taken the charge of; he is between five and six years old, very backward of his age, but good-tempered and orderly. He is the eldest son of Lord Portsmouth, who lives about ten miles from hence. . . . I have got a nice dairy fitted up, and am now worth a bull and six cows, and you would laugh to see them; for they are not much bigger than Jack-asses—and here I have got duckies and ducks and chickens for Phyllis's amusement. In short you must come, and, like Hezekiah, I will show you all my riches.

December 12, 1773.—I thank God we are all quite well and my little girl is almost ready to run away. Our new pupil, Master Vanderstegen, has been with us about a month, he is near fourteen years old, and is very good tempered and well disposed. Lord Lymington has left us, his mamma began to be alarmed at the hesitation in his speech, which certainly grew worse, and is going to take him to London in hopes a Mr. Angier (who undertakes to cure that disorder) may be of service to him.

A sixth child, Francis William, was born in April 1774.

August 20, 1775.—We are all, I thank God, in good health, and I am more nimble and active than I was last time, expect to be confined some time in November. My last boy is very stout, and has run alone these two months, and is not yet sixteen months old. My little girl talks all day long, and in my opinion is a very entertaining companion. Henry has been in breeches some months, and thinks himself near as good a man as his brother Neddy. Indeed no one would judge by their looks that there was above three years and a half difference in their ages, one is so little and the other so great. Master Van. is got very well again, and has been with us again these three months; he is gone home this morning for a few holidays.

The new infant, however, did not appear quite so soon as was expected, and the last letter of the series is written by George Austen on December 17, 1775.

Steventon: December 17, 1775.

DEAR SISTER,—You have doubtless been for some time in expectation of hearing from Hampshire, and perhaps wondered a little we were in our old age grown such bad reckoners, but so it was, for Cassy certainly expected to have been brought to bed a month ago; however, last night the time came, and without a great deal of warning, everything was soon happily over. We have now another girl, a present plaything for her sister Cassy, and a future companion. She is to be Jenny, and seems to me as if she would be as like Harry as Cassy is to Neddy. Your sister, thank God, is pure well after it.

George Austen's prediction was fully justified. Never were sisters more to each other than Cassandra and Jane; while in a particularly affectionate family there seems to have been a special link between Cassandra and Edward on the one hand, and between Jane and Henry on the other.

Jane's godparents were Mrs. Musgrave (a connexion of her mother's), Mrs. Francis Austen (another Jane), wife of George's kind uncle, and Samuel Cooke, Rector of Little Bookham. We may suppose that, like the rest of her family, she spent a considerable part of the first eighteen months of her existence at the good woman's at Deane.

We have, indeed, but little information about the household at Steventon for the next few years. Another child—the last—Charles, was born in June 1779. There must, as the children grew older, have been a bright and lively family party to fill the Rectory, all the more so because the boys were educated at home instead of being sent to any school. One of George Austen's sons has described him as being 'not only a profound scholar, but possessed of a most exquisite taste in every species of literature'; and, even if we allow for some filial exaggeration, there can be no doubt that it was a home where good teaching—in every sense of the word—good taste, and a general love of reading prevailed. To balance this characteristic the Austen nature possessed yet another—spread over many members of the family—namely, an enthusiastic love of sport. The boys hunted from an early age, in a scrambling sort of way, upon any pony or donkey that they could procure, or, in default of such luxuries, on foot; perhaps beginning the day with an early breakfast in the kitchen. A wonderful story is told, on good authority, of a piece of amateur horse-dealing accomplished by the youngest son but one, Francis, at the mature age of seven: how he bought on his own account (it must be supposed with his father's permission) a pony for £1 11*s*. 6*d*.; hunted it, jumping everything that the pony could get its nose over; and at the end of two years sold it again for £2 12*s.* 6*d.* It was a bright chestnut, and he called it 'Squirrel'; though his elder brothers, to plague him, called it 'Scug.' This was the boy for whose benefit his mother converted into a jacket and trousers the scarlet riding-habit which played so important a part in her early married life. If he mounted 'Squirrel' in this costume, the future Admiral of the Fleet was hunting 'in pink' with a vengeance, and must have contributed not a little to the gaiety of the field.

It is evident that part of the good training at Steventon consisted in making the boys, while quite young, manly, active, and self-reliant. When the time came for their leaving home they would not be found unprepared.

Mr. Austen found it a pleasant task to educate his own sons with his other pupils, and thereby to dispense with the cost of public schools. We get a glimpse of him as a teacher in a letter of his son Henry, written many years later to Warren Hastings. Henry, by the way, made use of a style that one is thankful Jane did not adopt.

Suffer me to say that among the earliest lessons of my infancy I was taught by precept and example to love and venerate your name. I cannot remember the time when I did not associate with your character the idea of everything great, amiable, and good. Your benevolence was a theme on which my young attention hung with truer worship than courtiers ever pay the throne. Your works of taste, both of the pencil and the pen, were continually offered to my notice as objects of imitation and spurs to exertion. I shall never forget the delight which I experienced when, on producing a translation of a well-known Ode of Horace to my father's criticism, he favoured me with a perusal of your manuscript, and as a high mark of commendation said that he was sure Mr. Hastings would have been pleased with the perusal of my humble essay.

There is also a pleasant picture of home life at Steventon drawn for us in the *History of the Leigh Family*, in which the writer speaks of Cassandra, 'wife of the truly respectable Mr. Austen,' and adds: 'With his sons (all promising to make figures in life), Mr. Austen educates a few youths of chosen friends and acquaintances.

When among this liberal society, the simplicity, hospitality, and taste which commonly prevail in affluent families among the delightful valleys of Switzerland ever recur to my memory.'

But though it might be an easy thing to educate his sons at home, it was another matter to teach his daughters, and, according to a family tradition, Cassandra and Jane were dispatched at a very early age to spend a year at Oxford with Mrs. Cawley, a sister of Dr. Cooper—a fact which makes it likely that their cousin, Jane Cooper, was also of the party. Mrs. Cawley was the widow of a Principal of Brasenose College, and is said to have been a stiff-mannered person. She moved presently to Southampton, and there also had the three girls under her charge. At the latter place Cassandra and Jane Austen were attacked by a putrid fever. Mrs. Cawley would not write word of this to Steventon, but Jane Cooper thought it right to do so, upon which Mrs. Austen and Mrs. Cooper set off at once for Southampton and took their daughters away. Jane Austen was very ill and nearly died. Worse befell poor Mrs. Cooper, who took the infection and died at Bath whither she had returned. As Mrs. Cooper died in October 1783, this fixes the date roughly when the sisters went to Oxford and Southampton. Jane would have been full young to profit from the instruction of masters at Oxford (she can hardly have been seven years old when she went there), and it must have been more for the sake of her being with Cassandra than for any other reason that she was sent.

On the same principle, she went to school at Reading soon after the Southampton experience. 'Not,' we are told, 'because she was thought old enough to profit much by the instruction there imparted, but because she would have been miserable without her sister'; her mother, in fact, observing that 'if Cassandra were going to have her head cut off, Jane would insist on sharing her fate.'

The school chosen was a famous one in its day—namely, the Abbey School in the Forbury at Reading, kept by a Mrs. Latournelle, an Englishwoman married to a Frenchman. Miss Butt, afterwards Mrs. Sherwood, who went to the same school in 1790, says in her Autobiography that Mrs. Latournelle never could speak a word of French; indeed, she describes her as 'a person of the old school, a stout woman, hardly under seventy, but very active, although she had a cork leg. . . . She was only fit for giving out clothes for the wash, and mending them, making tea, ordering dinner, and in fact doing the work of a housekeeper.'

But in Mrs. Sherwood's time she had a capable assistant in Madame St. Quentin, an Englishwoman, married to the son of a nobleman in Alsace, who in troubled times had been glad to accept the position of French teacher at Reading Grammar School under Dr. Valpy. Mrs. Sherwood says that the St. Quentins so entirely raised the credit of the seminary that when she went there it contained above sixty pupils. The history of the school did not end with Reading, for the St. Quentins afterwards removed to 22 Hans Place, where they had under their charge Mary Russell Mitford. Still later, after the fall of Napoleon, the St. Quentins moved to Paris, together with Miss Rowden, who had long been the mainstay of the school. It was while the school was here that it received Fanny Kemble among its pupils.

Mrs. Sherwood tells us that the school-house at Reading, 'or rather the abbey itself, was exceedingly interesting, . . . the ancient building . . . consisted of a gateway with rooms above, and on each side of it a vast staircase, of which the balustrades had originally been gilt. . . . The best part of the house was encompassed by a beautiful, old-fashioned garden, where the young ladies were allowed to wander under tall trees in hot summer evenings.'

Discipline was not severe, for the same lady informs us: 'The liberty which the first class had was so great that if we attended our tutor in his study for an hour or two every morning . . . no human being ever took the trouble to inquire where else we spent the rest of the day between our meals. Thus, whether we gossiped in one turret or another, whether we lounged about the garden, or out of the window above the gateway, no one so much as said "Where have you been, mademoiselle?"'

After reading this we are no longer surprised to be told that Cassandra and Jane, together with their cousin, Jane Cooper, were allowed to accept an invitation to dine at an inn with their respective brothers, Edward Austen and Edward Cooper, and some of their young friends.

School life does not appear to have left any very deep impression on Jane Austen. Probably she went at too youthful an age, and her stay was too short. At any rate, none of the heroines of her novels, except Anne Elliot, are sent to school, though it is likely enough, as several writers have pointed out, that her Reading experiences suggested Mrs. Goddard's school in *Emma*.

Mrs. Goddard was the mistress of a school—not of a seminary, or an establishment, or anything which professed, in long sentences of refined nonsense, to combine liberal acquirements with elegant morality upon new principles and new systems—and where young ladies for enormous pay might be screwed out of health and into vanity, but a real, honest, old-fashioned boarding-school, where a reasonable quantity of accomplishments were sold at a reasonable price, and where girls might be sent to be out of the way, and scramble themselves into a little education, without any danger of coming back prodigies. Mrs. Goddard's school was in high repute. . . . She had an ample house and garden, gave the children plenty of wholesome food, let them run about a great deal in the summer, and in winter dressed their chilblains with her own hands. It was no wonder that a train of twenty young couples now walked after her to church. She was a plain, motherly kind of woman.

Jane herself finished her schooling at the early age of nine. The rest of her education was completed at home. Probably her father taught her in his leisure hours, and James, when he was at home, gave her many useful hints. Father, mother, and eldest brother were all fully capable of helping her, and perhaps even Cassandra did her share. But for the most part her culture must have been self-culture, such as she herself imagined in the case of Elizabeth Bennet. Later on, the French of Reading Abbey school was corrected and fortified by the lessons of her cousin Eliza. On the whole, she grew up with a good stock of such accomplishments as might be expected of a girl bred in one of the more intellectual of the clerical houses of that day. She read French easily, and knew a little of Italian; and she was well read in the English literature of the eighteenth century. As a child, she had strong political opinions, especially on the affairs of the sixteenth and seventeenth centuries. She was a vehement defender of Charles I and his grandmother, Mary, and did not disdain to make annotations in this sense (which still exist) on the margin of her Goldsmith's *History*. As she grew up, the party politics of the day seem to have occupied very little of her attention, but she probably shared the feeling of moderate Toryism which prevailed in her family. Politics in their larger aspect—revolution and war—were of course very real at that date to every patriotic citizen, and came home with especial force to the Austens, whose cousin's husband perished by the guillotine, and whose brothers were constantly fighting on the sea. In her last published sentence at the end of *Persuasion* the author tells us how her Anne Elliot 'gloried' in being the wife of a sailor; and no doubt she had a similar feeling with regard to her two naval brothers. But there was then no daily authentic intelligence of events as they occurred. Newspapers were a luxury of the rich in those days, and it need excite no surprise to find that the events are very seldom mentioned in Jane's surviving letters.

We can be in no doubt as to her fervent, and rather exclusive, love for her own country. Writing to an old friend, within a few months of her own death, she says: 'I hope your letters from abroad are satisfactory. They would not be satisfactory to *me*, I confess, unless they breathed a strong spirit of regret for not being in England.'

Of her favourite authors and favourite pursuits, we will speak later.

CHAPTER III.

WARREN HASTINGS AND THE HANCOCKS
1752-1794

THE title of this chapter may seem at first sight to remove it far from the life of Jane Austen; but Mrs. Hancock (who had been Philadelphia Austen) was her aunt, and Eliza Hancock not only a cousin but also a close friend; and both were always welcome visitors at Steventon. The varying fortunes of these ladies would therefore be an object of constant thought and discussion at the Rectory, and Jane had an early opportunity of becoming interested in the affairs both of India and of France.

How the acquaintance of the family with Warren Hastings began, we cannot exactly say; but it certainly lasted long, and resulted on their side in an admiration for his genius and his kindness, and a readiness to defend him when he was attacked.

In one of Jane's early unpublished sketches occurs the following passage:—

The eldest daughter had been obliged to accept the offer of one of her cousins to equip her for the East Indies, and tho' infinitely against her inclinations, had been necessitated to embrace the only possibility that was offered to her of a maintenance; yet it was one so opposite to all her ideas of propriety, so contrary to her wishes, so repugnant to her feelings, that she would almost have preferred servitude to it, had choice been allowed her. Her personal attractions had gained her a husband as soon as she had arrived at Bengal, and she had now been married nearly a twelvemonth—splendidly, yet unhappily married. United to a man of double her own age, whose disposition was not amiable, and whose manners were unpleasing, though his character was respectable.

When Jane wrote this she may have been thinking of her father's sister, Philadelphia, whose fate is described not very incorrectly, though with a certain amount of exaggeration, in this passage. That Philadelphia Austen went to seek her fortune in India is certain, and that she did so reluctantly is extremely likely. She had at an early age been left an orphan without means or prospects, and the friends who brought her up may have settled the matter for her. Who those friends were, we do not know; but from the intimate terms on which she continued through life—not only with her brother, George Austen, but also, in a less degree, with her half-brother, William Walter—it is probable that she had spent much of her youth with her mother's family.

Her brother George, however, as a young man, was poor, and had no home to offer her; but the banishment which threatened entirely to separate the brother and sister proved in the end to have a contrary effect. Philadelphia did in time come back to England, as a wife and as the mother of one daughter, and her husband's subsequent return to India caused her to depend much for companionship upon her English relations. At Steventon little Betsy would find playfellows, somewhat younger than herself, in the elder Austen children, while her mother was discussing the last news from India with the heads of the family.

Our first definite information about Philadelphia is, that in November 1751 she petitioned the Court of East India Directors for leave to go to friends at Fort St. David by the *Bombay Castle;* but who these friends were, or what induced her to take so adventurous a journey in search of them, we cannot say. Her sureties were also sureties for a certain Mary Elliott, so they may have been friends intending to travel together. But, according to Sydney Grier's conjecture, Mary Elliott did not, after all, sail in the *Bombay Castle*, but remained behind to marry a certain Captain Buchanan, sailing with him to India the following year. Captain Buchanan lost his life in the Black Hole, and his widow (whether she was Mary Elliott or not) married Warren Hastings. By her second husband she had two children, a son, George, born about 1758, and a daughter born about 1759 who lived only three weeks.

The short history of the boy we have already told. Mrs. Hastings died on July 11, 1759, at Cossinbazar.

Philadelphia reached Madras on August 4, 1752. It is probable that in those days no girl was long in India without receiving offers of marriage. In fact, Dr. Hancock writing twenty years later, to deprecate his daughter's coming out to India, says to Philadelphia 'You know very well that no girl, tho' but fourteen years old, can arrive in India without attracting the notice of every coxcomb in the place; you yourself know how impossible it is for a young girl to avoid being attached to a young handsome man whose address is agreeable to her.' If there *was* any handsome young man in Philadelphia's case, it was probably not Mr. Hancock, who must have been forty or more when he married her at Cuddalore on February 22, 1753. The name of Tysoe Saul Hancock appears in the list of European inhabitants at Fort St. David for 1753, as surgeon, at £36 per annum; and at Fort St. David he and Philadelphia remained for three years after their marriage. Where the Hancocks were during the troublous times which began in 1757 is not known; but by the beginning of 1762 they were certainly in Calcutta, for their daughter Elizabeth—better known as Betsy—was born there in December 1761. Warren Hastings, at this time resident at Murshidabad, was godfather to Elizabeth, who received the name he had intended to give to his own infant daughter. The origin of the close intimacy that existed between the Hancocks and Warren Hastings is uncertain; but if Mary Elliott really became the wife of the latter, the friendship of the two women may perhaps explain the great obligation under which Hastings describes himself as being to Philadelphia.

The news of the death of his little son was the first thing Hastings heard on landing in England in 1765, and we are told it left a shadow on his face for years. He seems always to have been especially fond of children, and his intimate friends knew they could give no greater pleasure than by informing him of the welfare of his favourites, or by sending messages to them. Thus Marriott, writing to Hastings from India on August 15, 1765, sends his kisses and salaam to 'little (*"great"* I believe I should say) Betsy Hancock,' and a 'good hearty shake by the hand to George; I suppose if I were to go to kiss him he would give me a box on the ears.—Write me particularly how these little ones go.'

It seems likely that the Hancocks sailed with Warren Hastings for England in the *Medway* in 1764-5; but, whenever they went, we learn from Hancock's letters that the journey home cost them the large sum of £1500. He (Hancock) no doubt thought that he had amassed a sufficient fortune—perhaps from trading, or from private practice, for it can hardly have been from his official income—in India to enable him to end his days comfortably at home. But either his Indian investments turned out badly, or he discovered that living in good style in England cost much more than he had anticipated; and after three years he found himself under the disagreeable necessity of a second residence in Bengal, in order to secure a fresh provision for his wife and daughter. So low, indeed, were his finances at the time, that he was forced to borrow money from Hastings to pay for his passage out. He reached Calcutta in 1769, but did not prosper on this second visit. His health was bad, his trading ventures turned out amiss, and there were perpetual difficulties about remitting money home to Philadelphia. Hastings evidently foresaw how matters would end, and with his wonted generosity gave a sum amounting at first to £5000, and increased later to £10,000, in trust for Hancock and his wife during their lives, and, on the death of the survivor, to Betsy.

Mr. Hancock himself died in November 1775, 'universally beloved and deeply regretted' (in the words of a young man whom he had befriended), 'the patron of the widow and the fatherless.' He seems indeed to have been a man of affectionate and anxious disposition, strongly attached to his wife and daughter; but the last part of his life was passed away from them amid difficulties and disappointments, and his spirits were hardly high enough to enable him to bear up against unequal fortune. He alludes in his letters, with expressions of regard, to his brother-in-law, George Austen; but characteristically deplores his growing family, thinking that he will not be able to put them out in the world—a difficulty which did not eventually prove to be insuperable.

When the news of his death reached England—which would be in about six months' time—George Austen and his wife were, fortunately, present to comfort Philadelphia under the sad tidings. She and Betsy had now been living in England for ten years, and had seen, no doubt, much of the Steventon Austens. Warren Hastings's loyal attachment to the widow and daughter of his friend remained unchanged, and they lived on terms of intimacy with his brother-in-law Woodman and his family. As long as Hancock lived he wrote constantly to wife and child, and gave advice—occasionally, perhaps, of a rather embarrassing kind—about the education of the latter. He discouraged, however, an idea of his wife's that she should bring Betsy out to India at the age of twelve. At last Mrs. Hancock, who, though a really good woman, was over-indulgent to her daughter, was able to fulfil the chief desire of her own heart, and to take her abroad to finish her studies, and later to seek an entry into the great world in Paris. Her husband's affairs had been left in much confusion, but Hastings's generous gift of £10,000 put them above want.

Betsy, or rather 'Eliza' ('for what young woman of common gentility,' as we read in *Northanger Abbey*, 'will reach the age of sixteen without altering her name as far as she can?'), was just grown up when this great move was made. In years to come, her connexion with her Steventon cousins was destined to be a close one; at the present time she was a very pretty, lively girl, fond of amusements, and perhaps estimating her own importance a little too highly. But she had been carefully educated, and was capable of disinterested attachments. She seems to have had a special love for her uncle, George Austen, and one of her earliest letters from Paris, written May 16, 1780, announces that she is sending to him her picture in miniature, adding 'It is reckoned like what I am at present. The dress is quite the present fashion of what I usually wear.' This miniature is still in existence, and represents a charming, fresh young girl, in a low white dress edged with light blue ribbon, the hair turned up and powdered, with a ribbon of the same colour passed through it. Our knowledge of her character at this time is principally derived from a series of letters written by her to her cousin, Phila Walter—letters singularly frank and gossipy, and of especial interest to us from the sidelights they throw on the family circle at Steventon. There are also interesting letters from Phila to her own family.

Such a girl as Eliza was not likely to pass unnoticed in any society; and in August 1781 Mr. Woodman writes to tell Warren Hastings that she is on the point of marriage with a French officer, and that 'Mr. Austen is much concerned at the connexion, which he says is giving up all their friends, their country, and he fears their religion.' The intended husband was Jean Capotte, Comte de Feuillide, aged thirty, an officer in the Queen's Regiment of Dragoons, and owner of an estate called Le Marais, near Gaboret, in Guyenne. The marriage took place in the same year, and in the following March, Eliza, now Comtesse de Feuillide, writes Phila a long letter praising the Comte and his devotion to herself.

The man to whom I have given my hand is everyways amiable both in mind and person. It is too little to say he loves me, since he literally adores me; entirely devoted to me, and making my inclinations the guide of all his actions, the whole study of his life seems to be to contribute to the happiness of mine. My situation is everyways agreeable, certain of never being separated from my dear Mama, whose presence enhances every other blessing I enjoy, equally sure of my husband's affection, mistress of an easy fortune with the prospect of a very ample one, add to these the advantages of rank and title, and a numerous and brilliant acquaintance amongst whom I can flatter myself I have some sincere friends, and you will unite with me in saying I have reason to be thankful to Providence for the lot fallen to my share; the only thing which can make me uneasy is the distance I am from my relations and country, but this is what I trust I shall not always have to complain of, as the Comte has the greatest desire to see England, and even to make it his residence a part of the year. We shall certainly make you a visit as soon as possible after the peace takes place.

In the same letter she mentions how gay the season has been, on account of the birth of the Dauphin, and of the fêtes which accompanied that event. Neither she nor her 'numerous and brilliant acquaintance' had any prevision of the terrible days that awaited all their order, nor any knowledge of the existence of the irresistible forces which were soon to overwhelm them, and to put a tragical end to every hope cherished by the bride, except that of rejoining her English friends. For the present, she led a life of pleasure and gaiety; but that it did not make her forgetful of Steventon is shown by another letter to Phila, dated May 7, 1784:—

I experienced much pleasure from the account you gave me of my Uncle Geo: Austen's family; each of my cousins seems to be everything their parents could wish them; such intelligence would have given me the completest satisfaction had it not been accompanied by the melancholy news of the death of the valuable Mrs. Cooper. I sincerely lament her loss and sympathize with the grief it must have occasioned. Both Mama and myself were very apprehensive of the influence of this event on my aunt's health, but fortunately the last accounts from Steventon assure us that the whole family continue well.

On January 19, 1786, she again writes on the subject of a visit to England, about which she hesitates, partly because of the state of her health, and partly because she was expecting a long visit from her cousin, James Austen (eldest son of George Austen)—a young man who, having completed his undergraduate residence at Oxford, was spending some months in France.

To England, however, she came, hoping to see much of the Austen family. 'I mean,' she writes, 'to spend a very few days in London, and, if my health allows me, immediately to pay a visit to Steventon, because my uncle informs us that Midsummer and Christmas are the only seasons when his mansion is sufficiently at liberty to admit of his receiving his friends.' The rectory was certainly too small a 'mansion' to contain the Comtesse and her mother, in addition to its own large family party and various pupils; so it is to be hoped that Eliza carried out her project in June, before she was otherwise engaged. She settled for a time in London, at 3 Orchard Street, and there it must be supposed her one child—a little boy—was born in the autumn, to be named Hastings after her own godfather. The Comte, who was himself detained by business in France, had, for some unexplained reason, desired that their child might be born in England. Whether she went again to Steventon at Christmas is uncertain, for her next letter is dated April 9, 1787. Eliza was then in town and expecting a visit from her cousin, Henry Austen—by this time a youth of sixteen about to go into residence at Oxford. She had been indulging in such gaieties as London had to offer her.

As to me, I have been for some time past the greatest rake imaginable, and really wonder how such a meagre creature as I am can support so much fatigue, of which the history of one day will give you some idea, for I only stood from two to four in the drawing-room and of course loaded with a great hoop of no inconsiderable weight, went to the Duchess of Cumberland's in the evening and from thence to Almack's, where I staid till five in the morning: all this I did not many days ago, and am yet alive to tell you of it. I believe tho', I should not be able to support London hours, and all the racketing of a London life for a year together. You are very good in your enquiries after my little boy who is in perfect health, but has got no teeth yet, which somewhat mortifies his two Mamas.

Eliza's domestic cares and her gaieties must still have left her some time to think with anxiety and apprehension of the impeachment of her godfather and benefactor, Hastings. We have a glimpse of this in a letter of Phila Walter, who was staying with her aunt and cousin in Orchard Street, in April 1788. They went to the trial one day 'and sat from ten till four, completely tired; but I had the satisfaction of hearing all the celebrated orators—Sheridan, Burke, and Fox. The first was so low we could not hear him, the second so hot and hasty we could not understand, the third was highly superior to either, as we could distinguish every word, but not to our satisfaction, as he is so much against Mr. Hastings whom we all wish so well.'

In August 1788, Eliza writes:—

What has contributed to hurry me and take up my time is my having been obliged to pay some visits out of town. We spent a little time at Beaumont Lodge, and I am but just returned from an excursion into Berkshire, during which we made some little stay at Oxford. My cousin met us there, and as well as his brother was so good as to take the trouble of shewing us the lions. We visited several of the Colleges, the Museum, etc., and were very elegantly entertained by our gallant relations at St. John's, where I was mightily taken with the garden and longed to be a *Fellow* that I might walk in it every day; besides I was delighted with the black gown and thought the square cap mighty becoming. I do not think you would know Henry with his hair powdered in a very *tonish* style, besides he is at present taller than his father.

You mention the troubles in France, but you will easily imagine from what I have said concerning my approaching journey, that things are in a quieter state than they were some months ago. Had they continued as they were it is most probable M. de F. would have been called out, and it would have been a very unpleasant kind of duty because he must have borne arms against his own countrymen.

We hear but little of Eliza during the next two or three years, which she seems to have spent partly in France, partly in England. She must have been much engrossed by the stirring events in Paris, the result of which was eventually to prove fatal to her husband.

In January 1791 she is at Margate for the benefit of her boy, and, though the place is very empty, occupies herself with reading, music, drawing, &c. She adds:—

M. de F. had given me hopes of his return to England this winter, but the turn which the affairs of France have taken will not allow him to quit the Continent at this juncture. I know not whether I have already mentioned it to you, but my *spouse*, who is a strong *Aristocrate* or Royalist in his heart, has joined this latter party who have taken refuge in Piedmont, and is now at Turin where the French Princes of the Blood are assembled and watching some favourable opportunity to reinstate themselves in the country they have quitted. I am no politician, but think they will not easily accomplish their purpose; time alone can decide this matter, and in the interim you will easily imagine I cannot be wholly unconcerned about events which must inevitably in some degree influence my future destiny.

Eliza had another terrible anxiety in June 1791, in the failure of her mother's health. In September she is hoping for a visit from her husband, when, if her mother's health allows, they will all go to Bath,—

a journey from which I promise myself much pleasure, as I have a notion it is a place quite after my own heart; however, the accomplishment of this plan is very uncertain, as from the present appearance of things, France will probably be engaged in a war which will not admit of an officer's (whose services will certainly be required) quitting his country at such a period. . . . My mother has this very morning received a letter from Steventon, where they all enjoy perfect health. The youngest boy, Charles, is gone to the Naval Academy at Portsmouth. As to the young ladies, I hear they are perfect Beauties, and of course gain hearts by dozens.

In November she says:—

Edward A. I believe will . . . in another month or two take unto himself a spouse. He shewed me the lady's picture, which is that of a very pretty woman; as to Cassandra, it is very probable, as you observe, that some son of Neptune may have obtained her approbation as she probably experienced much homage from these gallant gentlemen during her acquatic excursions. I hear her sister and herself are two of the prettiest girls in England.

Mrs. Hancock died in the winter of 1791-2, and our next letter from Eliza is not till June 7, 1792. In the interval she had been—together with M. de Feuillide, who had perhaps come over to attend the death-bed of Philadelphia—to Bath, from which place she had derived little amusement owing to the state of her spirits. Returning to London, M. de Feuillide had hoped to stay there some time;—

but he soon received accounts from France which informed him that, having already exceeded his leave of absence, if he still continued in England he would be considered as one of the Emigrants, and consequently his whole property forfeited to the nation. Such advices were not to be neglected, and M. de F. was obliged to depart for Paris, but not, however, without giving me hopes of his return in some months, that is to say, when the state of affairs would let him, for at present it is a very difficult business, for a military man especially, to obtain leave to absent himself.

On September 26 she writes:—

I can readily believe that the share of sensibility I know you to be possessed of would not suffer you to learn the tragical events of which France has of late been the theatre, without being much affected. My private letters confirm the intelligence afforded by the public prints, and assure me that nothing we there read is exaggerated. M. de F. is at present in Paris. He had determined on coming to England, but finds it impossible to get away.

The crisis of her husband's fate was not far distant. How the tragedy was led up to by the events of 1793, we do not know; but in February 1794 he was arrested on the charge of suborning witnesses in favour of the Marquise de Marbœuf. The Marquise had been accused of conspiring against the Republic in 1793; one of the chief counts against her being that she had laid down certain arable land on her estate at Champs, near Meaux, in lucerne, sainfoin, and clover, with the object of producing a famine. The Marquise, by way of defence, printed a memorial of her case, stating, among other things, that she had not done what she was accused of doing, and further, that if she had, she had a perfect right to do what she liked with her own property. But it was evident that things were likely to go hard with the Marquise at her trial. The Comte de Feuillide then came upon the scene, and attempted to bribe Morel, one of the Secretaries of the Committee of Safety, to suppress incriminating documents, and even to bear witness in her favour. Morel drew the Count on, and then betrayed him. The Marquise, her agent and the Count were all condemned to death, and the Count suffered the penalty on February 22, 1794.

We cannot tell where Eliza was through this trying time. The tradition in the family is that she escaped through dangers and difficulties to England and found a refuge at Steventon; but we have no positive information of her having returned to France at all. It is quite possible that she was at Steventon, and if so, the horror-struck party must have felt as though they were brought very near to the guillotine. It was an event to make a lasting impression on a quick-witted and emotional girl of eighteen, and Eliza remained so closely linked with the family that the tragedy probably haunted Jane's memory for a long time to come.

CHAPTER IV.

FAMILY LIFE 1779-1792

THE eldest brother of the family, James, was nearly eleven years older than Jane, and had taken his degree at Oxford before she left school. He had matriculated at St. John's (where he obtained a 'founder's kin' Scholarship and, subsequently, a Fellowship) in 1779, at the early age of fourteen; his departure from home having been perhaps hastened in order to make room for the three or four pupils who were sharing his brothers' studies at that time. His was a scholarly type of mind; he was well read in English literature, had a correct taste, and wrote readily and happily, both in prose and verse. His son, the author of the *Memoir*, believes that he had a large share in directing the reading, and forming the taste, of his sister Jane. James was evidently in sympathy with Cowper's return to nature from the more artificial and mechanical style of Pope's imitators, and so was she; in *Sense and Sensibility*, Marianne, after her first conversation with Willoughby, had happily assured herself of his admiring Pope 'no more than is proper.' In 1786 we hear of James being in France; his cousin Eliza was hoping for a visit of some months from him; but in the next year he had returned, and he must have soon gone into residence at Oxford as a young Fellow of his College; for there, in 1789, he became the originator and chief author of a periodical paper called *The Loiterer*, modelled on *The Spectator* and its successors. It existed for more than a twelvemonth, and in the last number the whole was offered to the world as a 'rough, but not entirely inaccurate Sketch of the Character, the Manners, and the Amusements of Oxford, at the close of the eighteenth century.' In after life, we are told, he used to speak very slightingly of this early work, 'which he had the better right to do, as, whatever may have been the degree of their merits, the best papers had certainly been written by himself.'

Edward Austen's disposition and tastes were as different from James's as his lot in life proved to be. Edward, as his mother says, 'made no pretensions' to literary taste and scholarship; but he was an excellent man of business, kind-hearted and affectionate; and he possessed also a spirit of fun and liveliness, which made him—as time went on—especially delightful to all young people. His history was more like fiction than reality. Most children have at some time or other indulged in day-dreams, in which they succeed to unexpected estates and consequent power; and it all happened to Edward. Mr. Thomas Knight of Godmersham Park in Kent, and Chawton House in Hampshire, had married a second cousin of George Austen, and had placed him in his Rectory at Steventon. His son, another Thomas Knight, and his charming wife, Catherine Knatchbull, took a fancy to young Edward, had him often to their house, and eventually adopted him. The story remains in the family of Mr. and Mrs. Knight's asking for the company of young Edward during his holidays, of his father's hesitating in the interests of the Latin Grammar, and of his mother's clinching the matter by saying 'I think, my dear, you had better oblige your cousins and let the child go.' There was no issue of the marriage of Mr. and Mrs. Knight, and by degrees they made up their minds to adopt Edward Austen as their heir. This resolution was not only a mark of their regard for Edward but also a compliment to the Austen family in general, whose early promise their cousins had probably observed; the relationship not being near enough to constitute any claim. But Mr. Knight was most serious in his intentions, for in his will he left the estates in remainder to Edward's brothers in succession in case of the failure of his issue, and Mrs. Knight always showed the kindest interest in all the family. Edward was now more and more at Godmersham and less and less at home. Under the Knights' auspices, he was sent, not to the University, but on a 'grand tour,' which included Dresden and Rome. He was probably away on this tour at the date which we have now reached.

Jane's favourite brother, Henry, was nearly four years younger than Edward, and was no doubt still profiting by his father's instructions. By 1789 he was not only at Oxford but was contributing to *The Loiterer* a paper on the sentimental school of Rousseau, and considering 'how far the indulgence of the above-named sentiments affects the immediate happiness or misery of human life.' Henry, whose course in life was marked by sharper curves than that of any of his brothers, was no doubt a very attractive personality. His niece, Mrs. Lefroy, says of him:—

He was the handsomest of his family and, in the opinion of his own father, also the most talented. There were others who formed a different estimate, and considered his abilities greater in show than in reality; but for the most part he was greatly admired. Brilliant in conversation he was, and, like his father, blessed with a hopefulness of temper which in adapting itself to all circumstances, even the most adverse, seemed to create a perpetual sunshine. The race, however, is not all to the swift, it never has been, and, though so highly gifted by nature, my uncle was not prosperous in life.

There can be no doubt that by his bright and lovable nature he contributed greatly to the happiness of his sister Jane. She tells us that he could not help being amusing, and she was so good a judge of that quality that we accept her opinion of Henry's humour without demur; but he became so grandiloquent when wishing to be serious that he certainly must have wanted that last and rarest gift of a humorist—the art of laughing at himself.

Very different again was the self-contained and steadfast Francis—the future Admiral of the Fleet; who was born in April 1774, and divided in age from Henry by their sister Cassandra. He must have spent some time at home with his sisters, after their return from school, before he entered the Royal Naval Academy, established in 1775 at Portsmouth under the supreme direction of the Lords of the Admiralty. Francis joined it when he was just twelve, and, 'having attracted the particular notice of the Lords of the Admiralty by the closeness of his application, and been in consequence marked out for early promotion,' embarked two and a half years later as a volunteer on board the frigate *Perseverance* (captain, Isaac Smith), bound to the East Indies. His father on this occasion wrote him a long letter—of which a great part is given in *Jane Austen's Sailor Brothers*. Nothing in this wise and kind letter is more remarkable than the courtesy and delicacy with which the father addresses his advice to the son, who was but a boy, but whom he treats as an officer, and as a young man of whom he already cherished the highest hopes, consequent upon his previous good conduct. He speaks on many topics, religious duties being given the first place among them. He rejoices in the high character Francis had acquired in the academy and assures him that 'your good mother, brothers, sisters and myself will all exult in your reputation and rejoice in your happiness.' The letter concludes thus: 'I have nothing more to add but my blessing and best prayers for your health and prosperity, and to beg you would never forget you have not upon earth a more disinterested and warm friend than your truly affectionate father, Geo. Austen.' We need not be surprised to learn that this letter was found among the Admiral's private papers when he died at the age of ninety-one.

The remaining brother, Charles, his sisters' 'own particular little brother,' born in 1779, must have been still in the nursery when his sisters left school.

These brothers meant a great deal to Jane; 'but dearest of all to her heart was her sister Cassandra, about three years her senior. Their sisterly affection for each other could scarcely be exceeded.

Perhaps it began on Jane's side with the feeling of deference natural to a loving child towards a kind elder sister. Something of this feeling always remained; and even in the maturity of her powers, and in the enjoyment of increasing success, she would still speak of Cassandra as of one wiser and better than herself.' 'Their attachment was never interrupted or weakened; they lived in the same home, and shared the same bedroom, till separated by death. They were not exactly alike. Cassandra's was the colder and calmer disposition; she was always prudent and well-judging, but with less outward demonstration of feeling and less sunniness of temper than Jane possessed. It was remarked in the family that "Cassandra had the *merit* of having her temper always under command, but that Jane had the *happiness* of a temper which never required to be commanded."'

Such was the family party at Steventon; and 'there was so much that was agreeable in it that its members may be excused if they were inclined to live somewhat too exclusively within it. They might see in each other much to love and esteem, and something to admire. The family talk had abundance of spirit and vivacity, and was never troubled by disagreements even in little matters, for it was not their habit to dispute or argue with each other; above all, there was strong family affection and firm union, never to be broken but by death. It cannot be doubted that all this had its influence with the author in the construction of her stories,' in which family life often plays a large part.

The party which we have described was for many years 'unbroken by death and seldom visited by sorrow. Their situation had some peculiar advantages beyond those of ordinary rectories. Steventon was a family living. Mr. Knight, the patron, was also proprietor of nearly the whole parish. He never resided there, and, consequently, the Rector and his children came to be regarded in the neighbourhood as representatives of the family. They shared with the principal tenant the command of an excellent manor, and enjoyed, in this reflected way, some of the consideration usually awarded to landed proprietors. They were not rich, but, aided by Mr. Austen's power of teaching, they had enough to afford a good education to their sons and daughters, to mix in the best society of the neighbourhood, and to exercise a liberal hospitality to their own relations and friends.' 'A carriage and pair of horses were kept'; but this could be done more cheaply in the eighteenth century than in the nineteenth. 'There were then no assessed taxes; the carriage, once bought, entailed little further expense; and the horses, probably, like Mr. Bennet's (in *Pride and Prejudice*), were often employed on farm work. Moreover, it should be remembered that a pair of horses in those days were almost a necessity, if ladies were to move about at all; for neither the condition of the roads nor the style of carriage-building admitted of any comfortable vehicle being drawn by a single horse'; indeed, the object of the builders seems to have been 'to combine the greatest possible weight with the least possible amount of accommodation.'

Jane Austen lost no time in entering on the career of authorship. She wrote because she must, and with very little prevision of the path which her genius was afterwards to mark out for her. She was urged onward 'by the first stirrings of talent within her and the absorbing interest of early composition.

'It is impossible to say at how early an age she began. There are copy-books extant containing tales, some of which must have been composed while she was a young girl, as they had amounted to a considerable number by the time she was sixteen. Her earliest stories are of a slight and flimsy texture, and are generally intended to be nonsensical, but the nonsense has much spirit in it. They are usually preceded by a dedication of mock solemnity to some one of her family. It would seem that the grandiloquent dedications prevalent in those days had not escaped her youthful penetration. Perhaps the most characteristic feature in those early productions is that, however puerile the matter, they are always composed in pure simple English, quite free from the over-ornamented style which might be expected from so young a writer.' The following is a specimen:—

THE MYSTERY.

AN UNFINISHED COMEDY.

DEDICATION.
TO THE REV. GEORGE AUSTEN.

SIR,—I humbly solicit your patronage to the following Comedy, which, though an unfinished one, is, I flatter myself, as complete a *Mystery* as any of its kind.

> I am, Sir, your most humble Servant,
> THE AUTHOR.

THE MYSTERY, A COMEDY.

DRAMATIS PERSONÆ.

Men.	Women.
Col. ELLIOT.	FANNY ELLIOTT.
OLD HUMBUG.	MRS. HUMBUG
YOUNG HUMBUG.	*and*
Sir EDWARD SPANGLE	DAPHNE.

and

CORYDON.

ACT I.

SCENE I.—*A Garden.*
Enter CORYDON.

Corydon. But hush: I am interrupted. [*Exit* CORYDON.

Enter OLD HUMBUG *and his* SON, *talking.*

Old Hum. It is for that reason that I wish you to follow my advice. Are you convinced of its propriety?

Young Hum. I am, sir, and will certainly act in the manner you have pointed out to me.

Old Hum. Then let us return to the house. [*Exeunt.*

SCENE II.—*A parlour in* HUMBUG'S *house.* Mrs. HUMBUG *and* FANNY *discovered at work.*

Mrs. Hum. You understand me, my love?

Fanny. Perfectly, ma'am: pray continue your narration.

Mrs. Hum. Alas! it is nearly concluded; for I have nothing more to say on the subject.

Fanny. Ah! here is Daphne.

Enter DAPHNE.

Daphne. My dear Mrs. Humbug, how d'ye do? Oh! Fanny, it is all over.

Fanny. Is it indeed!

Mrs. Hum. I'm very sorry to hear it.

Fanny. Then 'twas to no purpose that I——

Daphne. None upon earth.

Mrs. Hum. And what is to become of——?

Daphne. Oh! 'tis all settled. (*Whispers* Mrs. HUMBUG.)

Fanny. And how is it determined?

Daphne. I'll tell you. (*Whispers* FANNY.)

Mrs. Hum. And is he to——?

Daphne. I'll tell you all I know of the matter. (*Whispers* Mrs. HUMBUG *and* FANNY.)

Fanny. Well, now I know everything about it, I'll go away.

Mrs. Hum. } } And so will I. [*Exeunt. Daphne.* }

SCENE III.—*The curtain rises, and discovers* Sir EDWARD SPANGLE *reclined in an elegant attitude on a sofa fast asleep.*

Enter Col. ELLIOTT.

Col. E. My daughter is not here, I see. There lies Sir Edward. Shall I tell him the secret? No, he'll certainly blab it. But he's asleep, and won't hear me, so I'll e'en venture. (*Goes up to* Sir EDWARD, *whispers him, and exit.*)

End of the First Act. Finis.

A somewhat later venture, pure extravaganza, called *Evelyn* is dedicated, by permission, to Miss Mary Lloyd.

The manuscript volume which contains *Evelyn* is grandly entitled on the outside 'Volume the Third'; on the inside 'Effusions of Fancy by a very Young Lady, consisting of Tales in a Style entirely new.' It contains one other tale, unfinished, but of considerable length, called *Kitty or the Bower*, which is preceded by the following dedication, dated 'Steventon, August 1792.'

TO MISS AUSTEN.

MADAM,—Encouraged by your warm patronage of *The Beautiful Cassandra* and *The History of England*, which, through your generous support, have obtained a place in every library in the Kingdom, and run through four score editions, I take the liberty of begging the same Exertions in favour of the following novel, which I humbly flatter myself possesses Merit beyond any already published, or any that will ever in future appear, except such as may proceed from the pen of your most grateful

Humble Servant,
THE AUTHOR.

The tale begins in characteristic style, which suggests the later *Northanger Abbey*.

Catharine had the misfortune, as many heroines have had before her, of losing her parents when she was very young, and of being brought up under the care of a maiden aunt, who, while she tenderly loved her, watched her conduct with so scrutinizing a severity as to make it very doubtful to many people, and to Catharine among the rest, whether she loved her or not.

Catharine lives with this aunt in Devonshire, five miles from Exeter. Some friends of her aunt, a Mr. Stanley, M.P., his wife and daughter (very foolish, and suggestive of Isabella Thorpe) come to visit them. Mr. Stanley's son turns up unexpectedly and pays great attention to Catharine, much to the disgust of the aunt, who has a detestation of all young men. The tale comes to an abrupt conclusion with the departure of the guests. The story is at times amusing, but obviously immature, and we need not regret that it was never finished.

Other early sketches are *Henry and Eliza*, dedicated to Miss Cooper, which must have been written before the latter's marriage at the end of 1792; *The Visit*, dedicated to the Rev. James Austen; *Jack and Alice*, and *Adventures of Mr. Harley*, dedicated to Francis William Austen, Esq., midshipman on board H.M.S. *Perseverance* (soon after 1788), and other pieces dedicated to Charles John Austen, Esq.

Evelyn and *Kitty* seem to mark a second stage in her literary education: when she was hesitating between burlesque and immature story-telling, and when indeed it seemed as if she were first taking note of all the faults to be avoided, and curiously considering how she ought *not* to write before she attempted to put forth her strength in the right direction. 'Her own mature opinion of the desirableness of such an early habit of composition is given in the following words of a niece:—

As I grew older, my aunt would talk to me more seriously of my reading and my amusements. I had taken early to writing verses and stories, and I am sorry to think how I troubled her with reading them. She was very kind about it, and always had some praise to bestow, but at last she warned me against spending too much time upon them. She said—how well I recollect it!—that she knew writing stories was a great amusement, and *she* thought a harmless one, though many people, she was aware, thought otherwise; but that at my age it would be bad for me to be much taken up with my own compositions. Later still—it was after she had gone to Winchester—she sent me a message to this effect, that if I would take her advice I should cease writing till I was sixteen; that she had herself often wished she had read more, and written less in the corresponding years of her own life.

'As this niece was only twelve years old at the time of her aunt's death, these words seem to imply that the juvenile tales which we have mentioned had, some of them at least, been written in her childhood; while others were separated only by a very few years from the period which included specimens of her most brilliant writing.'

In the summer of 1788, when the girls were fifteen and twelve respectively, they accompanied their parents on a visit to their great-uncle, old Mr. Francis Austen, at Sevenoaks. Though Jane had been to Oxford, Southampton, and Reading before, it is probable that this was her first visit into Kent, and, what must have been more interesting still, her first visit to London. We have no clue as to where the party stayed in town, but one of Eliza de Feuillide's letters to Philadelphia Walter mentions that they dined with Eliza and her mother on their way back to Hampshire.

They talked much of the satisfaction their visit into Kent had afforded them. What did you think of my uncle's looks? I was much pleased with them, and if possible he appeared more amiable than ever to me. What an excellent and pleasing man he is; I love him most sincerely, as indeed I do all the family. I believe it was your first acquaintance with Cassandra and Jane.

Though Philadelphia's reply to this letter has not been preserved, we have a letter of hers to her brother. Writing on July 23, she says:—

Yesterday I began an acquaintance with my two female cousins, Austens. My uncle, aunt, Cassandra, and Jane arrived at Mr. F. Austen's the day before. We dined with them there. As it's pure nature to love ourselves, I may be allowed to give the preference to the eldest, who is generally reckoned a most striking resemblance of me in features, complexion, and manners. I never found myself so much disposed to be vain, as I can't help thinking her very pretty, but fancied I could discover *she* was not so well pleased with the comparison, which reflection abated a great deal of the vanity so likely to arise and so proper to be suppres't. The youngest [Jane] is very like her brother Henry, not at all pretty and very prim, unlike a girl of twelve; but it is hasty judgment which you will scold me for. My aunt has lost several fore-teeth, which makes her look old; my uncle is quite white-haired, but looks vastly well; all in high spirits and disposed to be pleased with each other.

A day or two later, Philadelphia wrote further:—

I continue to admire my amiable likeness the best of the two in every respect; she keeps up conversation in a very sensible and pleasing manner. Yesterday they all spent the day with us, and the more I see of Cassandra the more I admire [her]. Jane is whimsical and affected.

'Not at all pretty,' 'whimsical and affected.' 'Poor Jane!' one is tempted to exclaim, but whatever she would have said to this estimate of herself, of one thing we may be perfectly sure: that she would have been the first to agree with her critic as to her own absolute inferiority to Cassandra.

There is a passage in a letter written from Southampton, February 1807, in which she says she is often 'all astonishment and shame' when she thinks of her own manners as a young girl and contrasts them with what she sees in the 'best children' of a later date.

One other mention of Jane at this period may be quoted—that of Sir Egerton Brydges, the author and genealogist. His sister had married Mr. Lefroy, who in 1783 had become rector of Ashe (the living which George Austen would have held, had it become vacant before Deane), in succession to Dr. Russell. Sir Egerton, on his marriage in 1788, had for two years rented Mr. Austen's parsonage at Deane in order to be near his sister.

The nearest neighbours of the Lefroys were the Austens at Steventon. I remember Jane Austen the novelist as a little child. She was very intimate with Mrs. Lefroy and much encouraged by her. Her mother was a Miss Leigh, whose paternal grandmother was sister to the first Duke of Chandos. Mr. Austen was of a Kentish family, of which several branches have been settled in the Weald of Kent, and some are still remaining there. When I knew Jane Austen I never suspected that she was an authoress, but my eyes told me that she was fair and handsome, slight and elegant, but with cheeks a little too full.

Sir Egerton's description is the more pleasing of the two; but it must be remembered that he was writing long after the time he mentions, and that his recollections were no doubt somewhat mellowed by Jane Austen's subsequent fame; whereas Philadelphia Walter's is an unvarnished contemporary criticism—the impression made by Jane on a girl a few years older than herself.

Fortunately, neither looks nor manners are stereotyped at the age of twelve, so we need not be surprised to find that Eliza, when writing in August 1791 in reference to a letter just received from Steventon, talks of the two sisters as 'perfect Beauties,' who were of course gaining 'hearts by dozens.' And again in November of the same year, she writes that she hears 'they are two of the prettiest girls in England.' When due allowance is made for family exaggeration, we may conclude that at eighteen and fifteen years of age both Cassandra and Jane had their fair share of good looks.

Eliza's letters give us another glimpse of the sisters in 1792, and indeed of the whole Steventon party. She writes on September 26:—

I have the real pleasure of informing you that our dear Uncle and Aunt are both in perfect health. The former looks uncommonly well, and in my opinion his likeness to my beloved mother is stronger than ever. Often do I sit and trace her features in his, till my heart overflows at my eyes. I always tenderly loved my Uncle, but I think he is now dearer to me than ever, as being the nearest and best beloved relation of the never to be sufficiently regretted parent I have lost; Cassandra and Jane are both very much grown (the latter is now taller than myself), and greatly improved as well in manners as in person, both of which are now much more formed than when you saw them. They are I think equally sensible and both so to a degree seldom met with, but still my heart gives the preference to Jane, whose kind partiality to me indeed requires a return of the same nature. Henry is now rather more than six feet high, I believe; he also is much improved, and is certainly endowed with uncommon abilities, which indeed seem to have been bestowed, though in a different way, upon each member of this family. As to the coolness which you know had taken place between H. and myself, it has now ceased, in consequence of due acknowledgement, on his part, and we are at present on very proper relationlike terms. You know that his family design him for the Church. Cassandra was from home when I arrived; she was then on a visit to Rowling, the abode of her brother Edward—from which she returned some time since, but is now once more absent, as well as her sister, on a visit to the Miss Lloyds, who live at a place called Ibthorp, about eighteen miles from hence. . . . There has been a Club Ball at Basingstoke and a private one in the neighbourhood, both of which my cousins say were very agreeable.

The date 1790 or 1791 must be assigned to the portrait—believed to be of Jane Austen, and believed to be by Zoffany—which has been chosen as the frontispiece for this book, as it was for Lord Brabourne's edition of the Letters. We are unable for want of evidence to judge of the likeness of the picture to Jane Austen as a girl; there is, so far as we have heard, no family tradition of her having been painted; and, as her subsequent fame could hardly have been predicted, we should not expect that either her great-uncle Frank, or her cousin, Francis Motley Austen, would go to the expense of a picture of her by Zoffany. Francis Motley had a daughter of his own, another Jane Austen, who became Mrs. Campion of Danny, and a confusion between the two Janes is a possible explanation.

On the other hand, we believe there is no tradition in either the Austen or the Campion family of any such portrait of *that* Jane Austen, and the *provenance* of our picture is well authenticated. The Rev. Morland Rice (grandson of Edward Austen) was a Demy of Magdalen College, Oxford. An old Fellow of Magdalen, Dr. Newman, many years before his death, told him that he had a portrait of Jane Austen the novelist, that had long been in his family. He stated that it was painted at Bath when she was about fifteen, and he promised to leave him (M. Rice) the picture. A few months before his death, Dr. Newman wrote to his friend, Dr. Bloxam, sending him a picture as a farewell present, and adding: 'I have another picture that I wish to go to your neighbour, Morland Rice. It is a portrait of Jane Austen the novelist, by Zoffany. The picture was given to my stepmother by her friend Colonel Austen of Kippington, Kent, because she was a great admirer of her works.' Colonel Austen was a son of Francis Motley, and it is hardly conceivable that he should give away to a stranger a portrait of his *sister* Jane as one of his *cousin* Jane. Our Jane became fifteen on December 16, 1790, and Zoffany returned from India in that year. Jane is believed to have visited her uncle, Dr. Cooper (who died in 1792), at Bath. There is nothing in these dates to raise any great difficulty, and, on the whole, we have good reason to hope that we possess in this picture an authentic portrait of the author.

The Austens seem to have been possessed of considerable histrionic talent, and they were decidedly ambitious in the plays they undertook. Their cousin Eliza was out of England in 1784 when their theatricals first began; but on a later occasion she was one of the principal performers. They had their summer theatre in the barn, and their winter theatre either there or within the narrow limits of the dining-room, where the number of listeners must have been very small. In 1784 Sheridan's *Rivals* was acted by 'some ladies and gentlemen at Steventon.' The same year they seem to have given also the tragedy of *Matilda*. It was the day of prologues and epilogues, and the young actors were careful to omit nothing that would make the performance complete. James, the eldest son, brought into play his skill in verse-making; and we read of Henry Austen speaking a prologue (from his brother's pen) to *The Rivals*, while the prologue to *Matilda* was given by Edward Austen, and the epilogue by Thomas Fowle.

Midsummer and Christmas were the two seasons when George Austen dismissed his pupils for their holidays, and it was at these two periods that the theatricals usually took place. For the year 1787 we have a few details as to contemplated performances. Eliza de Feuillide had come to England with her mother in the summer of 1786, and probably went to Steventon at midsummer. In September 1787 she was at Tunbridge Wells with her mother and her cousin Phila. In a letter to her brother, Phila tells us that they went to the theatre, where (as was the custom in those days) the Comtesse—presumably as a person of some importance—'bespoke' the play, which was *Which is the Man?* and *Bon Ton*. This is interesting, because later on in the same letter Phila says: 'They [i.e. the Comtesse and her mother] go at Christmas to Steventon and mean to act a play, *Which is the Man?* and *Bon Ton*. My uncle's barn is fitting up quite like a theatre, and all the young folks are to take their part. The Countess is Lady Bob Lardoon [*sic*] in the former and Miss Tittup in the latter. They wish me much of the party and offer to carry me, but I do not think of it. I should like to be a spectator, but am sure I should not have courage to act a part, nor do I wish to attain it.'

Eliza was, however, very urgent with Phila that she should send all diffidence *to Coventry*.

Your accommodations at Steventon are the only things my Aunt Austen and myself are uneasy about, as the house being very full of company, she says she can only promise you 'a place to hide your head in,' but I think you will not mind this inconvenience. I am sure I should not—to be with you. Do not let your dress neither disturb you, as I think I can manage it so that the *Green Room* should provide you with what is necessary for acting. We purpose setting out the 17th of December. . . . I assure you we shall have a most brilliant party and a great deal of amusement, the house full of company, frequent balls. You cannot possibly resist so many temptations, especially when I tell you your old friend James is returned from France and is to be of the acting party.

But Phila still stood out, and Eliza attacked her once more on November 23, begging her to come for a fortnight to Steventon, provided she could bring herself to act, 'for my Aunt Austen declares "she has not room for any *idle young people*."'

We hear no more news of these theatricals, but it is probable that there was a change in the selection of the plays, for there is extant a prologue by James Austen to *The Wonder*, acted at Steventon, December 26 and 28, 1787, as well as an epilogue 'spoken by a Lady in the character of Violante.' There is also a prologue to *The Chances*, acted at Steventon, January 1788.

The last Steventon performances of which we have any knowledge took place in January 1790, when a farce called *The Sultan* was acted. The leading lady on this last occasion was Miss Cooper, who spoke the epilogue in the character of Roxalana, Henry Austen playing the title-rôle. On the same occasion Townley's farce, *High Life below Stairs*, was also given.

Of Jane's own part in these performances there is no record, for she was only just fourteen when the last took place. But even if she took no more share than Fanny Price, she must have acquired a considerable acquaintance with the language of the theatre—knowledge that she was to turn to good account in *Mansfield Park*. She was an early observer, and it might reasonably be supposed that some of the incidents and feelings which are so vividly painted in the *Mansfield Park* theatricals are due to her recollections of these entertainments.

The talent and liveliness which she would show, if ever she had an opportunity of acting herself, may be imagined. The late Sir William Heathcote is said to have remembered being with her at a Twelfth Night party when he was a little boy, on which occasion she, having drawn the part of Mrs. Candour, acted it with appreciation and spirit.

CHAPTER V.

GROWTH AND CHANGE 1792-1796

THOUGH it may hardly be likely that the Austens could rival Mrs. Bennet of *Pride and Prejudice* by professing to dine with four-and-twenty families, there was, nevertheless (for a quiet country neighbourhood), a very fair amount of society to be had around Steventon.

Readers of Jane Austen's letters will come across the names of many Hampshire neighbours, with occasional indications of the estimate which she formed of their intellects and characters. Probably there were many different degrees of refinement in different families; and towards the bottom of the list must have come the squire of many acres, who, we are told, inquired of Mr. Austen whether Paris was in France or France in Paris, and who quoted a speech of the Rector's wife as beginning with a round oath, saying, when remonstrated with, that it was merely his 'way of telling the story.' When the author of the *Memoir* expresses his belief that a century and a half ago the improvement of manners in most country parishes began with the clergy, he was no doubt thinking of the more learned minority of that body, who would bring into the depths of the country something of the enlightenment of a university. To this minority Jane's father and brother belonged, and thus the family probably gave to the society around them at least as much culture as they received from it in return.

In the outer circle of their neighbourhood stood the houses of three peers—those of Lord Portsmouth at Hurstbourne, Lord Bolton at Hackwood, and Lord Dorchester at Greywell. The owners of these places now and then gave balls at home, and could also be relied upon to bring parties to some of the assemblies at Basingstoke. Hardly less important than these magnates were the

Mildmays of Dogmersfield and the Chutes of The Vyne. The Mr. Chute of that day was not only one of the two M.P.'s for the whole county of Hampshire, but was also a well-known and popular M.F.H., and the husband of an excellent and cultivated wife. Then came other squires—Portals at Freefolk, Bramstons at Oakley Hall, Jervoises at Herriard, Harwoods at Deane, Terrys at Dummer, Holders at Ashe Park—with several clerical families, and other smaller folk.

But there were three houses which meant to the Austen sisters far more than any of the others. The Miss Biggs of Manydown Park—a substantial old manor-house owned by their father, Mr. Bigg Wither, which stands between Steventon and Basingstoke—were especial friends of Cassandra and Jane. One of these, Elizabeth, became Mrs. Heathcote, and was the mother of Sir William Heathcote of Hursley Park—a fine specimen, morally and intellectually, of a country gentleman, and still remembered by many as Member for Oxford University, and as *sole* patron of John Keble. Catherine, another sister, married Southey's uncle, the Rev. Herbert Hill; and Alethea, who never married, was probably for that very reason all the more important to the Steventon sisters. One of the latest of Jane's extant letters is addressed to Alethea.

A still closer friendship united Jane and Cassandra to a family named Lloyd, who for a short time inhabited their father's second house, the parsonage at Deane. Mrs. Lloyd had been a Craven— one of the unhappy daughters of a beautiful and fashionable but utterly neglectful mother, who left them to shift for themselves and to marry where they could. In this respect Martha Craven had done better than some of her sisters, having become the wife of a beneficed clergyman of respectable character and good position. With him she had led a peaceful life, and, on his death in January 1789, she spent the first two or three years of a quiet widowhood at Deane. Her second daughter, Eliza, was then already married to a first cousin, Fulwar Craven Fowle; but the two others, Martha and Mary, were still at home. Both became fast friends of Cassandra and Jane, and both were destined eventually to marry into the Austen family. For the present, their near neighbourhood came to an end at the beginning of 1792, when Mrs. Lloyd removed to

Ibthorp, eighteen miles distant from Steventon. It was on the occasion of this removal that Jane, then just sixteen years old, presented to Mary Lloyd an interesting specimen of her own needlework—still existing. It is a very small bag, containing a yet smaller rolled-up housewife furnished with minikin needles and fine thread. In the housewife is a tiny pocket, and in the pocket is enclosed a slip of paper, on which, written as with a crow-quill, are these lines:—

> This little bag, I hope, will prove
>
> To be not vainly made;
>
> For should you thread and needles want,
>
> It will afford you aid.
>
> And, as we are about to part,
>
> 'Twill serve another end:
>
> For, when you look upon this bag,
>
> You'll recollect your friend. *January 1792.*

It is made of a scrap of old-fashioned gingham, and, having been carefully preserved, it is in as perfect a condition as when it was first made a hundred and twenty years ago; and shows that the same hand which painted so exquisitely with the pen could work as delicately with the needle.

Martha Lloyd also had her dedicatory poem. Some years later, when, it seems, she wanted to go to Harrogate, and hoped in vain for the escort of a Mr. Best, Jane presented her with a copy of doggerel—and probably almost extemporaneous—verses:—

> Oh! Mr. Best, you're very bad
>
> And all the world shall know it;

> Your base behaviour shall be sung
>
> By me, a tuneful poet.
>
> You used to go to Harrogate
>
> Each summer as it came,
>
> And why, I pray, should you refuse
>
> To go this year the same?
>
> The way's as plain, the road's as smooth,
>
> The posting not increased,
>
> You're scarcely stouter than you were,
>
> Not younger, Sir, at least.
>
> &c., &c.

We must mention one other intimate friendship—that which existed between the Austens and the Lefroys of Ashe. Mr. Lefroy was Rector of that parish; and his wife, known within it as 'Madam Lefroy,' was sister to Sir Egerton Brydges to whom we are indebted for the very early notice of Jane Austen as a girl which we have already given.

'Mrs. Lefroy was a remarkable person. Her rare endowments of goodness, talents, graceful person, and engaging manners were sufficient to secure her a prominent place in any society into which she was thrown; while her enthusiastic eagerness of disposition rendered her especially attractive to a clever and lively girl.' How intensely Jane loved and admired her is shown by some lines which she wrote on December 16, 1808—the anniversary both of her own birth and of the sudden death of her friend, killed by a fall from her horse in 1804. It has sometimes been assumed that the self-restraint in expressions of affection to be found throughout

Jane's published writings, and the self-control they display in matters of emotion, arises from the fact that in the writer's nature there were no very ardent affections to be restrained, and no overpowering emotions to be suppressed. These lines show the baselessness of such an assumption. It was not for the gaze of the public, but to relieve her own heart, that Jane, at the age of thirty-three, wrote thus, four years after the death of this elder friend. Here she dared to speak as she felt, striving in all the warmth and depth of enduring attachment and admiration to paint a character which she yet declares to have been 'past her power to praise.' The verses continue thus:—

But come, fond fancy, thou indulgent power;

Hope is desponding, chill, severe, to thee:

Bless thou this little portion of an hour;

Let me behold her as she used to be.

I see her here with all her smiles benign,

Her looks of eager love, her accents sweet,

That voice and countenance almost divine,

Expression, harmony, alike complete.

Listen! It is not sound alone, 'tis sense,

'Tis genius, taste, and tenderness of soul;

'Tis genuine warmth of heart without pretence,

And purity of mind that crowns the whole.

> Can aught enhance such goodness? Yes, to me
>
> Her partial favour from my earliest years
>
> Consummates all: ah! give me but to see
>
> Her smile of love! The vision disappears.

Time was now to bring changes to the Austens. The elder brothers married. James had a curacy at Overton, and near Overton was Laverstoke Manor House, now occupied by General and Lady Jane Mathew. James became engaged to their daughter Anne, five years older than himself. They were married in March 1792, and started life on an income of £300 (of which £100 was an allowance made by General Mathew), keeping, it is said, a small pack of harriers for the husband, and a close carriage for the wife. James afterwards moved to Deane, where he was his father's curate. The married life of the couple was but short. Their one child, always known as Anna, was born in April 1793, and the mother died suddenly in May 1795, leaving to her daughter only a shadowy recollection of 'a tall and slender lady dressed in white.' The poor little girl fretted in her solitude, till her father took the wise step of sending her to Steventon Rectory to be comforted by her aunts. She was admitted to the chocolate-carpeted dressing-room, which was now becoming a place of eager authorship. Anna was a very intelligent, quick-witted child, and, hearing the original draft of *Pride and Prejudice* read aloud by its youthful writer to her sister, she caught up the names of the characters and repeated them so much downstairs that she had to be checked; for the composition of the story was still a secret kept from the knowledge of the elders.

Anna also composed stories herself long before she could write them down, and preserved a vivid remembrance of her dear Aunt Jane performing that task for her, and then telling her others of endless adventure and fun, which were carried on from day to day, or from visit to visit.

Towards the end of 1796 James became engaged to Mary Lloyd, and they were married early in 1797. The marriage could hardly have happened had not General Mathew continued, for the sake of Anna, the £100 a year which he had allowed to his daughter. The event must have been most welcome to Jane; and Mrs. Austen wrote a very cheerful and friendly letter to her daughter-in-law elect, expressing the 'most heartfelt satisfaction at the prospect.' She adds: 'Had the selection been mine, you, my dear Mary, are the person I should have chosen for James's wife, Anna's mother and my daughter, being as certain as I can be of anything in this uncertain world, that you will greatly increase and promote the happiness of each of the three. . . . I look forward to you as a real comfort to me in my old age when Cassandra is gone into Shropshire, and Jane—the Lord knows where. Tell Martha she too shall be my daughter, she does me honour in the request.' There was an unconscious prophecy contained in the last words, for Martha became eventually the second wife of the writer's son Francis.

Edward Austen's marriage had preceded his brother's by a few months. His kind patrons, the Knights, would be sure to make this easy for him; and it must have been under their auspices that he married (before the end of 1791) Elizabeth, daughter of Sir Brook Bridges, and was settled at Rowling, a small house belonging to the Bridges family, about a mile away from their seat at Goodnestone. No doubt it was a suitable match; but it must also have been a marriage of affection, if one may judge from the happy life which ensued, and from the lovely features of Mrs. Edward Austen, preserved in the miniature by Cosway. Some of Jane's earliest extant letters were written from Rowling.

The place was not, however, to be the home of the Edward Austens for long. Mr. Thomas Knight died in 1794, leaving his large estates to his widow for her life. Three years later, in 1797, she determined to make them over, at once, to the adopted son, who was after her death to become their owner, retaining for herself only an income of £2000. On learning her intentions, he sent her a most grateful and affectionate letter, saying that he wrote because he felt himself incapable of speaking with her on the subject; that it was impossible for him and his wife to accede to her plan, for they should never be happy at Godmersham whilst she was living in a smaller and less comfortable house, having quitted a mansion where he had so often heard her say her whole happiness was centred. This protest by no means turned Mrs. Knight from her intentions; on the contrary, she expressed them still more strongly, and in so charming a spirit that we must quote a considerable part of her letter:—

Godmersham Park: Friday.

If anything were wanting, my dearest Edward, to confirm my resolution concerning the plan I propose executing, your letter would have that effect; it is impossible for any person to express their gratitude and affection in terms more pleasing and gratifying than you have chosen, and from the bottom of my heart I believe you to be perfectly sincere when you assure me that your happiness is best secured by seeing me in the full enjoyment of everything that can contribute to my ease and comfort, and that happiness, my dear Edward, will be yours by acceding to my wishes. From the time that my partiality for you induced Mr. Knight to treat you as our adopted child I have felt for you the tenderness of a mother, and never have you appeared more deserving of affection than at this time; to reward your merit, therefore, and to place you in a situation where your many excellent qualities will be call'd forth and render'd useful to the neighbourhood is the fondest wish of my heart. Many circumstances attached to large landed possessions, highly gratifying to a man, are entirely lost on me at present; but when I see you in enjoyment of them, I shall, if possible, feel my gratitude to my beloved husband redoubled, for having placed in my hands the power of bestowing happiness on one so very dear to me. If my income had not been sufficient to enable us both to live in affluence I should never have proposed this plan, for nothing would have given me more pain than to have seen a rigid economy take the place of that liberality which the poor have always experienced from the family; but with the income I have assigned you, I trust, my dear Edward, you will feel yourself rich. . . . You may assure yourself and my dear Lizzie, that the pain I shall feel in quitting this dear place will no longer be remembered when I see you in possession of it. My attachment to it can, I think, only cease with my life; but if I am near enough to be your frequent daily visitor and within reach of the sight of you and your boys and Lizzie and her girls, I trust I shall be as happy, perhaps happier, than I am now. . . .

Your most sincere friend,
C. K.

Meanwhile, Francis Austen had made a good start in his profession. Going out to the East Indies, according to the custom of those days as a 'volunteer,' he became a midshipman, but remained one for four years only. Promotion—'that long thought of, dearly earned, and justly valued blessing'—was bestowed upon him two years sooner than it fell to the lot of William Price in *Mansfield Park*, and he became a lieutenant at the age of seventeen—a sufficient testimony to that steadiness of character which distinguished him throughout the course of a very long life. As lieutenant he remained another year in the East Indies, and then returned to serve on the Home Station. The result of this last move was that in 1793, rather more than a year after the marriages of James and Edward, their parents had the delight of welcoming back a son, who, having quitted them as a boy not yet fifteen years old, reappeared as a young man and successful officer, of whom his family might be justly proud.

Other events, grave and gay, were now happening at Steventon. Besides Eliza de Feuillide, who took refuge there with her young son while the clouds were gathering round her husband in France, the rectory had another visitor in the summer of 1792, in Jane Cooper, daughter of Mrs. Austen's only sister, who came here after her father's death. Dr. Cooper had set out in June with his son and daughter, and his neighbours, the Lybbe Powyses, on a tour to the Isle of Wight. The tour had important results for the young Coopers, as Edward became engaged to Caroline Lybbe Powys, and his sister to Captain Thomas Williams, R.N., whom she met at Ryde. Dr. Cooper, whose health had been the chief reason for the tour, did not long survive his return, dying at Sonning (of which he had been vicar since 1784) on August 27. The date of his daughter's wedding was already fixed, but had of course to be postponed. She went immediately to Steventon, and was married from the Rectory on December 11 of the same year. One happy result of this marriage was to provide an opening for the naval career of the youngest of the Austens, Charles, who was three years younger than Jane, and whom we last met in the nursery. As he was also five years junior to Francis, the latter must have quitted the Naval Academy some time before his brother entered it. Charles Austen was one of those happy mortals destined to be loved from childhood to old age by every one with whom they come in contact. How great a favourite he was at home is easily to be read between the lines of his sister's letters; and when he died at the age of seventy-three as Admiral of the British Fleet in the Burmese waters, one who was with him wrote that 'his death was a great grief to the whole fleet—I know I cried bitterly when I found he was dead.' The charming expression of countenance in the miniatures still existing of this youngest brother makes such feelings quite comprehensible.

On leaving the Academy he served under his cousin's husband, Captain Thomas Williams, and was fortunate enough to witness and take part in a most gallant action when, in June 1796, Captain Williams's frigate, the *Unicorn*, gave chase to a French frigate, *La Tribune*, and, after a run of two hundred and ten miles, succeeded in capturing her. To Charles, at the age of seventeen, this must have been a very exciting experience; while to Captain Williams it brought the honour of knighthood.

What with their visitors and their dances, and with a wedding to prepare for, life must have been gay enough for the Miss Austens during the autumn of 1792. Cassandra and Jane were now of an age to enjoy as much dancing as they could get: in fact, if Jane began dancing as early as she made Lydia Bennet begin, she may already have been going for a year or two to the monthly assemblies that Basingstoke (like every other town of any size) boasted of during the winter months.

Unfortunately, we know very little of Jane's personal history from 1792 to 1796. Most of her time would naturally be spent at home; but we catch an occasional glimpse of her, now dancing at Southampton, now travelling with Cassandra one hot summer's day from London to stay with her brother Edward at Rowling (in 1794), now visiting in Gloucestershire.

Early in 1794 came the shock of the execution of the Comte de Feuillide; and Eliza, widowed and motherless, and with an invalid boy, must have become more of a serious care to her relations. Over the acquittal of her benefactor and godfather, Warren Hastings, there was but one feeling in the family. They all admired him as a high-minded patriot, a warm and disinterested friend, and a scholar whose approbation was an honour. The event inspired Henry Austen with more than his usual grandeur of language. 'Permit me,' he says (writing to Hastings) 'to congratulate my country and myself as an Englishman; for right dear to every Englishman must it be to behold the issue of a combat where forms of judicature threatened to annihilate the essence of justice.'

One event of the deepest interest occurred during this period—namely, Cassandra's engagement to Thomas Fowle (brother of Eliza Lloyd's husband), which probably took place in 1795 when she was twenty-three years old. She had known him from childhood, as he was a pupil at Steventon Rectory in 1779. Mr. Fowle had taken Orders, and was at this time Rector of Allington in Wiltshire. An immediate marriage did not seem prudent, but advancement was hoped for from his kinsman, Lord Craven; and, as one of the livings in his gift was Ryton in Shropshire, it must have been to this place that Mrs. Austen alluded as the future home of Cassandra in the letter to her intended daughter-in-law, Mary Lloyd. At present, however, Lord Craven could only show his interest in Mr. Fowle by taking him out with him to the West Indies as chaplain to his own regiment.

Jane's literary projects were now assuming a more definite shape, although the process of selection and elimination both in subjects and method was not yet finished. To this period belongs *Elinor and Marianne*, a first sketch for *Sense and Sensibility*, but written in letters. We know that it was read aloud, but no details have come down to us, and it is difficult to guess between whom the letters can have passed, for in the novel Elinor and Marianne are never parted, even for a single day. It seems therefore as if the alterations subsequently made must have been radical; and the difficulty and labour which such a complete transformation would involve make the author's unfavourable judgment on her own earlier method of writing all the stronger. If she decided against using letters as a vehicle for story-telling in the future, it seems all the more probable that the only other instance of her use of this style was at least as early as the date we have now reached.

The author of the *Memoir* yielded with reluctance to many solicitations asking him to include *Lady Susan* in his second edition; while he himself agreed with other critics that the work was 'scarcely one on which a literary reputation could be founded.' As a stage in the development of the author it has great interest. Strictly speaking, it is not a story but a study. There is hardly any attempt at a plot, or at the grouping of various characters; such as exist are kept in the background, and serve chiefly to bring into bolder relief the one full-length, highly finished, wholly sinister figure which occupies the canvas, but which seems, with the completion of the study, to have disappeared entirely from the mind of its creator. It is equally remarkable that an inexperienced girl should have had independence and boldness enough to draw at full length a woman of the type of Lady Susan, and that, after she had done so, the purity of her imagination and the delicacy of her taste should have prevented her from ever repeating the experiment.

But if Jane Austen never again wrote a story in letters, no one was ever more successful in using them for exhibitions of character. The letters of Lucy Steele, Mr. Collins, Isabella Thorpe,

Lady Bertram, and Mary Musgrove are all masterpieces of unconscious humour—and some of the more serious letters are not far behind them.

The extant letters of Jane herself begin in 1796, and will accompany us through the rest of the story. They are far the most important additions that can be made to the short history contained in the *Memoir;* and the little notices which we have given—it may have seemed with needless particularity—of her relations and neighbours have been given partly in order to enable the readers of her letters to follow the numerous personal allusions to be found in them. We must not, however, try to extract more out of the letters than they will yield. The bulk of them belong to the collection published by Lord Brabourne, and nearly the whole of this collection consists of letters from Jane to Cassandra. But the normal condition of the sisters' lives was to be together—residing in one house, sleeping in one room. We can therefore only learn from this source what happened on the comparatively rare occasions when they were separated. Nor is this all, for a good deal of their correspondence is missing. Some of it is probably lost by accident; a great deal was certainly destroyed by Cassandra of set purpose. The Austens had a great hatred and dread of publicity. Cassandra felt this with especial force, and the memory of Jane was to her so sacred that to allow the gaze of strangers to dwell upon the actions or the feelings of so precious a being would have seemed to her nothing short of profanation. In her old age she became aware that Jane's fame had not only survived but increased, and that a time might come when the public would wish to know more details of her life than had been given in the short memoir, written by Henry Austen, and prefixed to her posthumous works. Cassandra would not indeed be likely to think it possible that the letters themselves should be published, but they might be made use of as materials, and so she determined to do what must have been a great sacrifice, and burn all those which were specially dear to herself, feeling confident that the remainder would not be disturbed. The destroyed MSS. without doubt included much that would have been of particular value to the biographer.

We must also remember that the correspondence was between sisters who knew, each of them, what the other was thinking, and could feel sure that nothing one might say would be misapprehended by the other; and the sort of freemasonry which results from such a situation adds to the difficulty of perfect comprehension by outsiders. Jane, too, was a mistress of subtle irony: the inveterate playfulness which is constantly cropping up in her books appears also in her letters. Secure of her correspondent, she could pass criticisms, impute motives, and imagine circumstances which would have been very far from her nature had she thought it possible that any less perfectly informed third person could see them.

All our authorities agree in describing her as one of the most considerate and least censorious of mortals. 'She was singularly free,' says one of her nieces, 'from the habit . . . of looking out for people's foibles for her own amusement, or the entertainment of her hearers. . . . I do not suppose she ever in her life said a sharp thing.' We may be sure, therefore, that when she seems to imply that her mother's ailments were imaginary, or that Mrs. Knight's generosity to Edward was insignificant, or that Mrs. Knight herself was about to contract a second marriage, she is no more serious than when she describes herself as having taken too much wine, as a hardened flirt, or as a selfish housekeeper ordering only those things which she herself preferred.

We must therefore take the letters as they are, without expecting to find any expression of views on such important subjects as religion, politics, or literature—subjects which might better be discussed in conversation with Cassandra; and with these limitations in our minds we shall probably agree with Mr. A. C. Bradley, who does not find the letters disappointing because 'the Jane Austen who wrote the novels is in them.'

CHAPTER VI.

ROMANCE 1795-1802

MISS MITFORD, in a paragraph showing some hostility to Jane Austen, tells us that her own mother spent her maiden life in the neighbourhood of the Austens and knew Jane as 'the prettiest, silliest, most affected, husband-hunting butterfly she ever remembers.' It is perhaps a sufficient answer to this attack if we remark that when Mrs. Mitford married and left her home Jane was barely ten years old, and that at a date two years later she was accused by a cousin of being 'prim.' It is probable that on growing up she, like other girls, enjoyed admiration, and it is certain that she attracted a good deal of it; but she says so much to her elder sister and mentor about one particular flirtation that we may be sure that it was neither a serious nor a frequent occupation with her.

In a letter written from Steventon, November 17, 1798, she mentions a visit from her friend Mrs. Lefroy, and adds that she had enough private conversation with her to hear all that was interesting,—

> which you will easily credit when I tell you that of her nephew she said nothing at all, and of her friend very little. She did not once mention the name of the former to *me*, and I was too proud to make any enquiries; but on my father's afterwards asking where he was, I learnt that he was gone back to London in his way to Ireland, where he is called to the Bar and means to practise.

She showed me a letter which she had received from her friend a few weeks ago (in answer to one written by her to recommend a nephew of Mrs. Russell to his notice at Cambridge) towards the end of which was a sentence to this effect: 'I am very sorry to hear of Mrs. Austen's illness. It would give me particular pleasure to have an opportunity of improving my acquaintance with that family with a hope of creating to myself a nearer interest. But at present I cannot indulge any expectation of it.' This is rational enough; there is less love and more sense in it than sometimes appeared before, and I am very well satisfied. It will all go on exceedingly well, and decline away in a very reasonable manner. There seems no likelihood of his coming into Hampshire this Christmas, and it is therefore most probable that our indifference will soon be mutual, unless his regard, which appeared to spring from knowing nothing of me at first, is best supported by never seeing me.

Mrs. Lefroy's 'friend,' though Jane was interested to hear of him, had evidently not touched her heart, and we should know nothing more of him if it were not for a letter of hers to her brother Frank, written more than fourteen years afterwards, and published in the *Sailor Brothers*.

I wonder whether you happened to see Mr. Blackall's marriage in the papers last January. We did. He was married at Clifton to a Miss Lewis, whose father had been late of Antigua. I should very much like to know what sort of a woman she is. He was a piece of perfection—noisy perfection—himself, which I always recollect with regard. We had noticed a few months before his succeeding to a College living, the very living which we recollected his talking of, and wishing for; an exceeding good one, Great Cadbury in Somersetshire. I could wish Miss Lewis to be of a silent turn and rather ignorant, but naturally intelligent and wishing to learn, fond of cold veal pies, green tea in the afternoon, and a green window-blind at night.

North Cadbury is an Emmanuel College living, and Mr. Blackall was a Fellow of that society, who, after the fashion of the times, had waited long for his living and his wife. Jane had known him well and liked him much, though with sufficient detachment to remember and to criticise his demonstrative manners, his love of instructing others, and other little peculiarities. The 'friend' of 1798 must have been a young Cambridge don; and she was not likely to have had an opportunity of knowing individually more than one of that limited community, who did not naturally come in the Austens' way. It seems obvious to link the two allusions together; and if this is correct, we have identified one of the admirers of our heroine.

More serious—but not *very* serious—was the attachment between her and Mrs. Lefroy's nephew, Tom Lefroy, afterwards Chief Justice of Ireland, which is mentioned somewhat cautiously in the *Memoir*, and the end of which is alluded to in the letter already quoted.

The young people became acquainted in the winter of 1795-6, and took to each other from the first. In a lively letter to Cassandra on January 9, 1796, Jane describes a ball at Manydown:—

Mr. H[eathcote] began with Elizabeth, and afterwards danced with her again; but *they* do not know how *to be particular*. I flatter myself, however, that they will profit by the three successive lessons which I have given them.

You scold me so much in the nice long letter which I have this moment received from you, that I am almost afraid to tell you how my Irish friend and I behaved. Imagine to yourself everything most profligate and shocking in the way of dancing and sitting down together. I *can* expose myself, however, only *once more*, because he leaves the country soon after next Friday, on which day we *are* to have a dance at Ashe after all. He is a very gentlemanlike, good-looking, pleasant young man, I assure you. But as to our having ever met, except at the three last balls, I cannot say much; for he is so excessively laughed at about me at Ashe, that he is ashamed of coming to Steventon, and ran away when we called on Mrs. Lefroy a few days ago. . . . After I had written the above, we received a visit from Mr. Tom Lefroy and his cousin George. The latter is really very well-behaved now; and as to the other, he has but *one* fault, which time will I trust entirely remove; it is that his morning coat is a great deal too light. He is a very great admirer of Tom Jones, and therefore wears the same coloured clothes, I imagine, which *he* did when he was wounded.

A few days later she is writing again:—

Our party to Ashe to-morrow night will consist of Edward Cooper, James (for a ball is nothing without *him*), Buller, who is now staying with us, and I. I look forward with great impatience to it, as I rather expect to receive an offer from my friend in the course of the evening. I shall refuse him, however, unless he promises to give away his white coat.

Friday.—At length the day is come on which I am to flirt my last with Tom Lefroy, and when you receive this it will be over. My tears flow as I write at the melancholy idea.

Truly the 'prim' little girl of twelve had made considerable progress by the time she was twenty! Unfortunately, there is no further letter to tell us whether Tom made the expected proposal or not; but it is pretty certain that he did not, and indeed there is a good deal of doubt whether it was really expected. Possibly lack of means prevented its ever being a serious matter on his side. They can never have met again on the same intimate terms. If he visited Ashe at all in 1798, the conditions must have been different, for he was by that time tacitly engaged to the lady whom he married in March 1799. Tom Lefroy accordingly disappears from Jane's life, though he never forgot her till his death at the age of ninety. When he was an old man he told a young relation that 'he had been in love with Jane Austen, but it was a boy's love.'

As for Jane's feelings, the opinion in the family seems to have been that it was a disappointment, but not a severe one. Had it been severe, either Jane would not have joked about it, or Cassandra would have destroyed the letters.

But the day of Jane's one real romance was still to come: a romance which probably affected the flow of her spirits, and helped to disincline her for literary composition, for some time after its occurrence. In this case, as in the other, the author of the *Memoir* was rather reticent; but shortly after its publication his sister, Caroline Austen, was induced to put down in writing the facts as she knew them. No one could be better qualified to do this, for she was a person of great ability, and endowed with a wonderfully accurate and retentive memory. It will be seen also that she has the unimpeachable authority of Cassandra to support her; we can therefore feel confidence in the truth of the story, although date, place, and even the name of the gentleman are missing.

Caroline Austen's account is as follows:—

All that I know is this. At Newtown, Aunt Cassandra was staying with us [i.e. with the writer and her mother, Mrs. James Austen] when we made acquaintance with a certain Mr. H. E., of the Engineers. He was very pleasing and very good-looking. My aunt was very much struck with him, and *I* was struck by her commendation; she so rarely admired strangers. Afterwards, at another time—I do not remember exactly when—she spoke of him as of one so unusually gifted with all that was agreeable, and said that he reminded her strongly of a gentleman whom they had met one summer when they were by the sea—I think she said in Devonshire; I don't think she named the place, and I am sure she did not say Lyme, for that I should have remembered—that he seemed greatly attracted by my Aunt Jane—I suppose it was an intercourse of some weeks—and that when they had to part (I imagine he was a visitor also, but his family might have lived near) he was urgent to know where they would be the next summer, implying or perhaps saying that he should be there also, wherever it might be. I can only say that the impression left on Aunt Cassandra was that he had fallen in love with her sister, and was quite in earnest. Soon afterwards they heard of his death. Mr. H. E. also died of a sudden illness soon after we had seen him at Newtown, and I suppose it was that coincidence of early death that led my aunt to speak of him—the unknown—at all. I am sure she thought he was worthy of her sister, from the way in which she recalled his memory, and also that she did not doubt, either, that he would have been a successful suitor.

This short history contains all the facts that are known. The rest must be left to imagination; but of two things we may be sure: the man whom Cassandra deemed worthy of her sister can have been no ordinary person, and the similarity in the ending of romance in the case of both sisters must have added a strong link of sympathy to the chain of love which bound their lives together.

A story is given in the *Reminiscences of Sir Francis H. Doyle*, to the effect that Mr. Austen, accompanied by Cassandra and Jane, took advantage of the Peace of Amiens, in 1802, to undertake a foreign tour. Whilst in Switzerland, they fell in with a young naval officer, who speedily became attached to Jane. His love was returned, and all seemed to be going smoothly. The party were making for Chamonix; but while the Austens kept to such high road as there was, their friend was to make his way thither over the mountains. The Austens reached Chamonix safely, but their friend never arrived, and at last news came that he had over-tired himself and died of brain fever on the way. The Austens returned to England, and Jane resumed her ordinary life, never referring to her adventures abroad. This story is given on the authority of a Miss Ursula Mayow, who heard it thirty or forty years later from a niece of Jane Austen's. Who this niece was we do not know, but she cannot have been either of the two who were grown up before their aunt's death, for they knew nothing of any such journey. As it stands, the story is impossible for many reasons. We give three:—

1. Such an important and unusual event as a tour in Switzerland could not have taken place without leaving traces behind, and there is no shadow of a tradition of it remaining in the family.

2. They could not possibly have afforded it. George Austen had given up his living, and was hoping to have £600 a year as a maximum for the family party of four persons, and they had just had the expense of setting up house in Bath.

3. We can almost prove an alibi. We know that they were at Dawlish in the year of the Peace of Amiens, and they certainly could not have made another lengthened absence.

The story, however, is interesting, for it fits in (so far as its main theme is concerned) with the authentic account given above of Jane's romance in the west, although the setting is completely different. It is quite possible that the fiction originated in an incorrect account—mis-heard or mis-repeated—of the true tale, mixed up with the fact (mentioned below) that the Henry Austens went abroad at this time.

One more incident shall be narrated: an incident which, though full of discomfort and inconvenience for the actors, yet lacks the note of tragedy contained in the last. It rests on the same excellent authority, with the additional safeguard that Caroline Austen's own mother must have known the circumstances exactly. The story is as follows:—

In November 1802 Cassandra and Jane came from Bath to pay a visit to their old home—then in the possession of their eldest brother James and his wife Mary. In the course of it, they went to spend a few days with some old friends in the neighbourhood. On the morning of Friday, December 3, they suddenly reappeared—their friends having driven them back—at an unlooked-for moment. All got out, and to Mrs. James Austen's surprise a tender scene of embraces and tears and distressing farewells took place in the hall. No sooner had the carriage disappeared than Cassandra and Jane, without offering any explanation, turned to her and said that they must at once go back to Bath—the very next day—it was absolutely necessary, and (as an escort for young ladies travelling by coach was also necessary) their brother James must take them—although Saturday was a day on which it was most inconvenient for a single-handed rector to go far from his parish; for he could not return till Monday, and there was hardly any time to provide for his Sunday duty. But Cassandra and Jane, in a manner very unlike their usual considerate selves, refused to remain till Monday, nor would they give any reason for this refusal. James was therefore obliged to yield and to go with them to Bath. In course of time the mystery was solved. One of the family with whom they had been staying had made Jane an offer of marriage, which she accepted—only to repent of her action deeply before many hours had passed. Her niece Caroline's remarks are as follows:—

I conjecture that the advantages he could offer, and her gratitude for his love, and her long friendship with his family, induced my aunt to decide that she would marry him when he should ask her, but that having accepted him she found she was miserable. To be sure, she should not have said 'Yes' overnight; but I have always respected her for her courage in cancelling that 'Yes' the next morning; all worldly advantages would have been to her, and she was of an age to know this quite well (she was nearly twenty-seven). My aunts had very small fortunes; and on their father's death, they and their mother would be, they were aware, but poorly off. I believe most young women so circumstanced would have gone on trusting to love after marriage.

If this event occurred after the more romantic incident in the west of England it is possible that Jane had hardly as yet regained her wonted balance of mind and calmness of judgment. We have no further tale of the sort to tell. As time went on, she acquiesced cheerfully in the gradual disappearance of youth. She did not eschew balls, but was indifferent whether she was asked to dance or not: 'It was the same room in which we danced fifteen years ago; I thought it all over, and in spite of the shame of being so much older, felt with thankfulness that I was quite as happy now as then. . . . You will not expect to hear that *I* was asked to dance, but I was.'

She was to spend the remainder of her life in the centre of family interests, and by degrees to become engrossed in the exciting business of authorship. She could afford to laugh at the suggestion that she should marry the Rector of Chawton, and promise to do so, whatever his reluctance or her own. She retained to the end her freshness and humour, her sympathy with the young: '*We* do not grow older, of course,' she says in one of her latest letters; and it is evident that this was the impression left with the rising generation of nephews and nieces from their intercourse with her.

CHAPTER VII.

AUTHORSHIP AND CORRESPONDENCE
1796-1798

THE appearance of Jane Austen's name among the list of subscribers to Madame d'Arblay's *Camilla*, in 1796, marks the beginning of her literary career. Her father must have paid the necessary subscription for her: and he probably did so believing that his daughter's talent deserved encouragement. Jane's cousins, the Cookes of Bookham, were some of Madame d'Arblay's closest friends while the latter was living in that neighbourhood, from 1793 to 1797, and it is quite likely that they were active in getting subscribers. One likes to think that—as Miss Hill has suggested—Jane may have met Madame d'Arblay when paying a visit to Bookham.

Jane was destined to have two periods of active authorship: periods of unequal length, and divided from each other by eight or ten nearly barren years. This unfruitful time has been accounted for in several different ways: as arising from personal griefs, literary disappointment, or want of a settled home. These disturbing causes all existed, and it is probable that each contributed its share to her unwillingness to write; but at present she enjoyed hope and happiness, the vigour and cheerfulness of youth among congenial companions, and a home as yet unvisited by any acute sorrows.

No precise date has been assigned to the writing of *Elinor and Marianne;* but after the completion of that sketch her time has been fully mapped out as follows:—

First Impressions (original of *Pride and Prejudice*), begun October 1796, ended August 1797.

Sense and Sensibility, begun November 1797.

Northanger Abbey (probably called *Susan*), written in 1797 and 1798.

It has been usual to dwell on the precocity of intellect shown in the composition of the first two of these works by a young and inexperienced girl, and no doubt there is much justice in the observation; but we venture to think that it is in *Northanger Abbey* that we get the best example of what she could produce at the age of three- or four-and-twenty. In the two others, the revision they underwent before publication was so complete that it is impossible now to separate the earlier from the later work; whereas in *Northanger Abbey*, while there is good evidence from the author's preface of a careful preparation for the press before she sold it in 1803, there is no mention of any radical alteration at a subsequent date. On the contrary, she apologises for what may seem old-fashioned in the social arrangements of the story by alleging the length of time that had elapsed since its completion. There is internal evidence to the same effect: she has not quite shaken off the tendency to satirise contemporary extravagances; and it is not until several chapters are past that she settles herself down to any serious creation of characters. The superiority also in interest and fun of the first volume over the second, though no doubt inherent in the scheme of the story, is a defect which she would hardly have tolerated at a later date. Nevertheless, we think her admirers may be satisfied with this example of her youthful style. The charm with which she manages to invest a simple ingenuous girl like Catherine, the brightness of Henry Tilney—even the shallowness of Isabella and the boorishness of John Thorpe—are things we part from with regret. And in parting with our friends at the end of one of her novels, we part with them for good and all; they never reappear in another shape elsewhere; even Mrs. Allen and Lady Bertram are by no means the same.

It seems to have been only a happy accident (though no doubt an accident very likely to occur) which prevented *First Impressions* from appearing in its immature shape.

George Austen was ready, and indeed anxious, that his daughter's work should be published; and when she had finished the story in August 1797, he took steps to find a publisher. Years afterwards (probably in 1836), at the sale of the effects of Mr. Cadell, the famous London publisher, the following letter was purchased by a connexion of the family:—

> SIR,—I have in my possession a manuscript novel, comprising 3 vols., about the length of Miss Burney's *Evelina*. As I am well aware of what consequence it is that a work of this sort sh$^{d.}$ make its first appearance under a respectable name, I apply to you. I shall be much obliged, therefore, if you will inform me whether you choose to be concerned in it, what will be the expense of publishing it at the author's risk, and what you will venture to advance for the property of it, if on perusal it is approved of. Should you give any encouragement, I will send you the work.
>
> I am, Sir, your humble servant,
> GEORGE AUSTEN.

Steventon, near Overton, Hants.: November 1, 1797.

This proposal, we are told, was declined by return of post.

The earliest of Jane's letters which have survived date from the year 1796. They begin at Steventon in the middle of their winter engagements, and when Tom Lefroy was in the foreground.

Steventon: Saturday [January 9, 1796].

In the first place, I hope you will live twenty-three years longer. Mr. Tom Lefroy's birthday was yesterday, so that you are very near of an age.

After this necessary preamble I shall proceed to inform you that we had an exceeding good ball last night, and that I was very much disappointed at not seeing Charles Fowle of the party, as I had previously heard of his being invited.

We were so terrible good as to take James in our carriage, though there were three of us before; but indeed he deserves encouragement for the very great improvement which has lately taken place in his dancing. Miss Heathcote is pretty, but not near so handsome as I expected.

Henry is still hankering after the Regulars, and as his project of purchasing the adjutancy of the Oxfordshire is now over, he has got a scheme in his head about getting a lieutenancy and adjutancy in the 86th, a new-raised regiment, which he fancies will be ordered to the Cape of Good Hope. I heartily hope that he will, as usual, be disappointed in this scheme.

Steventon: Thursday [January 14, 1796].

I am very much flattered by your commendation of my last letter, for I write only for fame, and without any view to pecuniary emolument.

Tell Mary that I make over Mr. Heartley and all his estate to her for her sole use and benefit in future, and not only him, but all my other admirers into the bargain wherever she can find them, even the kiss which C. Powlett wanted to give me, as I mean to confine myself in future to Mr. Tom Lefroy, for whom I don't care sixpence. Assure her also as a last and indubitable proof of Warren's indifference to me, that he actually drew that gentleman's picture for me, and delivered it to me without a sigh.

The next batch of letters date from a visit paid by Jane, in August 1796, to Rowling, the Kent home of her brother Edward. She seems to have experienced a difficulty in finding an escort for her return journey. Henry kept changing his plans; and Frank, the sailor, was liable to be sent for at a day's notice. She had evidently been studying her copy of *Camilla*.

Cork Street: Tuesday morn [August 1796].

MY DEAR CASSANDRA,—Here I am once more in this scene of dissipation and vice, and I begin already to find my morals corrupted. We reached Staines yesterday, I do not [know] when, without suffering so much from the heat as I had hoped to do. We set off again this morning at seven o'clock, and had a very pleasant drive, as the morning was cloudy and perfectly cool. I came all the way in the chaise from Hartford Bridge.

Edward and Frank are both gone out to seek their fortunes; the latter is to return soon and help us seek ours. The former we shall never see again. We are to be at Astley's to-night, which I am glad of. Edward has heard from Henry this morning. He has not been at the races at all, unless his driving Miss Pearson over to Rowling one day can be so called. We shall find him there on Thursday.

I hope you are all alive after our melancholy parting yesterday, and that you pursued your intended avocation with success. God bless you! I must leave off, for we are going out.

Yours very affectionately,
J. AUSTEN.

Everybody's love.

> Rowling: Thursday [September 1, 1796].

MY DEAREST CASSANDRA,—The letter which I have this moment received from you has diverted me beyond moderation. I could die of laughter at it, as they used to say at school. You are indeed the finest comic writer of the present age.

I am sorry that you found such a conciseness in the strains of my first letter. I must endeavour to make you amends for it, when we meet, by some elaborate details, which I shall shortly begin composing.

Our men had but indifferent weather for their visit to Godmersham, for it rained great part of the way there and all the way back. They found Mrs. Knight remarkably well and in very good spirits. It is imagined that she will shortly be married again. I have taken little George once in my arms since I have been here, which I thought very kind.

To-morrow I shall be just like Camilla in Mr. Dubster's summer-house; for my Lionel will have taken away the ladder by which I came here, or at least by which I intended to get away, and here I must stay till his return. My situation, however, is somewhat preferable to hers, for I am very happy here, though I should be glad to get home by the end of the month. I have no idea that Miss Pearson will return with me.

What a fine fellow Charles is, to deceive us into writing two letters to him at Cork! I admire his ingenuity extremely, especially as he is so great a gainer by it.

I am glad to hear so good an account of Mr. Charde, and only fear that my long absence may occasion his relapse. I practise every day as much as I can—I wish it were more for his sake. . . .

Frank has turned a very nice little butter-churn for Fanny. I do not believe that any of the party were aware of the valuables they had left behind; nor can I hear anything of Anna's gloves. Indeed I have not enquired at all about them hitherto.

We are very busy making Edward's shirts, and I am proud to say that I am the neatest worker of the party.

Rowling: Monday [September 5, 1796].

MY DEAR CASSANDRA,—I shall be extremely anxious to hear the event of your ball, and shall hope to receive so long and minute an account of every particular that I shall be tired of reading it. . . . I hope John Lovett's accident will not prevent his attending the ball, as you will otherwise be obliged to dance with Mr. Tincton the whole evening. Let me know how J. Harwood deports himself without the Miss Biggs, and which of the Marys will carry the day with my brother James.

We were at a ball on Saturday, I assure you. We dined at Goodnestone, and in the evening danced two country-dances and the Boulangeries. I opened the ball with Edward Bridges; the other couples were Lewis Cage and Harriet, Frank and Louisa, Fanny and George. Elizabeth played one country-dance, Lady Bridges the other, which she made Henry dance with her, and Miss Finch played the Boulangeries.

In reading over the last three or four lines, I am aware of my having expressed myself in so doubtful a manner that, if I did not tell you to the contrary, you might imagine it was Lady Bridges who made Henry dance with her at the same time that she was playing, which, if not impossible, must appear a very improbable event to you. But it was Elizabeth who danced. We supped there and walked home at night under the shade of two umbrellas.

We have just got some venison from Godmersham, which the two Mr. Harveys are to devour to-morrow, and on Friday or Saturday the Goodnestone people are to finish their scraps. Henry went away on Friday, as he purposed, *without fayl*. You will hear from him soon, I imagine, as he talked of writing to Steventon shortly. Mr. Richard Harvey is going to be married; but as it is a great secret, and only known to half the neighbourhood, you must not mention it. The lady's name is Musgrave.

Pray remember me to everybody who does not enquire after me; those who do, remember me without bidding. Give my love to

Mary Harrison, and tell her I wish, whenever she is attached to a young man, some *respectable* Dr. Marchmont may keep them apart for five volumes.

Rowling: Thursday [September 15, 1796].

At Nackington we met Lady Sondes' picture over the mantelpiece in the dining-room, and the pictures of her three children in an ante-room, besides Mr. Scott, Miss Fletcher, Mr. Toke, Mr. J. Toke, and the Archdeacon Lynch. Miss Fletcher and I were very thick, but I am the thinnest of the two. She wore her purple muslin, which is pretty enough, though it does not become her complexion. There are two traits in her character which are pleasing—namely, she admires *Camilla*, and drinks no cream in her tea. If you should ever see Lucy, you may tell her that I scolded Miss Fletcher for her negligence in writing, as she desired me to do, but without being able to bring her to any proper sense of shame—that Miss Fletcher says in her defence, that as everybody whom Lucy knew when she was in Canterbury has now left it, she has nothing at all to write to her about. By *everybody*, I suppose Miss Fletcher means that a new set of officers have arrived there. But this is a note of my own.

So His Royal Highness Sir Thomas Williams has at length sailed; the papers say 'on a cruise.' But I hope they are gone to Cork, or I shall have written in vain. Give my love to Jane, as she arrived at Steventon yesterday, I dare say.

Edward and Frank went out yesterday very early in a couple of shooting jackets, and came home like a couple of bad shots, for they killed nothing at all. They are out again to-day, and are not yet returned. Delightful sport! They are just come home, Edward with his two brace, Frank with his two and a half. What amiable young men!

Rowling: Sunday [September 18, 1796].

This morning has been spent in doubt and deliberation, in forming plans and removing difficulties, for it ushered in the day with an event which I had not intended should take place so soon by a week. Frank has received his appointment on board the *Captain John Gore* commanded by the Triton and will therefore be obliged to be in town on Wednesday; and though I have every disposition in the world to accompany him on that day, I cannot go on the uncertainty of the Pearsons being at home, as I should not have a place to go to in case they were from home.

My father will be so good as to fetch home his prodigal daughter from town, I hope, unless he wishes me to walk the hospitals, enter at the Temple, or mount guard at St. James'. It will hardly be in Frank's power to take me home—nay, it certainly will not. I shall write again as soon as I get to Greenwich.

I am very glad that the idea of returning with Frank occurred to me; for as to Henry's coming into Kent again, the time of its taking place is so very uncertain that I should be waiting for *dead men's shoes*. I had once determined to go with Frank to-morrow and take my chance, &c., but they dissuaded me from so rash a step, as I really think on consideration it would have been; for if the Pearsons were not at home, I should inevitably fall a sacrifice to the arts of some fat woman who would make me drunk with small beer.

In some way or other, Jane managed to reach Steventon, and at once set to work on *First Impressions*. From that point the letters cease for two years—namely, till October 1798. Several family events occurred during the interval. In January 1797 came the wedding of James Austen and Mary Lloyd. Owing to the friendship which had long existed between the Austens and the Lloyds, this marriage gave great pleasure at Steventon, and Eliza de Feuillide remarks on it as follows:—

James has chosen a second wife in the person of Miss Mary Lloyd, who is not either rich or handsome, but very sensible and good humoured. . . . Jane seems much pleased with the match, and it is natural she should, having long known and liked the lady.

Not long after this happy event, the rectory at Steventon was plunged into deep grief, for news came that Cassandra's intended husband, Thomas Fowle, who was expected home from St. Domingo in a few weeks, had died in February of yellow fever.

Our chief informant is again Eliza de Feuillide, who writes on May 3:—

This is a very severe stroke to the whole family, and particularly to poor Cassandra, for whom I feel more than I can express. Indeed I am most sincerely grieved at this event, and the pain which it must occasion our worthy relations. Jane says that her sister behaves with a degree of resolution and propriety which no common mind could evince in so trying a situation.

His kinsman, Lord Craven, who had taken him out as chaplain to his regiment, said afterwards that, had he known of his engagement, he would not have allowed him to go to so dangerous a climate.

After such a blow as this, Jane was hardly likely to leave Cassandra, and the absence of letters at this time is easily understood. In November of this same year, Mrs. Austen, whose health was not good determined to go to Bath with her daughters. The route from Steventon was by Andover and Devizes, one night being usually spent at the latter place. Mrs. Austen's brother, Mr. Leigh Perrot, was a regular visitor to Bath, and there is every reason to suppose that Jane had already visited the Leigh Perrots or the Coopers, or both, at this still fashionable resort, whose place was only gradually being usurped by Brighton. Owing to the absence of contemporary letters our knowledge of her stay there in 1797 is chiefly derived from reminiscences in later correspondence. Thus in May 1799, when visiting Bath again, Jane remarks that it rained almost all the way from Devizes; 'and our first view of Bath has been just as gloomy as it was last November twelve-month.' We may therefore imagine them 'entering Bath on a wet afternoon'—like Lady Russell, in *Persuasion*—'and driving through the long course of streets . . . amidst the dash of other carriages, the heavy rumble of carts and drays, the bawling of newsmen, muffin-men and milkmen, and the ceaseless clink of pattens.' The Austens probably stayed with the Perrots at their house, No. 1 Paragon Buildings.

Writing in April 1805, Jane describes a visit to a riding-school, and says: 'Seven years and four months ago we went to the same riding-house to see Miss Lefroy's performance. What a different set are we now moving in!' It would be interesting to know in what way the set differed, whether in kind or only in the individuals composing it. In this earlier visit Jane was likely to have seen plenty of company, as the Leigh Perrots had a large acquaintance. The Austens stayed at Bath into December, for Elizabeth de Feuillide mentions, on December 11, that she had heard very lately from Jane, 'who is still at Bath with her mother and sister. Mr. Hampson, whom I saw yesterday . . . told me he had heard Cassandra was going to be married, but Jane says not a word of it.' When we think of Jane's silence, and still more of Cassandra's recent grief, we may safely discredit this extremely improbable rumour.

On returning home for Christmas, they received a piece of news which, even if it did not come entirely as a surprise, can hardly have given unmixed pleasure. This was the engagement of Henry Austen to his cousin, Eliza de Feuillide—his senior by some ten years. Intended originally for the Church, Henry Austen had abandoned the idea of taking Orders, and had joined the Oxford Militia as lieutenant, in 1793, becoming adjutant and captain four years later. Though he was endowed with many attractive gifts there was a certain infirmity of purpose in his character that was hardly likely to be remedied by a marriage to his very pleasure-loving cousin.

In default of Eliza's letter on the occasion to her uncle, we may quote that which she wrote to Warren Hastings:—

DEAR SIR,—As I flatter myself you still take an interest in my welfare, I think it incumbent on me to acquaint you with a circumstance by which it must be materially influenced. I have consented to an Union with my Cousin, Captain Austen, who has the honour of being known to you. He has been for some time in Possession of a comfortable income, and the excellence of his Heart, Temper and Understanding, together with steady attachment to me, his Affection for my little Boy, and disinterested concurrence in the disposal of my Property in favour of this latter, have at length induced me to an acquiescence which I have withheld for more than two years. Need I say, my dear Sir, that I most earnestly wish for your approbation on this occasion, and that it is with the sincerest attachment I shall ever remain

> Your much obliged
> and affectionate God-daughter,
> ELIZABETH DE FEUILLIDE.

I beg leave to present my affectionate compliments to Mrs. Hastings.

December 26, 1797.

Neither side wished for a long engagement, and they were married on December 31. Henry continued with the Militia regiment probably till the Peace of 1802. By 1804 he had joined a brother Militia officer of the name of Maunde, and set up as banker and army agent, with offices in Albany, Piccadilly; removing in or before 1808 to 10 Henrietta Street, Covent Garden. Poor little Hastings de Feuillide became subject to epilepsy, and died on October 9, 1801, while the Henry Austens were living in Upper Berkeley Street.

During the first half of 1798, Jane, fresh from her late visit to Bath, was able to devote some happy months of unbroken leisure to writing the first draft of the book known to us as *Northanger Abbey;* but her comedy was once more interrupted by one of the tragedies of real life. On August 9 occurred the death of her cousin, Lady Williams (Jane Cooper): while she was driving herself in a whiskey, a dray-horse ran away and drove against the chaise. She was thrown out and killed on the spot: 'never spoke again,' so Mrs. Lybbe Powys records the news on August 14. Jane Williams had been married from Steventon Rectory, and had been, both before and after that event, so frequent a visitor there that her death must have been severely felt by the Austens—especially by the daughters of the family, her friends and contemporaries.

CHAPTER VIII.

GODMERSHAM AND STEVENTON 1798-1799

SOME change after this shock must have been desirable; and at the end of the same month Mr. and Mrs. Austen, with Cassandra and Jane, started on a visit to the Edward Austens—no longer at Rowling but at Godmersham, which, by the generosity of Mrs. Knight, was now become their residence. Edward would naturally wish for a visit from his parents and sisters in his new and beautiful home. We know very little of Jane's doings there, except that she attended a ball at Ashford; but, on her parting from Cassandra (who was left behind) and returning to Steventon with her father and mother, we find ourselves fortunately in the company of the letters once more. Mrs. Austen was at this time in poor health, and Jane evidently felt the responsibility of taking charge of her in Cassandra's absence.

'Bull and George,' Dartford: Wednesday [October 24, 1798].

MY DEAR CASSANDRA,—You have already heard from Daniel, I conclude, in what excellent time we reached and quitted Sittingbourne, and how very well my mother bore her journey thither. I am now able to send you a continuation of the same good account of her. She was very little fatigued on her arrival at this place, has been refreshed by a comfortable dinner, and now seems quite stout. It wanted five minutes of twelve when we left Sittingbourne, from whence we had a famous pair of horses, which took us to Rochester in an hour and a quarter; the postboy seemed determined to show my mother that Kentish drivers were not always tedious, and really drove as fast as *Cax*.

Our next stage was not quite so expeditiously performed; the load was heavy and our horses very indifferent. However, we were in such good time, and my mother bore her journey so well, that expedition was of little importance to us; and as it was, we were very little more than two hours and a half coming hither, and it was scarcely past four when we stopped at the inn.

I should have begun my letter soon after our arrival but for a little adventure which prevented me. After we had been here a quarter of an hour it was discovered that my writing and dressing boxes had been by accident put into a chaise which was just packing off as we came in, and were driven away towards Gravesend in their way to the West Indies. No part of my property could have been such a prize before, for in my writing box was all my worldly wealth, £7, and my dear Harry's deputation. Mr. Nottley immediately despatched a man and horse after the chaise, and in half an hour's time I had the pleasure of being as rich as ever; they were got about two or three miles off.

My day's journey has been pleasanter in every respect than I expected. I have been very little crowded and by no means unhappy. Your watchfulness with regard to the weather on our accounts was very kind and very effectual. We had one heavy shower on leaving Sittingbourne, but afterwards the clouds cleared away, and we had a very bright *chrystal* afternoon.

My father is now reading the *Midnight Bell* which he has got from the library, and mother sitting by the fire. Our route tomorrow is not determined. We have none of us much inclination for London, and if Mr. Nottley will give us leave, I think we shall go to Staines through Croydon and Kingston, which will be much pleasanter than any other way; but he is decidedly for Clapham and Battersea. God bless you all!

Yours affectionately,
J. A.

I flatter myself that *itty Dordy* will not forget me at least under a week. Kiss him for me.

Steventon: Saturday [October 27, 1798].

We arrived here yesterday between four and five, but I cannot send you quite so triumphant an account of our last day's journey as of the first and second. Soon after I had finished my letter from Staines, my mother began to suffer from the exercise or fatigue of travelling, and she was a good deal indisposed.

James called on us just as we were going to tea, and my mother was well enough to talk very cheerfully to him before she went to bed. . . . They [James and Mary] were to have dined here to-day, but the weather is too bad. I have had the pleasure of hearing that Martha is with them. James fetched her from Ibthorp on Thursday, and she will stay with them till she removes to Kintbury.

I am very grand indeed; I had the dignity of dropping out my mother's laudanum last night. I carry about the keys of the wine and closet, and twice since I began this letter have had orders to give in the kitchen. Our dinner was very good yesterday and the chicken boiled perfectly tender; therefore I shall not be obliged to dismiss Nanny on that account.

Your letter was chaperoned here by one from Mrs. Cooke, in which she says that *Battleridge* is not to come out before January, and she is so little satisfied with Cawthorn's dilatoriness that she never means to employ him again.

Mrs. Hall, of Sherborne, was brought to bed yesterday of a dead child, some weeks before she expected, owing to a fright. I suppose she happened unawares to look at her husband.

There has been a great deal of rain here for this last fortnight, much more than in Kent, and indeed we found the roads all the way from Staines most disgracefully dirty. Steventon Lane has its full share of it, and I don't know when I shall be able to get to Deane.

My dear *itty Dordy's* remembrance of me is very pleasing to me—foolishly pleasing, because I know it will be over so soon. My attachment to him will be more durable. I shall think with tenderness and delight on his beautiful and smiling countenance and interesting manner until a few years have turned him into an ungovernable ungracious fellow.

The books from Winton are all unpacked and put away; the binding has compressed them most conveniently, and there is now very good room in the bookcase for all that we wish to have there. I believe the servants were all very glad to see us. Nanny was, I am sure. She confesses that it was very dull, and yet she had her child with her till last Sunday. I understand that there are some grapes left, but I believe not many; they must be gathered as soon as possible, or this rain will entirely rot them.

Saturday [November 17, 1798].

My mother desires me to tell you that I am a very good housekeeper, which I have no reluctance in doing, because I really think it my peculiar excellence, and for this reason—I always take care to provide such things as please my own appetite, which I consider as the chief merit in housekeeping. I have had some ragout veal, and I mean to have some haricot mutton to-morrow. We are to kill a pig soon.

There is to be a ball at Basingstoke next Thursday. Our assemblies have very kindly declined ever since we laid down the carriage, so that dis-convenience and dis-inclination to go have kept pace together.

Sunday.—I have just received a note from James to say that Mary was brought to bed last night, at eleven o'clock, of a fine little boy, and that everything is going on very well. My mother had desired to know nothing of it before it should be all over, and we were clever enough to prevent her having any suspicion of it, though Jenny, who had been left here by her mistress, was sent for home.

Steventon: Sunday [November 25, 1798].

MY DEAR SISTER,—I expected to have heard from you this morning, but no letter is come. I shall not take the trouble of announcing to you any more of Mary's children, if, instead of thanking me for the intelligence, you always sit down and write to

James. I am sure nobody can desire your letters so much as I do, and I don't think anybody deserves them so well.

Having now relieved my heart of a great deal of malevolence, I will proceed to tell you that Mary continues quite well, and my mother tolerably so. I saw the former on Friday, and though I had seen her comparatively hearty the Tuesday before, I was really amazed at the improvement which three days had made in her. She looked well, her spirits were perfectly good, and she spoke much more vigorously than Elizabeth did when we left Godmersham. I had only a glimpse at the child, who was asleep; but Miss Debary told me that his eyes were large, dark, and handsome. *She* looks much as she used to do, is netting herself a gown in worsteds, and wears what Mrs. Birch would call a *pot hat*. A short and compendious history of Miss Debary!

We have got *Fitz-Albini;* my father has bought it against my private wishes, for it does not quite satisfy my feelings that we should purchase the only one of Egerton's works of which his family are ashamed. That these scruples, however, do not at all interfere with my reading it, you will easily believe. We have neither of us yet finished the first volume. My father is disappointed—*I* am not, for I expected nothing better. Never did any book carry more internal evidence of its author. Every sentiment is completely Egerton's. There is very little story, and what there is is told in a strange, unconnected way. There are many characters introduced, apparently merely to be delineated. We have not been able to recognise any of them hitherto, except Dr. and Mrs. Hey and Mr. Oxenden, who is not very tenderly treated. . . .

We have got Boswell's *Tour to the Hebrides*, and are to have his *Life of Johnson;* and as some money will yet remain in Burdon's hands, it is to be laid out in the purchase of Cowper's works. This would please Mr. Clarke, could he know it.

Steventon: [December 1, 1798.]

MY DEAR CASSANDRA,—I am so good as to write you again thus speedily, to let you know that I have just heard from Frank.

He was at Cadiz, alive and well, on October 19, and had then very lately received a letter from you, written as long ago as when the *London* was at St. Helen's. But his *raly* latest intelligence of us was in one from me of September 1st, which I sent soon after we got to Godmersham. He had written a packet full for his dearest friends in England, early in October, to go by the *Excellent;* but the *Excellent* was not sailed, nor likely to sail, when he despatched this to me. It comprehended letters for both of us, for Lord Spencer, Mr. Daysh, and the East India Directors. Lord St. Vincent had left the fleet when he wrote, and was gone to Gibraltar, it was said to superintend the fitting out of a private expedition from thence against some of the enemies' ports; Minorca or Malta were conjectured to be the objects.

Frank writes in good spirits, but says that our correspondence cannot be so easily carried on in future as it has been, as the communication between Cadiz and Lisbon is less frequent than formerly. You and my mother, therefore, must not alarm yourselves at the long intervals that may divide his letters. I address this advice to you two as being the most tender-hearted of the family.

My mother made her *entrée* into the dressing-room through crowds of admiring spectators yesterday afternoon, and we all drank tea together for the first time these five weeks. She has had a tolerable night, and bids fair for a continuance in the same brilliant course of action to-day. . . .

Mr. Lyford was here yesterday; he came while we were at dinner, and partook of our elegant entertainment. I was not ashamed at asking him to sit down to table, for we had some pease-soup, a sparerib, and a pudding. He wants my mother to look yellow and to throw out a rash, but she will do neither.

We live entirely in the dressing-room now, which I like very much; I always feel so much more elegant in it than in the parlour.

I have made myself two or three caps to wear of evenings since I came home, and they save me a world of torment as to hair-dressing, which at present gives me no trouble beyond washing and brushing, for my long hair is always plaited up out of sight, and my short hair curls well enough to want no papering.

Sunday.—My father is glad to hear so good an account of Edward's pigs, and desires he may be told, as encouragement to his taste for them, that Lord Bolton is particularly curious in *his* pigs, has had pigstyes of a most elegant construction built for them, and visits them every morning as soon as he rises.

This and the following letter contain allusions to Jane's wearing caps. Those intended for use at balls, &c. would be smart head-dresses, worn at that period by younger as well as older women. In later life, the Miss Austens seem to have been rather indifferent to fashion and beauty in their clothing, although always very neat.

Steventon: Tuesday [December 18, 1798].

I took the liberty a few days ago of asking your black velvet bonnet to lend me its cawl, which it very readily did, and by which I have been enabled to give a considerable improvement of dignity to my cap, which was before too *nidgetty* to please me. I shall wear it on Thursday, but I hope you will not be offended with me for following your advice as to its ornaments only in part. I still venture to retain the narrow silver round it, put twice round without any bow, and instead of the black military feather shall put in the coquelicot one as being smarter, and besides, coquelicot is to be all the fashion this winter. After the ball I shall probably make it entirely black.

I am sorry that our dear Charles begins to feel the dignity of ill-usage. My father will write to Admiral Gambier. He must have already received so much satisfaction from his acquaintance and patronage of Frank, that he will be delighted, I dare say, to have another of the family introduced to him.

I am very much obliged to my dear little George for his message—for his *love* at least; his *duty*, I suppose, was only in consequence of some hint of my favourable intentions towards him from his father or mother. I am sincerely rejoiced, however, that I ever was born, since it has been the means of procuring him a dish of tea. Give my best love to him.

I have received a very civil note from Mrs. Martin, requesting my name as a subscriber to her library, which opens January 14, and my name, or rather yours, is accordingly given. My mother finds the money. Mary subscribes too, which I am glad of, but hardly expected. As an inducement to subscribe, Mrs. Martin tells me that her collection is not to consist only of novels, but of every kind of literature, &c. She might have spared this pretension to *our* family, who are great novel-readers and not ashamed of being so; but it was necessary, I suppose, to the self-consequence of half her subscribers.

I enjoyed the hard black frosts of last week very much, and one day while they lasted walked to Deane by myself. I do not know that I ever did such a thing in my life before.

We dine now at half-past three, and have done dinner, I suppose, before you begin. We drink tea at half-past six. I am afraid you will despise us. My father reads Cowper to us in the morning, to which I listen when I can. How do you spend your evenings? I guess that Elizabeth works, that you read to her, and that Edward goes to sleep.

Wednesday.—I have changed my mind, and changed the trimmings of my cap this morning; they are now such as you suggested. I felt as if I should not prosper if I strayed from your directions, and I think it makes me look more like Lady Conyngham now than it did before, which is all that one lives for now. I believe I *shall* make my new gown like my robe, but the back of the latter is all in a piece with the tail, and will seven yards enable me to copy it in that respect?

People get so horribly poor and economical in this part of the world that I have no patience with them. Kent is the only place for happiness; everybody is rich there. I must do similar justice, however, to the Windsor neighbourhood.

Steventon: Monday night [December 24, 1798].

MY DEAR CASSANDRA,—I have got some pleasant news for you which I am eager to communicate, and therefore begin my letter sooner, though I shall not *send* it sooner than usual.

Admiral Gambier, in reply to my father's application, writes as follows:—'As it is usual to keep young officers in small vessels, it being most proper on account of their inexperience, and it being also a situation where they are more in the way of learning their duty, your son has been continued in the *Scorpion;* but I have mentioned to the Board of Admiralty his wish to be in a frigate, and when a proper opportunity offers and it is judged that he has taken his turn in a small ship, I hope he will be removed. With regard to your son now in the *London* I am glad I can give you the assurance that his promotion is likely to take place very soon, as Lord Spencer has been so good as to say he would include him in an arrangement that he proposes making in a short time relative to some promotions in that quarter.'

There! I may now finish my letter and go and hang myself, for I am sure I can neither write nor do anything which will not appear insipid to you after this. *Now*, I really think he will soon be made, and only wish we could communicate our foreknowledge of the event to him whom it principally concerns. My father has written to Daysh to desire that he will inform us, if he can, when the commission is sent. Your chief wish is now ready to be accomplished; and could Lord Spencer give happiness to Martha at the same time, what a joyful heart he would make of yours!

I have sent the same extract of the sweets of Gambier to Charles, who, poor fellow, though he sinks into nothing but an humble attendant on the hero of the piece, will, I hope, be contented with the prospect held out to him. By what the Admiral says, it appears as if he had been designedly kept in the *Scorpion*. But I will not torment myself with conjectures and suppositions; facts shall satisfy me.

Frank had not heard from any of us for ten weeks when he wrote me on November 12 in consequence of Lord St. Vincent being removed to Gibraltar. When his commission is sent, however, it will not be so long on its road as our letters, because all the

Government despatches are forwarded by land to his lordship from Lisbon with great regularity.

I spent my time [at Manydown] very quietly and very pleasantly with Catherine. Miss Blachford is agreeable enough. I do not want people to be very agreeable, as it saves me the trouble of liking them a great deal.

Our ball was very thin, but by no means unpleasant. There were thirty-one people, and only eleven ladies out of the number, and but five single women in the room. Of the gentlemen present you may have some idea from the list of my partners—Mr. Wood, G. Lefroy, Rice, a Mr. Butcher (belonging to the Temples, a sailor and not of the 11th Light Dragoons), Mr. Temple (not the horrid one of all), Mr. Wm. Orde (cousin to the Kingsclere man), Mr. John Harwood, and Mr. Calland, who appeared as usual with his hat in his hand, and stood every now and then behind Catherine and me to be talked to and abused for not dancing. We teased him, however, into it at last. I was very glad to see him again after so long a separation, and he was altogether rather the genius and flirt of the evening. He enquired after you.

There were twenty dances, and I danced them all, and without any fatigue. I was glad to find myself capable of dancing so much, and with so much satisfaction as I did; from my slender enjoyment of the Ashford balls (as assemblies for dancing) I had not thought myself equal to it, but in cold weather and with few couples I fancy I could just as well dance for a week together as for half an hour. My black cap was openly admired by Mrs. Lefroy, and secretly I imagine by everybody else in the room.

Tuesday.—I thank you for your long letter, which I will endeavour to deserve by writing the rest of this as closely as possible. I am full of joy at much of your information; that you should have been to a ball, and have danced at it, and supped with the Prince, and that you should meditate the purchase of a new muslin gown, are delightful circumstances.

Poor Edward! It is very hard that he, who has everything else in the world that he can wish for, should not have good health too.

I know no one more deserving of happiness without alloy than Edward is.

Of my charities to the poor since I came home you shall have a faithful account. I have given a pair of worsted stockings to Mary Hutchins, Dame Kew, Mary Steevens, and Dame Staples; a shift to Hannah Staples, and a shawl to Betty Dawkins; amounting in all to about half a guinea. But I have no reason to suppose that the *Battys* would accept of anything, because I have not made them the offer.

The Lords of the Admiralty will have enough of our applications at present, for I hear from Charles that he has written to Lord Spencer himself to be removed. I am afraid his Serene Highness will be in a passion, and order some of our heads to be cut off.

Steventon: Friday [December 28, 1798].

MY DEAR CASSANDRA,—Frank is made. He was yesterday raised to the rank of Commander, and appointed to the *Peterel* sloop, now at Gibraltar. A letter from Daysh has just announced this, and as it is confirmed by a very friendly one from Mr. Mathew to the same effect, transcribing one from Admiral Gambier to the General, we have no reason to suspect the truth of it.

As soon as you have cried a little for joy, you may go on, and learn farther that the India House have taken *Captain Austen's* petition into consideration—this comes from Daysh—and likewise that Lieutenant Charles John Austen is removed to the *Tamar* frigate—this comes from the Admiral. We cannot find out where the *Tamar* is, but I hope we shall now see Charles here at all events.

This letter is to be dedicated entirely to good news. If you will send my father an account of your washing and letter expenses, &c., he will send you a draft for the amount of it, as well as for your next quarter, and for Edward's rent. If you don't buy a muslin gown now on the strength of this money and Frank's promotion, I shall never forgive you.

Mrs. Lefroy has just sent me word that Lady Dorchester meant to invite me to her ball on January 8, which, though an humble blessing compared with what the last page records, I do not consider as any calamity.

I cannot write any more now, but I have written enough to make you very happy, and therefore may safely conclude.

Steventon: Tuesday [January 8, 1799].

I am tolerably glad to hear that Edward's income is a good one—as glad as I can be at anybody's being rich except you and me—and I am thoroughly rejoiced to hear of his present to you.

I assure you that I dread the idea of going to Brighton as much as you do, but I am not without hopes that something may happen to prevent it.

[*Wednesday.*]—You express so little anxiety about my being murdered under Ashe Park Copse by Mrs. Hulbert's servant, that I have a great mind not to tell you whether I was or not, and shall only say that I did not return home that night or the next, as Martha kindly made room for me in her bed, which was the shut-up one in the new nursery. Nurse and the child slept upon the floor, and there we all were in some confusion and great comfort. The bed did exceedingly well for us, both to lie awake in and talk till two o'clock, and to sleep in the rest of the night. I love Martha better than ever, and I mean to go and see her, if I can, when she gets home. We all dined at the Harwoods' on Thursday, and the party broke up the next morning.

My sweet little George! I am delighted to hear that he has such an inventive genius as to face-making. I admired his yellow wafer very much, and hope he will choose the wafer for your next letter. I wore my green shoes last night, and took my *white fan* with me; I am very glad he never threw it into the river.

Mrs. Knight giving up the Godmersham estate to Edward was no such prodigious act of generosity after all, it seems, for she has reserved herself an income out of it still; this ought to be known, that her conduct may not be overrated. I rather think Edward shows the most magnanimity of the two, in accepting her resignation with such incumbrances.

The more I write, the better my eye gets, so I shall at least keep on till it is quite well, before I give up my pen to my mother.

I do not think I was very much in request [at the Kempshot ball]. People were rather apt not to ask me till they could not help it; one's consequence, you know, varies so much at times without any particular reason. There was one gentleman, an officer of the Cheshire, a very good-looking young man, who, I was told, wanted very much to be introduced to me; but as he did not want it quite enough to take much trouble in effecting it, we never could bring it about.

I danced with Mr. John Wood again, twice with a Mr. South, a lad from Winchester, who, I suppose, is as far from being related to the bishop of that diocese as it is possible to be, with G. Lefroy, and J. Harwood, who I think takes to me rather more than he used to do. One of my gayest actions was sitting down two dances in preference to having Lord Bolton's eldest son for my partner, who danced too ill to be endured. The Miss Charterises were there, and played the parts of the Miss Edens with great spirit. Charles never came. Naughty Charles! I suppose he could not get superseded in time.

I do not wonder at your wanting to read *First Impressions* again, so seldom as you have gone through it, and that so long ago.

I *shall* be able to send this to the post to-day, which exalts me to the utmost pinnacle of human felicity, and makes me bask in the sunshine of prosperity, or gives me any other sensation of pleasure in studied language which you may prefer. Do not be angry with me for not filling my sheet, and believe me yours affectionately,

J. A.

Steventon: Monday [January 21, 1799].

Charles leaves us to-night. The *Tamar* is in the Downs, and Mr. Daysh advises him to join her there directly, as there is no chance of her going to the westward. Charles does not approve of this at all, and will not be much grieved if he should be too late for her before she sails, as he may then hope to get into a better station. He attempted to go to town last night, and got as far on his road thither as Deane Gate, but both the coaches were full, and we had the pleasure of seeing him back again.

Martha writes me word that Charles was very much admired at Kintbury, and Mrs. Lefroy never saw anyone so much improved in her life, and thinks him handsomer than Henry. He appears to far more advantage here than he did at Godmersham, not surrounded by strangers and neither oppressed by a pain in his face or powder in his hair.

Yesterday came a letter to my mother from Edward Cooper to announce, not the birth of a child, but of a living; for Mrs. Leigh has begged his acceptance of the Rectory of Hamstall-Ridware in Staffordshire, vacant by Mr. Johnson's death. We collect from his letter that he means to reside there, in which he shows his wisdom. Staffordshire is a good way off; so we shall see nothing more of them till, some fifteen years hence, the Miss Coopers are presented to us, fine, jolly, handsome, ignorant girls. The living is valued at £140 a year, but perhaps it may be improvable. How will they be able to convey the furniture of the dressing-room so far in safety?

Our first cousins seem all dropping off very fast. One is incorporated into the family, another dies, and a third goes into Staffordshire. . . .

[*Tuesday.*]—Our own particular brother got a place in the coach last night, and is now, I suppose, in town. I have no objection at all to your buying our gowns there, as your imagination has pictured to you exactly such a one as is necessary to make me happy. You quite abash me by your progress in notting, for I am still without silk. You must get me some in town or in Canterbury; it should be finer than yours.

I thought Edward would not approve of Charles being a crop, and rather wished you to conceal it from him at present, lest it might fall on his spirits and retard his recovery.

Wednesday.—I have just heard from Charles, who is by this time at Deal. He is to be Second Lieutenant, which pleases him very well. The *Endymion* is come into the Downs, which pleases him likewise. He expects to be ordered to Sheerness shortly, as the *Tamar* has never been refitted.

My father and mother made the same match for you last night, and are very much pleased with it. *He* is a beauty of my mother's.

CHAPTER IX.

THE LEIGH PERROTS AND BATH 1799-1800

MRS. AUSTEN'S brother, James Leigh Perrot, and his wife had for many years led a prosperous and uneventful life at Scarlets, enjoying the respect and friendship of a large circle of acquaintances. Scarlets was a small property on the Bath road, about thirty miles from London, adjoining the hamlet of Hare Hatch, where (as was often the case on a great highroad) a number of gentlemen's places of moderate size were congregated within easy reach of each other. Among those who sooner or later were neighbours of the Leigh Perrots were Maria Edgeworth's father Richard Lovell Edgeworth (who speaks of the help he received from Mr. Perrot in his experiments of telegraphing from Hare

Hatch to Nettlebed by means of windmills), and Thomas Day, the author of *Sandford and Merton*. The house at Scarlets in its then existing shape was the work of Mr. Leigh Perrot, and was of a suitable size for a childless couple in easy circumstances. Its owner had abilities which might have stood him in good stead in any profession, had he adopted one; and he was of a kind and affectionate disposition, combining an easy temper with ready wit, and much resolution of character. His wife was hardly formed for popularity, but she was highly respected. She was not exactly open-handed, but she had a great idea of the claims of family ties, and a keen sense of justice as between herself and others. The couple were unusually devoted to each other. The only crook in their lot appeared to be the constant gout attacks from which the husband suffered, and the necessity for frequent visits to Bath: visits, by the way, which had helped to give to their niece, Jane Austen, such good opportunities for studying the Bath varieties of human nature.

The journey, however, of the Austens to Bath in the spring of 1799 (described in our next letters) was independent of the Leigh Perrots. Edward Austen had been suffering, like his uncle, from gout, and determined to try the waters of Bath; his mother and Jane accompanying his family party thither. But the Perrots were already settled in Paragon Buildings when the Austens arrived, and the two families would be constantly meeting.

The Austens took up their quarters in Queen Square, which Jane seems to have liked much better than she made her Miss Musgroves like it when she wrote *Persuasion*, sixteen years later.

13 Queen Square: Friday [May 17, 1799].

MY DEAREST CASSANDRA,—Our journey yesterday went off exceedingly well; nothing occurred to alarm or delay us. We found the roads in excellent order, had very good horses all the way, and reached Devizes with ease by four o'clock. I suppose John has told you in what manner we were divided when we left Andover, and no alteration was afterwards made. At Devizes we had comfortable rooms and a good dinner, to which we sat down about five; amongst other things we had asparagus and a lobster, which made me wish for you, and some cheesecakes, on which the children made so delightful a supper as to endear the town of Devizes to them for a long time.

Well, here we are at Bath; we got here about one o'clock, and have been arrived just long enough to go over the house, fix on our rooms, and be very well pleased with the whole of it. Poor Elizabeth has had a dismal ride of it from Devizes, for it has rained almost all the way, and our first view of Bath has been just as gloomy as it was last November twelvemonth.

I have got so many things to say, so many things equally important, that I know not on which to decide at present, and shall therefore go and eat with the children.

We stopped in Paragon as we came along, but as it was too wet and dirty for us to get out, we could only see Frank, who told us that his master was very indifferent, but had had a better night last night than usual.

We are exceedingly pleased with the house; the rooms are quite as large as we expected. Mrs. Bromley is a fat woman in mourning, and a little black kitten runs about the staircase. Elizabeth has the apartment within the drawing-room; she wanted my mother to have it, but as there was no bed in the inner one, and the stairs are so much easier of ascent, or my mother so much stronger than in Paragon as not to regard the double flight, it is settled for us to be above, where we have two very nice-sized rooms, with dirty quilts and everything comfortable. I have the outward and larger apartment, as I ought to have; which is quite as large as our bed-room at home, and my mother's is not materially less. The beds are both as large as any at Steventon, and I have a very nice chest of drawers and a closet full of shelves—so full indeed that there is nothing else in it, and it should therefore be called a cupboard rather than a closet, I suppose.

There was a very long list of arrivals here in the newspaper yesterday, so that we need not immediately dread absolute solitude; and there is a public breakfast in Sydney Gardens every morning, so that we shall not be wholly starved.

Yours very affectionately,
JANE.

13 Queen Square: Sunday [June 2, 1799].

Flowers are very much worn, and fruit is still more the thing. Elizabeth has a bunch of strawberries, and I have seen grapes, cherries, plums, and apricots. There are likewise almonds and raisins, French plums, and tamarinds at the grocers', but I have never seen any of them in hats. A plum or greengage would cost three shillings; cherries and grapes about five, I believe, but this is at some of the dearest shops. My aunt has told me of a very cheap one, near Walcot Church, to which I shall go in quest of something for you. I have never seen an old woman at the pump-room.

I spent Friday evening with the Mapletons, and was obliged to submit to being pleased in spite of my inclination. We took a very charming walk from six to eight up Beacon Hill, and across some fields, to the village of Charlecombe, which is sweetly situated in a little green valley, as a village with such a name ought to be. Marianne is sensible and intelligent, and even Jane, considering how fair she is, is not unpleasant. We had a Miss North and a Mr. Gould of our party; the latter walked home with me after tea. He is a very young man, just entered Oxford, wears spectacles, and has heard that *Evelina* was written by Dr. Johnson.

There is to be a grand gala on Tuesday evening in Sydney Gardens, a concert, with illuminations and fireworks. To the latter Elizabeth and I look forward with pleasure, and even the concert will have more than its usual charm for me, as the gardens are large enough for me to get pretty well beyond the reach of its sound. In the morning Lady Willoughby is to present the colours to some corps, or Yeomanry, or other, in the Crescent.

13 Queen Square: Tuesday [June 11, 1799].

I would not let Martha read *First Impressions* again upon any account, and am very glad that I did not leave it in your power. She is very cunning, but I saw through her design; she means to publish it from memory, and one more perusal must enable her to do it. As for *Fitz-Albini*, when I get home she shall have it, as soon as ever she will own that Mr. Elliott is handsomer than Mr. Lance, that fair men are preferable to black; for I mean to take every opportunity of rooting out her prejudices.

I am very glad you liked my lace, and so are you, and so is Martha, and we are all glad together. I have got your cloak home, which is quite delightful—as delightful at least as half the circumstances which are called so.

I do not know what is the matter with me to-day, but I cannot write quietly; I am always wandering away into some exclamation or other. Fortunately I have nothing very particular to say.

Fanny desires her love to you, her love to grandpapa, her love to Anna, and her love to Hannah; the latter is particularly to be remembered. Edward desires his love to you, to grandpapa, to Anna, to little Edward, to Aunt James and Uncle James, and he hopes all your turkeys and ducks, and chicken and guinea fowls are very well; and he wishes you very much to send him a printed letter, and so does Fanny—and they both rather think they shall answer it.

13 Queen Square: Wednesday [June 19, 1799].

Last Sunday we all drank tea in Paragon; my uncle is still in his flannels, but is getting better again.

Last night we were in Sydney Gardens again, as there was a repetition of the gala which went off so ill on the 4th. We did not go till nine, and then were in very good time for the fireworks, which were really beautiful, and surpassing my expectation; the illuminations too were very pretty. The weather was as favourable as it was otherwise a fortnight ago. The play on Saturday is, *I hope*, to conclude our gaieties here, for nothing but a lengthened stay will make it otherwise. We go with Mrs. Fellowes.

The Austens quitted Bath on Wednesday, June 26, reaching Steventon on the following day, and leaving the Leigh Perrots to an unexpected fate—which they had done nothing whatever to deserve.

On Thursday, August 8, Mrs. Leigh Perrot went into a milliner's shop at the corner of Bath and Stall Streets, kept by a certain Mrs. Gregory (but known as Smith's), and bought a piece of *black* lace. She paid for it, and took it away wrapped up in a piece of paper. After leaving the shop, Mrs. Perrot met her husband and strolled about with him. As they re-passed the same shop a quarter of an hour later, Mrs. Gregory rushed out and accused Mrs. Perrot of having in her possession a piece of *white* lace. Mrs. Perrot replied that if so it must have been put up in her parcel by mistake. She then handed her parcel to Mrs. Gregory to examine, when a piece of *white* lace was found therein as well as a piece of *black*. Mrs. Gregory at once accused Mrs. Perrot of having stolen it, and, refusing to listen to any protest, made off with the incriminating piece of lace. A little later, as the Perrots were turning the corner of the Abbey Churchyard, Charles Filby, the shop assistant who had actually sold the black lace, came up and asked Mr. Perrot his name. Mr. Perrot replied that he lived at No. 1 Paragon Buildings, and that his name was on the door.

On the same day, Mrs. Gregory and Filby went to the town hall to lay information before the magistrates; but found them so busily engaged in dealing with the excesses of the soldiers who were at that time passing through Bath, that the information could not be taken before August 14. Meanwhile, the piece of *white* lace was lodged—at any rate, for the night of August 8—at the house of a certain printer named Gye.

The result of the magistrates' inquiry may be discovered in *The Times* of August 20, where we read:—

The Lady of a Gentleman of Bath, possessed of a good fortune, and respected by a numerous circle of acquaintance, was committed on Thursday by G. Chapman, Esq., the Mayor, to the County Gaol at Ilchester, on a charge of privately stealing a card of lace from a haberdasher's shop.

As Mrs. Perrot did not come up for trial until the end of the following March, she had to undergo a long and trying confinement. It appears that she was not lodged actually in the gaol, but in some neighbouring house, kept by a man of the name of Scadding.

The charge was a monstrous one; the accused had ample means to indulge every wish, and nothing short of lunacy (of which she never showed the slightest sign) could have induced her to commit so petty a theft. Her high character and the absence of motive combined to render it incredible, and, had she been capable of such a deed, she would not have courted detection by walking quietly past the shop, a quarter of an hour later, with the parcel in her hand. There were also strong reasons for thinking that the accusation was the result of a deep-laid plot. Gye, the printer, who lived in the market-place, was believed to be the chief instigator. His character was indifferent, and he had money invested in Gregory's shop; and the business was in so bad a way that there was a temptation to seek for some large haul by way of blackmail. Mrs. Leigh Perrot was selected as the victim, people thought, because her husband was so extremely devoted to her that he would be sure to do anything to save her from the least vexation. If so, the conspirators were mistaken in their man. Mr. Perrot resolved to see the matter through, and, taking no notice of the many suggestions as to hush-money that were apparently circulated, engaged the best counsel possible, secured his most influential acquaintance as witnesses to his wife's character, and spent the terrible intervening period in confinement with her at Ilchester. He was well aware that the criminal law of England, as it then existed, made the lot of untried prisoners as hard, and the difficulty of proving their innocence as great, as possible; he knew also that in the seething disquiet of men's minds, brought about by the French Revolution, it was quite possible they might encounter a jury anxious to cast discredit on the well-to-do classes. He was therefore prepared for a failure of justice; and, we are told, had arranged that in case of an adverse verdict, followed by transportation, he would sell his property and accompany his wife across the seas.

Among the warmest supporters of the Leigh Perrots was Mr. Morris—a lawyer of eminence, well used to dealing with evidence, but now living as an invalid at Bath. He was a total stranger to the accused, but maintained most energetically that, apart from her well-known character, the nature of the evidence adduced against her would have been sufficient to prove her innocence.

The amazement and indignation of the Steventon party may be imagined. They were too sensible to believe that so mean and objectless a crime should really have been committed by a respectable woman—a near relation of their own, whom they knew intimately; but it was not easy to determine how to show their sympathy. Mr. and Mrs. Austen seem at last to have come (no doubt with their daughters' good-will) to the momentous decision mentioned in the following letter, which was addressed to Mrs. Leigh Perrot on January 11, 1800, by her cousin, Montague Cholmeley.

You tell me that your good sister Austen has offered you one or both of her daughters to continue with you during your stay in that vile place, but you decline the kind offer, as you cannot procure them accommodation in the house with you, and you cannot let those elegant young women be your inmates in a prison, nor be subjected to the inconveniences which you are obliged to put up with.

So Cassandra and Jane just escaped a residence in gaol and contact with criminals.

Another letter written about this time must have given much pleasure to the Leigh Perrots:—

White Hart, Bath. [No date.]

HONORED SIR,—You may have forgot your old postillon Ben Dunford but I shall never forget yours and my mistresses great goodness to me when I was taken with the small pox in your sarvice. You sent me very careful to mothers, and paid a nurse and my doctor, and my board for a long time as I was bad, and when I was too bad with biles all over my head so as I could not go to sarvice for a many weeks you maintained me. the famaly as I lives with be a going thro' Bath into Devonshire and we stops two days at the Inn and there I heard of the bad trick as those bad shopkeepers has sarved my mistress and I took the libarty of going to your house to enquire how you both do and the housekeeper said she sent a pasel to you every week and if I had anything to say she could send a letter. I hope Honored Sir you will forgive my taking such a libarty to write but I wish anybody could tell me how to do you and mistress any good. I would travel night and day to serve you both. I be at all times with my humble duty to mistress and you Honored Sir your dutifull sarvant

BEN DUNFORD.

James Leigh Perrot Esq.

The trial took place at Taunton on Saturday, March 29. The old Castle Hall—where Judge Jeffreys once sat on his 'Bloody Assizes'—said to be capable of containing 2000 persons, was filled at an early hour. So urgent was the curiosity, even of the Bar, that the 'Nisi Prius' Court, which stood at the opposite end of the hall, was not opened for business that morning—all the counsel on the circuit surrounding the table of the Crown Bar; while the rest of the hall was thronged with anxious spectators, many hundreds of whom could not possibly have heard a word that was said, and were almost crushed to death and suffocated with heat. Between seven and eight o'clock, Mrs. Leigh Perrot, who had been conveyed from Ilchester, appeared in the dock, attended by Mr. Leigh Perrot and three ladies, and the proceedings commenced.

After the evidence for the prosecution was closed, the prisoner was invited by the judge to make her defence.

She attempted to address the Court; but, after speaking a few sentences, became so much agitated that her voice failed her; whereupon Mr. Jekyll, one of her counsel, was requested to repeat to the Court what she wished to address to them. She then dictated as follows:—

MY LORD AND GENTLEMEN OF THE JURY,—

I am informed by my counsel, that they cannot be permitted to offer any observations to you on my case. The circumstances of it do not render it necessary to detain you long. I shall therefore take this opportunity of troubling you with a few words.

Placed in a situation the most eligible that any woman could desire, with supplies so ample that I was left rich after every wish was gratified; blessed in the affections of the most generous man as a husband, what could induce me to commit such a crime? Depraved indeed must that mind be that under such circumstances could be so culpable.

You will hear from my noble and truly respectable friends what has been my conduct and character for a long series of years; you will hear what has been, and what is now, their opinion of me. Can you suppose that disposition so totally altered, as to lose all recollection of the situation I held in society—to hazard for this meanness my character and reputation, or to endanger the health and peace of mind of a husband whom I would die for?

Here her voice faltered; she seemed to be on the point of fainting, and Mr. Leigh Perrot, who had sustained all this trying scene with wonderful resolution, put his handkerchief to his face and wept in agony; many persons in Court, even amongst the counsel, participating in his emotion.

The prisoner continued:—

You have heard their evidence against me. I shall make no comment upon it—I shall leave that task where I am certain it will be executed with justice and mercy. I know my own oath in this case is inadmissible, but I call upon that God whom we all adore to attest that I am innocent of this charge, and may He reward or punish me as I speak true or false in denying it. I call that God to witness that I did not know that I had the lace in my possession, nor did I know it when Mrs. Gregory accosted me in the street. I have nothing more to add.

Then followed the evidence for the prisoner, which was chiefly evidence to character, and came from persons occupying prominent positions who knew her well, either at her Berkshire home or at Bath.

The judge's summing up occupied nearly an hour. In it he said that it was impossible that any person should have a higher character than the prisoner; but if the jury were satisfied with the evidence for the prosecution and believed it, that character ought not to avail her. If, however, upon taking all the circumstances of the case into consideration, the jury should see any reason to disbelieve the witnesses for the prosecution, or which led them to doubt of the prisoner's guilt, they should recollect the very excellent character which had been given her, and in that case it ought to bear great weight with them towards an acquittal. He also alluded to the conduct of the accused after leaving the shop as not being that of a guilty person, and commented on the ease with which she could have secreted the parcel before it was discovered.

The jury evidently saw great reason to disbelieve the witnesses for the prosecution, and, after only fifteen minutes, returned a verdict of 'Not Guilty.'

The *Star* tells us that 'the trial lasted seven hours, and the scene of the acquittal was extremely affecting; the agitation and embraces of Mr. and Mrs. Perrot may be more easily conceived than described. The Court was crowded with elegantly dressed women.'

Throughout the long months over which the affair extended, the Leigh Perrots had acted as persons convinced of the baselessness of the charge, and determined to confront the accusers, and, as far as the existing state of the law allowed, to establish the innocence of the accused.

Among the quantity of congratulatory letters received by Mr. Leigh Perrot, we must content ourselves with quoting the following from Mr. R. L. Edgeworth:—

Edgeworthstown, Ireland: [April 7, 1800.]

MY DEAR SIR,—I do not think that I ever felt so much astonishment or indignation as at the abominable transaction which was related in the *Star* of March 31st.

Among my numerous friends and acquaintance, if there was a couple whom I could have selected as the farthest removed from being the objects of such a villainous attack it would have been yourselves! But I too well know, that neither perfect innocence nor consummate prudence are sufficient shields against conspiracy and folly, and that bankrupt fortune and bankrupt character prepare men for the most desperate attempts.

I trouble you, my Dear Sir, with a few lines to express the deep sense that I have of regard and esteem for you and the amiable partner of your happiness; for so many as thirty-four years we have been acquainted, and during that time I do not think that I have met any man of such singularly nice feelings of honour and justice.

I am sensible that there is some impropriety in this address—but you must excuse it as I snatched this piece of paper the moment I had read the paragraph I allude to—and with tears of indignation in my eyes—aye Sir!—with actual, not sentimental, tears in my eyes I sat down to write to you.

Perhaps, after all, you are not the objects of this transaction!

Even if that should be the fact you will pardon me for renewing my claim to your remembrance and for assuring you that you possess my esteem and affection.

Yours sincerely,
RICHD LOVELL EDGEWORTH.

James Leigh Perrot, Esq., Bath, England.

This strange and painful episode in the life of the family was thus brought to a satisfactory ending. An accusation of petty and purposeless theft had been made against a woman whose uprightness was known to all those around her; a wife who enjoyed (then and always) the absolute confidence of an upright husband. It had been found baseless by a jury after only a few minutes' deliberation; and the Leigh Perrots had the pleasure of seeing the high estimation in which they were held by their neighbours exhibited in a strong light. This estimation was to be theirs for the remainder of their lives, extending in his case over seventeen, and in hers over thirty-five years. For our particular purpose the story seems worth narrating, because it shows that the peaceful and well-ordered progress of Jane Austen's life was not beyond the reach of tragic possibilities. Indeed, at or near this time there were three particular occurrences which, when taken together, might well disturb the serenity and cheerfulness of her mind, and indispose her for writing—especially writing of a humorous character. One of these events, which has already been recorded, was her love story in the West; another was Mrs. Leigh Perrot's trouble; and the third—the loss of her old home—will form part of the subject of the next two chapters.

CHAPTER X.

CHANGE OF HOME 1800-1801

THOUGH we can guess what was constantly occupying the thoughts of the Austens in the autumn and winter of 1799-1800, nothing remains to tell us how they employed themselves during these anxious months. Perhaps the sisters were at home, and exchanged no letters; but had any been written, we may be pretty sure they would be among those destroyed by Cassandra. When we meet the family again, in October 1800, we find that they have returned to everyday life with its little incidents, its duties, and its pleasures; that Edward and his eldest son have lately left Steventon for Godmersham, taking Cassandra with them, and that Jane is remaining at home with her parents.

Steventon: Saturday evening [October 25, 1800].

MY DEAR CASSANDRA,— . . . You have had a very pleasant journey of course, and have found Elizabeth and all the children very well on your arrival at Godmersham, and I congratulate you on it. Edward is rejoicing this evening, I dare say, to find himself once more at home, from which he fancies he has been absent a great while. His son left behind him the very fine chestnuts which had been selected for planting at Godmersham, and the drawing of his own which he had intended to carry to George; the former will therefore be deposited in the soil of Hampshire instead of Kent, the latter I have already consigned to another element.

We have been exceedingly busy ever since you went away. In the first place we have had to rejoice two or three times every day at your having such very delightful weather for the whole of your journey, and in the second place we have been obliged to take advantage of the very delightful weather ourselves by going to see almost all our neighbours.

On Thursday we walked to Deane, yesterday to Oakley Hall and Oakley, and to-day to Deane again. At Oakley Hall we did a great deal—eat some sandwiches all over mustard, admired Mr. Bramston's porter, and Mrs. Bramston's transparencies, and gained a promise from the latter of two roots of heartsease, one all yellow and the other all purple, for you. At Oakley we bought ten pair of worsted stockings and a shift; the shift is for Betty Dawkins, as we find she wants it more than a rug; she is one of the most grateful of all whom Edward's charity has reached, or at least she expresses herself more warmly than the rest, for she sends him a 'sight of thanks.'

This morning we called at the Harwoods', and in their dining-room found 'Heathcote and Chute for ever'—Mrs. William Heathcote and Mrs. Chute—the first of whom took a long ride yesterday morning with Mrs. Harwood into Lord Carnarvon's park, and fainted away in the evening, and the second walked down from Oakley Hall attended by Mrs. Augusta Bramston; they had meant to come on to Steventon afterwards, but we knew a trick worth two of that.

James called by my father's desire on Mr. Bayle to inquire into the cause of his being so horrid. Mr. Bayle did not attempt to deny his being horrid, and made many apologies for it; he did not plead his having a drunken self, he talked only of a drunken foreman, &c., and gave hopes of the tables being at Steventon on Monday se'nnight next. We have had no letter since you left us, except one from Mr. Serle, of Bishopstoke, to inquire the character of James Elton.

Sunday.—Our improvements have advanced very well; the bank along the *elm walk* is sloped down for the reception of thorns and lilacs, and it is settled that the other side of the path is to continue turfed, and to be planted with beech, ash, and larch.

Steventon: Saturday [November 1, 1800].

You have written, I am sure, though I have received no letter from you since your leaving London; the post, and not yourself, must have been unpunctual.

We have at last heard from Frank; a letter came from him to you yesterday, and I mean to send it on as soon as I can get a ditto (*that* means a frank), which I hope to do in a day or two. *En attendant*, you must rest satisfied with knowing that on the 8th of July the *Peterel* with the rest of the Egyptian squadron was off the Isle of Cyprus, whither they went from Jaffa for provisions, &c., and whence they were to sail in a day or two for Alexandria, there to wait the result of the English proposals for the evacuation of Egypt. The rest of the letter, according to the present fashionable style of composition, is chiefly descriptive. Of his promotion he knows nothing; of prizes he is guiltless.

Did you think of our ball [probably at Basingstoke] on Thursday evening, and did you suppose me at it? You might very safely, for there I was. On Wednesday morning it was settled that Mrs. Harwood, Mary, and I should go together, and shortly afterwards a very civil note of invitation for me came from Mrs. Bramston, who wrote I believe as soon as she knew of the ball. I might likewise have gone with Mrs. Lefroy, and therefore, with three methods of going, I must have been more at the ball than anyone else. I dined and slept at Deane; Charlotte and I did my hair, which I fancy looked very indifferent; nobody abused it, however, and I retired delighted with my success.

It was a pleasant ball, and still more good than pleasant, for there were nearly sixty people, and sometimes we had seventeen couple. The Portsmouths, Dorchesters, Boltons, Portals, and Clerks were there, and all the meaner and more usual &c., &c.'s. There was a scarcity of men in general, and a still greater scarcity of any that were good for much. I danced nine dances out of ten—five with Stephen Terry, T. Chute, and James Digweed, and four with Catherine. There was commonly a couple of ladies standing up together, but not often any so amiable as ourselves.

You were inquired after very prettily, and I hope the whole assembly now understands that you are gone into Kent, which the families in general seemed to meet in ignorance of. Lord Portsmouth surpassed the rest in his attentive recollection of you, inquired more into the length of your absence, and concluded by desiring to be 'remembered to you when I wrote next.'

Lady Portsmouth had got a different dress on, and Lady Bolton is much improved by a wig. The three Miss Terries were there, but no Annie; which was a great disappointment to me. I hope the poor girl had not set her heart on her appearance that evening so much as I had. Mr. Terry is ill, in a very low way. I said civil things for Edward to Mr. Chute, who amply returned them by declaring that, had he known of my brother's being at Steventon, he should have made a point of calling upon him to thank him for his civility about the Hunt.

Steventon: Saturday evening [November 8, 1800].

Having just finished *Les Veillées du Château* I think it a good opportunity for beginning a letter to you while my mind is stored with ideas worth transmitting.

I thank you for so speedy a return to my two last, and particularly thank you for your anecdote of Charlotte Graham and her cousin, Harriet Bailey, which has very much amused both my mother and myself. If you can learn anything farther of that interesting affair, I hope you will mention it. I have two messages; let me get rid of them, and then my paper will be my own. Mary fully intended writing to you by Mr. Chute's frank, and only happened entirely to forget it, but will write soon; and my father wishes Edward to send him a memorandum in your next letter of the price of the hops. The tables are come, and give general contentment. I had not expected that they would so perfectly suit the fancy of us all three, or that we should so well agree in the disposition of them; but nothing except their own surface can have been smoother. The two ends put together form one constant table for everything, and the centre piece stands exceedingly well under the glass, and holds a great deal most commodiously, without looking awkwardly. They are both covered with green baize, and send their best love. The Pembroke has got its destination by the sideboard, and my mother has great delight in keeping her money and papers locked up. The little table which used to stand there has most conveniently taken itself off into the best bedroom; and we are now in want only of the chiffonniere, which is neither finished nor come. So much for that subject; I now come to another, of a very different nature, as other subjects are very apt to be. Earle Harwood has been again giving uneasiness to his family and talk to the neighbourhood; in the present instance, however, he is only unfortunate, and not in fault.

About ten days ago, in cocking a pistol in the guard-room at Marcau (?) he accidentally shot himself through the thigh. Two young Scotch surgeons in the island were polite enough to propose taking off the thigh at once, but to that he would not consent; and accordingly in his wounded state was put on board a cutter and conveyed to Haslar Hospital, at Gosport, where the bullet was extracted, and where he now is, I hope, in a fair way of doing well. The surgeon of the hospital wrote to the family on the occasion, and John Harwood went down to him immediately, attended by James, whose object in going was to be the means of bringing back the earliest intelligence to Mr. and Mrs. Harwood, whose anxious sufferings, particularly those of the latter, have of course been dreadful. They went down on Tuesday, and James came back the next day, bringing such favourable accounts as greatly to lessen the distress of the family at Deane, though it will probably be a long while before Mrs. Harwood can be quite at ease. *One* most material comfort, however, they have: the assurance of its being really an accidental wound, which is not only positively declared by Earle himself, but is likewise testified by the particular direction of the bullet. Such a wound could not have been received in a duel. At present he is going on very well, but the surgeon will not declare him to be in no danger. . . . James had not time at Gosport to take any other steps towards seeing Charles, than the very few which conducted him to the door of the assembly room in the Inn, where there happened to be a Ball on the night of their arrival; a likely spot enough for the discovery of a Charles: but I am glad to say that he was not of the party, for it was in general a very ungenteel one, and there was hardly a pretty girl in the room.

Yesterday was a day of great business with me; Mary drove me all in the rain to Basingstoke, and still more all in the rain back again, because it rained harder; and soon after our return to Deane a sudden invitation and an own postchaise took us to Ashe Park to dine *tête-à-tête* with Mr. Holder, Mr. Gauntlet, and James Digweed; but our *tête-à-tête* was cruelly reduced by the non-attendance of the two latter. We had a very quiet evening. I believe Mary found it dull, but I thought it very pleasant. To sit in idleness over a good fire in a well-proportioned room is a luxurious sensation. Sometimes we talked, and sometimes we were quite silent; I said two or three amusing things, and Mr. Holder made a few infamous puns.

Mr. Heathcote met with a genteel little accident the other day in hunting; he got off to lead his horse over a hedge, or a house, or something, and his horse in his haste trod upon his leg, or rather ancle, I believe, and it is not certain whether the small bone is not broke.

. . . Martha has accepted Mary's invitation for Lord Portsmouth's ball. He has not yet sent out his *own* invitations, but *that* does not signify; Martha comes, and a ball there must be. I think it will be too early in her mother's absence for me to return with her.

Sunday Evening.—We have had a dreadful storm of wind in the fore part of this day, which has done a great deal of mischief among our trees. I was sitting alone in the dining-room when an odd kind of crash startled me—in a moment afterwards it was repeated; descend into the Sweep!!!!! The other, which had fallen, I suppose, in the first crash, and which was the nearest to the pond, taking a more easterly direction, sunk among our screen of chestnuts and firs, knocking down one spruce-fir, beating off the head of another, and stripping the two corner chestnuts of several branches in its fall. This is not all. One large elm out of the two on the left-hand side as you enter what I call the elm walk, was likewise blown down; the maypole bearing the weathercock was broke in two, and what I regret more than all the rest is, that all the three elms which grew in Hall's meadow, and gave such ornament to it, are gone; two were blown down, and the other so much injured that it cannot stand. I am happy to add, however, that no greater evil than the loss of trees has been the consequence of the storm in this place, or in our immediate neighbourhood. We grieve, therefore, in some comfort.

Mr. Holder's paper tells us that some time in last August Captain Austen and the *Peterel* were very active in securing a Turkish ship (driven into Port in Cyprus by bad weather) from the French. He was forced to burn her, however.

I am yours ever,
J. A.

Next in order comes a letter to Martha Lloyd:—

Steventon: Wednesday evening [November 12, 1800].

MY DEAR MARTHA,—I did not receive your note yesterday till after Charlotte had left Deane, or I would have sent my answer by her, instead of being the means, as I now must be, of lessening the elegance of your new dress for the Hurstbourne ball by the value of 3*d*. You are very good in wishing to see me at Ibthorp so soon, and I am equally good in wishing to come to you. I believe our merit in that respect is much upon a par, our self-denial mutually strong. Having paid this tribute of praise to the virtue of both, I shall here have done with panegyric, and proceed to plain matter of fact. In about a fortnight's time I hope to be with you. I have two reasons for not being able to come before. I wish so to arrange my visit as to spend some days with you after your mother's return. In the 1st place, that I may have the pleasure of seeing her, and in the 2nd, that I may have a better chance of bringing you back with me. Your promise in my favour was not quite absolute, but if your will is not perverse, you and I will do all in our power to overcome your scruples of conscience. I hope we shall meet next week to talk all this over, till we have tired ourselves with the very idea of my visit before my visit begins. Our invitations for the 19th are arrived, and very curiously are they worded. Mary mentioned to you yesterday poor Earle's unfortunate accident, I dare say. He does not seem to be going on very well. The two or three last posts have brought less and less favourable accounts of him. John Harwood has gone to Gosport again to-day. We have two families of friends now who are in a most anxious state; for though by a note from Catherine this morning there seems now to be a revival of hope at Manydown, its continuance may be too reasonably doubted. Mr. Heathcote, however, who has broken the small bone of his leg, is so good as to be going on very well. It would be really too much to have three people to care for.

You distress me cruelly by your request about books. I cannot think of any to bring with me, nor have I any idea of our wanting them. I come to you to be talked to, not to read or hear reading; I can do that at home; and indeed I am now laying in a stock of intelligence to pour out on you as my share of the conversation. I am reading Henry's *History of England*, which I will repeat to you in any manner you may prefer, either in a loose, desultory, unconnected stream, or dividing my recital, as the historian divides it himself, into seven parts:—The Civil and Military: Religion: Constitution: Learning and Learned Men: Arts and Sciences: Commerce, Coins, and Shipping: and Manners. So that for every evening in the week there will be a different subject. The Friday's lot—Commerce, Coins, and Shipping—you will find the least entertaining; but the next evening's portion will make amends. With such a provision on my part, if you will do yours by repeating the French Grammar, and Mrs. Stent will now and then ejaculate some wonder about the cocks and hens, what can we want? Farewell for a short time. We all unite in best love, and I am your very affectionate

J. A.

The Hurstbourne ball took place on November 19, and was graced by the presence of Lieutenant Charles Austen. He had distinguished himself on the *Endymion*, especially in the capture of the *Scipio* in a heavy gale. His ship was now at Portsmouth waiting for orders.

Steventon: Thursday [November 20, 1800].

MY DEAR CASSANDRA,—Your letter took me quite by surprise this morning; you are very welcome, however, and I am very much obliged to you. I believe I drank too much wine last night at Hurstbourne; I know not how else to account for the shaking of my hand to-day. You will kindly make allowance therefore for any indistinctness of writing, by attributing it to this venial error.

Naughty Charles did not come on Tuesday, but good Charles came yesterday morning. About two o'clock he walked in on a Gosport hack. His feeling equal to such a fatigue is a good sign, and his feeling no fatigue in it a still better. He walked down to Deane to dinner; he danced the whole evening, and to-day is no more tired than a gentleman ought to be.

Your desire to hear from me on Sunday will, perhaps, bring you a more particular account of the ball than you may care for, because one is prone to think much more of such things the morning after they happen, than when time has entirely driven them out of one's recollection.

It was a pleasant evening; Charles found it remarkably so, but I cannot tell why, unless the absence of Miss Terry, towards whom his conscience reproaches him with being now perfectly indifferent, was a relief to him. There were only twelve dances, of which I danced nine, and was merely prevented from dancing the rest by the want of a partner. We began at ten, supped at one, and were at Deane before five. There were but fifty people in the room; very few families indeed from our side of the county, and not many more from the other. My partners were the two St. Johns, Hooper, Holder, and very prodigious Mr. Mathew, with whom I called the last, and whom I liked the best of my little stock.

There were very few beauties, and such as there were not very handsome. Miss Iremonger did not look well, and Mrs. Blount was the only one much admired. She appeared exactly as she did in September, with the same broad face, diamond bandeau, white shoes, pink husband, and fat neck. The two Miss Coxes were there; I traced in one the remains of the vulgar, broad-featured girl who danced at Enham eight years ago; the other is refined into a nice, composed-looking girl, like Catherine Bigg. I looked at Sir Thomas Champneys and thought of poor Rosalie; I looked at his daughter, and thought her a queer animal with a white neck.

Mary said that I looked very well last night. I wore my aunt's gown and handkerchief, and my hair was at least tidy, which was all my ambition. I will now have done with the ball, and I will moreover go and dress for dinner.

The young lady whom it is expected that Sir Thomas is to marry is Miss Emma Wabshaw; she lives somewhere between Southampton and Winchester, is handsome, accomplished, amiable, and everything but rich. He is certainly finishing his house in a great hurry. Perhaps the report of his being to marry a Miss Fanshawe might originate in his attentions to this very lady—the names are not unlike.

The three Digweeds all came on Tuesday, and we played a pool at commerce. James Digweed left Hampshire to-day. I think he must be in love with you, from his anxiety to have you go to the Faversham balls, and likewise from his supposition that the two elms fell from their grief at your absence. Was not it a gallant idea? It never occurred to me before, but I dare say it was so.

I rejoice to say that we have just had another letter from our dear Frank. It is to you, very short, written from Larnica in Cyprus, and so lately as October 2nd. He came from Alexandria, and was to return there in three or four days, knew nothing of his promotion, and does not write above twenty lines, from a doubt of the letter's ever reaching you, and an idea of all letters being opened at Vienna. He wrote a few days before to you from Alexandria by the *Mercury* sent with despatches to Lord Keith. Another letter must be owing to us besides this, *one* if not *two;* because none of these are to me. Henry comes to-morrow, for one night only.

The visit to Ibthorp came off, as is shown by the following letter:—

Ibthorp: Sunday [November 30, 1800].

MY DEAR CASSANDRA,—Shall you expect to hear from me on Wednesday or not? I think you will, or I should not write, as the three days and half which have passed since my last letter have not produced many materials towards filling another sheet of paper. But, like Mr. Hastings, 'I do not despair,' and you perhaps, like the faithful Maria, may feel still more certain of the happy event. I have been here ever since a quarter after three on Thursday last, by the Shrewsbury clock, which I am fortunately enabled absolutely to ascertain because Mrs. Stent once lived at Shrewsbury, or at least at Tewksbury. I have the pleasure of thinking myself a very welcome guest, and the pleasure of spending my time very pleasantly. Martha looks well, and wants me to find out that she grows fat; but I cannot carry my complaisance farther than to believe whatever she asserts on the subject. Mrs. Stent gives us quite as much of her company as we wish for, and rather more than she used to do; but perhaps not more than is to our advantage in the end, because it is too dirty even for such desperate walkers as Martha and I to get out of doors, and we are therefore confined to each other's society from morning till night, with very little variety of books or gowns. Three of the Miss Debaries called here the morning after my arrival, but I have not yet been able to return their civility. You know it is not an uncommon circumstance in this parish to have the road from Ibthorp to the Parsonage much dirtier and more impracticable for walking than the road from the Parsonage to Ibthorp. I left my Mother very well when I came away, and left her with strict orders to continue so.

The endless Debaries are of course very well acquainted with the lady who is to marry Sir Thomas, and all her family. I pardon them, however, as their description of her is favourable. Mrs. Wapshire is a widow, with several sons and daughters, a good fortune, and a house in Salisbury; where Miss Wapshire has been for many years a distinguished beauty. She is now seven or eight and twenty, and tho' still handsome, less handsome than she has been. This promises better than the bloom of seventeen; and in addition to this they say that she has always been remarkable for the propriety of her behaviour distinguishing her far above the general classes of town misses, and rendering her of course very unpopular among them.

Martha has promised to return with me, and our plan is to have a nice black frost for walking to Whitchurch, and then throw ourselves into a post chaise, one upon the other, our heads hanging out at one door and our feet at the opposite one. If you have never heard that Miss Dawes has been married these two months, I will mention it in my next. Pray do not forget to go to the Canterbury Ball; I shall despise you all most insufferably if you do.

I have charged my myrmidons to send me an account of the Basingstoke Ball; I have placed my spies at different places that they may collect the more; and by so doing, by sending Miss Bigg to the Town-hall itself, and posting my mother at Steventon I hope to derive from their various observations a good general idea of the whole.

Miss Austen, Yours ever,
Godmersham Park, J. A.
Faversham, Kent.

While Jane was away on this visit, Mr. and Mrs. Austen came to a momentous decision—namely, to leave Steventon and retire to Bath. There can be little doubt that the decision was a hasty one. Some of Jane's previous letters contain details of the very considerable improvements that her father had just begun in the Rectory garden; and we do not hear that these improvements were concerted with the son who was to be his successor. So hasty, indeed, did Mr. Austen's decision appear to the Perrots that they suspected the reason to be a growing attachment between Jane and one of the three Digweed brothers. There is not the slightest evidence of this very improbable supposition in Jane's letters, though she *does* occasionally suggest that James Digweed must be in love with Cassandra, especially when he gallantly supposed that the two elms had fallen from grief at her absence. On the whole it seems most probable that Mrs. Austen's continued ill-health was the reason for the change.

Tradition says that when Jane returned home accompanied by Martha Lloyd, the news was abruptly announced by her mother, who thus greeted them: 'Well, girls, it is all settled; we have decided to leave Steventon in such a week, and go to Bath'; and that the shock of the intelligence was so great to Jane that she fainted away. Unfortunately, there is no further direct evidence to show how far Jane's feelings resembled those she has attributed to Marianne Dashwood on leaving Norland; but we have the negative evidence arising from the fact that none of her letters are preserved between November 30, 1800, and January 3, 1801, although Cassandra was at Godmersham during the whole of the intervening month. Silence on the part of Jane to Cassandra for so long a period of absence is unheard of: and according to the rule acted on by Cassandra, destruction of her sister's letters was a proof of their emotional interest. We cannot doubt, therefore, that she wrote in a strain unusual for her more than once in that month; but as she says of Elizabeth Bennet 'it was her business to be satisfied—and certainly her temper to be happy'; and the next letter that we have shows that she was determined to face a new life in a new place with cheerfulness.

Steventon: Saturday [January 3, 1801].

MY DEAR CASSANDRA,. . .—My mother looks forward with as much certainty as you can do to our keeping two maids; my father is the only one not in the secret. We plan having a steady cook and a young, giddy housemaid, with a sedate middle-aged man, who is to undertake the double office of husband to the former and sweetheart to the latter.

There are three parts of Bath which we have thought of as likely to have houses in them—Westgate Buildings, Charles Street, and some of the short streets leading from Laura Place or Pulteney Street.

Westgate Buildings, though quite in the lower part of the town, are not badly situated themselves. The street is broad, and has rather a good appearance. Charles Street, however, I think is preferable. The buildings are new, and its nearness to Kingsmead Fields would be a pleasant circumstance. Perhaps you may remember, or perhaps you may forget, that Charles Street leads from the Queen Square Chapel to the two Green Park Streets.

The houses in the streets near Laura Place I should expect to be above our price. Gay Street would be too high, except only the lower house on the left-hand side as you ascend. Towards that my mother has no disinclination; it used to be lower rented than any other house in the row, from some inferiority in the apartments. But above all others her wishes are at present fixed on the corner house in Chapel Row, which opens into Prince's Street. Her knowledge of it, however, is confined only to the outside, and therefore she is equally uncertain of its being really desirable as of its being to be had. In the meantime she assures you that she will do everything in her power to avoid Trim Street, although you have not expressed the fearful presentiment of it which was rather expected.

We know that Mrs. Perrot will want to get us into Oxford Buildings, but we all unite in particular dislike of that part of the town, and therefore hope to escape. Upon all these different situations you and Edward may confer together, and your opinion of each will be expected with eagerness.

I have now attained the true art of letter-writing, which we are always told is to express on paper exactly what one would say to the same person by word of mouth. I have been talking to you almost as fast as I could the whole of this letter.

My mother bargains for having no trouble at all in furnishing our house in Bath, and I have engaged for your willingly undertaking to do it all. I get more and more reconciled to the idea of our removal. We have lived long enough in this neighbourhood; the Basingstoke balls are certainly on the decline, there is something interesting in the bustle of going away, and the prospect of spending future summers by the sea or in Wales is very delightful. For a time we shall now possess many of the advantages which I have often thought of with envy in the wives of sailors or soldiers. It must not be generally known, however, that I am not sacrificing a great deal in quitting the country, or I can expect to inspire no tenderness, no interest, in those we leave behind.

The threatened Act of Parliament does not seem to give any alarm.

My father is doing all in his power to increase his income, by raising his tithes, &c., and I do not despair of getting very nearly six hundred a year.

Steventon: Thursday [January 8, 1801].

Mr. Peter Debary has declined Deane curacy; he wishes to be settled near London. A foolish reason! as if Deane were not near London in comparison of Exeter or York. Take the whole world through, and he will find many more places at a greater distance from London than Deane than he will at a less. What does he think of Glencoe or Lake Katherine?

I feel rather indignant that any possible objection should be raised against so valuable a piece of preferment, so delightful a situation!—that Deane should not be universally allowed to be as near the metropolis as any other country villages. As this is the case, however, as Mr. Peter Debary has shown himself a Peter in the blackest sense of the word, we are obliged to look elsewhere for an heir; and my father has thought it a necessary compliment to James Digweed to offer the curacy to him, though without considering it as either a desirable or an eligible situation for him.

Eliza has seen Lord Craven at Barton, and probably by this time at Kintbury, where he was expected for one day this week. She found his manners very pleasing indeed. The little flaw of having a mistress now living with him at Ashdown Park seems to be the only unpleasing circumstance about him. From Ibthorp, Fulwar and Eliza are to return with James and Mary to Deane.

Pray give my love to George; tell him that I am very glad to hear he can skip so well already, and that I hope he will continue to send me word of his improvement in the art.

Friday.—Sidmouth is now talked of as our summer abode. Get all the information, therefore, about it that you can from Mrs. C. Cage.

My father's old ministers are already deserting him to pay their court to his son. The brown mare, which as well as the black, was to devolve on James at our removal, has not had patience to wait for that, and has settled herself even now at Deane. The death of Hugh Capet, which, like that of Mr. Skipsey, though undesired, was not wholly unexpected, being purposely effected, has made the immediate possession of the mare very convenient, and everything else I suppose will be seized by degrees in the same manner. Martha and I work at the books every day.

Steventon: Wednesday [January 14, 1801].

Your letter to Mary was duly received before she left Deane with Martha yesterday morning, and it gives us great pleasure to know that the Chilham ball was so agreeable, and that you danced four dances with Mr. Kemble. Desirable, however, as the latter circumstance was, I cannot help wondering at its taking place.

Why did you dance four dances with so stupid a man? why not rather dance two of them with some elegant brother officer who was struck with your appearance as soon as you entered the room?

At present the environs of Laura Place seem to be his [my father's] choice. His views on the subject are much advanced since I came home; he grows quite ambitious, and actually requires now a comfortable and a creditable-looking house.

This morning brought my aunt's reply, and most thoroughly affectionate is its tenor. She thinks with the greatest pleasure of our being settled in Bath—it is an event which will attach her to the place more than anything else could do, &c., &c. She is, moreover, very urgent with my mother not to delay her visit in Paragon, if she should continue unwell, and even recommends her spending the whole winter with them. At present and for many days past my mother has been quite stout, and she wishes not to be obliged by any relapse to alter her arrangements.

Mention is made in several letters of Frank's promotion and his ignorance of it. In 1799, while commanding the sloop *Peterel*, he had been entrusted by Lord St. Vincent with dispatches conveying to Nelson at Palermo the startling news of Admiral Bruix's escape from Brest with a considerable fleet, and his entry into the Mediterranean. So important did Francis Austen believe this intelligence to be, that he landed his first lieutenant with the dispatches on the coast of Sicily some way short of Palermo, the wind being unfavourable for the approach to the capital by sea. Nelson next employed him in taking orders to the squadron blockading Malta. Frank spent the autumn and winter cruising about the Mediterranean, and taking various prizes; the most important capture being that of the *Ligurienne*—a French national brig convoying two vessels laden with corn for the French forces in Egypt. This exploit took place in March 1800, and was considered of such importance that he was made a post-captain for it; but so slow and uncertain was communication to and from the seat of war that he knew nothing of his promotion till October—long after his friends at home had become acquainted with it. His being 'collared and thrust out of the *Peterel* by Captain Inglis' (his successor) is of course a graphic way of describing his change of vessel and promotion.

Steventon: Wednesday [January 21, 1801].

MY DEAR CASSANDRA,—Expect a most agreeable letter, for not being overburdened with subject (having nothing at all to say), I shall have no check to my genius from beginning to end.

Well, and so Frank's letter has made you very happy, but you are afraid he would not have patience to stay for the *Haarlem* which you wish him to have done as being safer than the merchantman. Poor fellow! to wait from the middle of November to the end of December, and perhaps even longer, it must be sad work; especially in a place where the ink is so abominably pale. What a surprise to him it must have been on October 20, to be visited, collared, and thrust out of the *Peterel* by Captain Inglis. He kindly passes over the poignancy of his feelings in quitting his ship, his officers, and his men.

What a pity it is that he should not be in England at the time of his promotion, because he certainly would have had an appointment, so everybody says, and therefore it must be right for me to say it too. Had he been really here, the certainty of the appointment, I dare say, would not have been half so great, but as it could not be brought to the proof his absence will be always a lucky source of regret.

Eliza talks of having read in a newspaper that all the First Lieutenants of the frigates whose Captains were to be sent into line-of-battle ships were to be promoted to the rank of Commanders. If it be true, Mr. Valentine may afford himself a fine Valentine's knot, and Charles may perhaps become First of the *Endymion*, though I suppose Captain Durham is too likely to bring a villain with him under that denomination.

I join with you in wishing for the environs of Laura Place, but do not venture to expect it. My mother hankers after the Square dreadfully, and it is but natural to suppose that my uncle will take *her* part. It would be very pleasant to be near Sydney Gardens; we might go into the labyrinth every day.

Steventon: Sunday [January 25, 1801].

Your unfortunate sister was betrayed last Thursday into a situation of the utmost cruelty. I arrived at Ashe Park before the party from Deane, and was shut up in the drawing-room with Mr. Holder alone for ten minutes. I had some thoughts of insisting on the housekeeper or Mary Corbett being sent for, and nothing could prevail on me to move two steps from the door, on the lock of which I kept one hand constantly fixed. We met nobody but ourselves, played at *vingt-un* again, and were very cross.

Your brother Edward makes very honourable mention of you, I assure you, in his letter to James, and seems quite sorry to part with you. It is a great comfort to me to think that my cares have not been thrown away, and that you are respected in the world. Perhaps you may be prevailed on to return with him and Elizabeth into Kent, when they leave us in April, and I rather suspect that your great wish of keeping yourself disengaged has been with that view. Do as you like; I have overcome my desire of your going to Bath with my mother and me. There is nothing which energy will not bring one to.

On her way back from Godmersham, Cassandra spent some time with the Henry Austens now in Upper Berkeley Street; and while she was there, Jane sent her a letter, of which the following was a part. Information respecting the sailor brothers on active service was always rare, and proportionately valuable.

Manydown: Wednesday [February 11, 1801].

MY DEAR CASSANDRA,— . . . I should not have thought it necessary to write to you so soon, but for the arrival of a letter from Charles to myself. It was written last Saturday from off the Start, and conveyed to Popham Lane by Captain Boyle, on his way to Midgham. He came from Lisbon in the *Endymion*. I will copy

Charles's account of his conjectures about Frank: 'He has not seen my brother lately, nor does he expect to find him arrived, as he met Captain Inglis at Rhodes, going up to take command of the *Peterel* as he was coming down; but supposes he will arrive in less than a fortnight from this time, in some ship which is expected to reach England about that time with despatches from Sir Ralph Abercrombie.' The event must show what sort of a conjuror Captain Boyle is. The *Endymion* has not been plagued with any more prizes. Charles spent three pleasant days in Lisbon.

They were very well satisfied with their royal passenger whom they found jolly, fat, and affable, who talks of Lady Augusta as his wife, and seems much attached to her.

When this letter was written the *Endymion* was becalmed, but Charles hoped to reach Portsmouth by Monday or Tuesday. . . . He received my letter, communicating our plans, before he left England, was much surprised, of course, but is quite reconciled to them, and means to come to Steventon once more while Steventon is ours.

After this, we have no letters of Jane till she wrote from Bath; so we may suppose that the sisters were soon united. The months of March and April were spent in making the final preparations for leaving Steventon, and in receiving farewell visits from Edward Austen and his wife, as well as from Frank and Charles and Martha Lloyd. At the beginning of May, Mrs. Austen and her two daughters left their old home and went to Ibthorp; two days later, leaving Cassandra behind them, Jane and her mother went in a single day from Ibthorp to Bath, where they stayed with the Leigh Perrots in Paragon Buildings.

CHAPTER XI.

BATH AGAIN 1801-1805

In the separation of Jane and Cassandra, the letters begin again.

Paragon: Tuesday [May 5, 1801].

MY DEAR CASSANDRA,— . . . Our journey here was perfectly free from accident or event; we changed horses at the end of every stage, and paid at almost every turnpike. We had charming weather, hardly any dust, and were exceedingly agreeable, as we did not speak above once in three miles.

We had a very neat chaise from Devizes; it looked almost as well as a gentleman's, at least as a very shabby gentleman's; in spite of this advantage, however, we were above three hours coming from thence to Paragon, and it was half after seven by your clocks before we entered the house.

Frank, whose black head was in waiting in the hall window, received us very kindly; and his master and mistress did not show less cordiality. They both look very well, though my aunt has a violent cough. We drank tea as soon as we arrived, and so ends the account of our journey, which my mother bore without any fatigue.

There is to be only one more ball—next Monday is the day. The Chamberlaynes are still here. I begin to think better of Mrs. C., and upon recollection believe she has rather a long chin than otherwise, as she remembers us in Gloucestershire, when we were very charming young women.

The first view of Bath in fine weather does not answer my expectations; I think I see more distinctly through rain. The sun was got behind everything, and the appearance of the place from the top of Kingsdown was all vapour, shadow, smoke, and confusion.

I fancy we are to have a house in Seymour Street, or thereabouts. My uncle and aunt both like the situation. I was glad to hear the former talk of all the houses in New King Street as too small; it was my own idea of them. I had not been two minutes in the dining-room before he questioned me with all his accustomary eager interest about Frank and Charles, their views and intentions. I did my best to give information.

Tuesday Night.—When my uncle went to take his second glass of water I walked with him, and in our morning's circuit we looked at two houses in Green Park Buildings, one of which pleased me very well. We walked all over it except into the garret; the dining-room is of a comfortable size, just as large as you like to fancy it; the second room about 14ft. square. The apartment over the drawing-room pleased me particularly, because it is divided into two, the smaller one a very nice-sized dressing-room, which upon occasion might admit a bed. The aspect is south-east. The only doubt is about the dampness of the offices, of which there were symptoms.

Paragon: Tuesday [May 12, 1801].

Sixty-one guineas and a-half for the three cows gives one some support under the blow of only eleven guineas for the tables. Eight for my pianoforte is about what I really expected to get; I am more anxious to know the amount of my books, especially as they are said to have sold well.

In the evening, I hope you honoured my toilette and ball with a thought; I dressed myself as well as I could, and had all my finery much admired at home. By nine o'clock my uncle, aunt, and I entered the rooms, and linked Miss Winstone on to us. Before tea it was rather a dull affair; but then the before tea did not last long, for there was only one dance, danced by four couple. Think of four couple, surrounded by about an hundred people, dancing in the Upper Rooms at Bath.

After tea we *cheered up;* the breaking up of private parties sent some scores more to the ball, and though it was shockingly and inhumanly thin for this place, there were people enough, I suppose, to have made five or six very pretty Basingstoke assemblies.

I then got Mr. Evelyn to talk to, and Miss T. to look at; and I am proud to say that though repeatedly assured that another in the same party was the *She,* I fixed upon the right one from the first. A resemblance to Mrs. L. was my guide. She is not so pretty as I expected; her face has the same defect of baldness as her sister's, and her features not so handsome; she was highly rouged, and looked rather quietly and contentedly silly than anything else.

Mrs. B. and two young women were of the same party, except when Mrs. B. thought herself obliged to leave them to run round the room after her drunken husband. His avoidance, and her pursuit, with the probable intoxication of both, was an amusing scene.

Wednesday.—Another stupid party last night; perhaps if larger they might be less intolerable, but here there were only just enough to make one card table, with six people to look on and talk nonsense to each other. Lady Fust, Mrs. Busby, and a Mrs. Owen sat down with my uncle to whist, within five minutes after the three old *Toughs* came in, and there they sat, with only the exchange of Adm. Stanhope for my uncle, till their chairs were announced.

I cannot anyhow continue to find people agreeable; I respect Mrs. Chamberlayne for doing her hair well, but cannot feel a more tender sentiment. Miss Langley is like any other short girl, with a broad nose and wide mouth, fashionable dress and exposed bosom. Adm. Stanhope is a gentlemanlike man, but then his legs are too short and his tail too long.

Paragon: Thursday [May 21, 1801].

The friendship between Mrs. Chamberlayne and me which you predicted has already taken place, for we shake hands whenever we meet. Our grand walk to Weston was again fixed for yesterday, and was accomplished in a very striking manner. Every one of the party declined it under some pretence or other except our two selves and we had therefore a *tête-à-tête*, but *that* we should equally have had, after the first two yards, had half the inhabitants of Bath set off with us.

It would have amused you to see our progress. We went up by Sion Hill, and returned across the fields. In climbing a hill Mrs. Chamberlayne is very capital; I could with difficulty keep pace with her, yet would not flinch for the world. On plain ground I was quite her equal. And so we posted away under a fine hot sun, *she* without any parasol or any shade to her hat, stopping for nothing and crossing the churchyard at Weston with as much expedition as if we were afraid of being buried alive. After seeing what she is equal to, I cannot help feeling a regard for her. As to agreeableness, she is much like other people.

I went with my mother to help look at some houses in New King Street, towards which she felt some kind of inclination, but their size has now satisfied her. They were smaller than I expected to find them; one in particular out of the two was quite monstrously little; the best of the sitting-rooms not so large as the little parlour at Steventon, and the second room in every floor about capacious enough to admit a very small single bed.

You will be sorry to hear that Marianne Mapleton's disorder has ended fatally. She was believed out of danger on Sunday, but a sudden relapse carried her off the next day. So affectionate a family must suffer severely; and many a girl on early death has been praised into an angel, I believe, on slighter pretensions to beauty, sense, and merit, than Marianne.

Paragon: Tuesday [May 26, 1801].

. . . .

The *Endymion* came into Portsmouth on Sunday and I have sent Charles a short letter by this day's post. My adventures since I wrote you three days ago have been such as the time would easily contain. I walked yesterday morning with Mrs. Chamberlayne to Lyncombe and Widcombe, and in the evening I drank tea with the Holders. Mrs. Chamberlayne's pace was not quite so magnificent on this second trial as on the first: it was nothing more than I could keep up with, without effort, and for many many yards together on a raised narrow footpath I led the way. The walk was very beautiful, as my companion agreed whenever I made the observation. And so ends our friendship, for the Chamberlaynes leave Bath in a day or two. Prepare likewise for the loss of Lady Fust, as you will lose before you find her. My evening visit was by no means disagreeable. Mrs. Lillingston came to engage Mrs. Holder's conversation, and Miss Holder and I adjourned after tea to the inner drawing-room to look over prints and talk pathetically. She is very unreserved and very fond of talking of her deceased brother and sister, whose memories she cherishes with an enthusiasm which, though perhaps a little affected, is not unpleasing. She has an idea of your being remarkably lively, therefore get ready the proper selection of adverbs and due scraps of Italian and French. I must now pause to make some observation on Mrs. Heathcote's having got a little boy. I wish her well to wear it out—and shall proceed. Frank writes me word that he is to be in London to-morrow: some money negotiation, from which he hopes to derive advantage, hastens him from Kent and will detain him a few days behind my father in town. I have seen the Miss Mapletons this morning. Marianne was buried yesterday, and I called without expecting to be let in to enquire after them all. On the servant's invitation, however, I sent in my name, and Jane and Christiana, who were walking in the garden, came to me immediately, and I sat with them about ten minutes. They looked pale and dejected but were more composed than I had thought probable. When I mentioned your coming here on Monday they said they should be very glad to see you.

We drink tea to-night with Mrs. Lysons: now this, says my Master, will be mighty dull. . . .

I assure you in spite of what I might choose to insinuate in a former letter, that I have seen very little of Mr. Evelyn since my coming here; I met him this morning for only the fourth time, and as to my anecdote about Sydney Gardens, I made the most of the story because it came into advantage, but in fact he only asked me whether I were to be in Sydney Gardens in the evening or not. There is now something like an engagement between us and the Phaeton, which to confess my frailty I have a great desire to go out in; but whether it will come to anything must remain with him. I really believe he is very harmless; people do not seem afraid of him here, and he gets groundsel for his birds and all that. . . .

Yours affectionately,
J. A.

Wednesday.—I am just returned from my airing in the very bewitching Phaeton and four for which I was prepared by a note from Mr. E., soon after breakfast. We went to the top of Kingsdown, and had a very pleasant drive. One pleasure succeeds another rapidly. On my return I found your letter, and a letter from Charles, on the table. The contents of yours I suppose I need not repeat to you; to thank you for it will be enough. I give Charles great credit for remembering my uncle's direction, and he seems rather surprised at it himself. He has received £30 for his share of the privateer, and expects £10 more, but of what avail is it to take prizes if he lays out the produce in presents to his sisters? He has been buying gold chains and topaze crosses for us—he must be well scolded. The *Endymion* has already received orders for taking troops to Egypt—which I should not like at all if I did not trust to Charles being removed from her somehow or other before she sails. He knows nothing of his own destination he says—but desires me to write directly—as the *Endymion* will probably sail in three or four days. He will receive my yesterday's letter to-day, and I shall write again by this post to thank and reproach him. We shall be unbearably fine.

So began the five years' residence at Bath.

Cassandra and her father (the latter having been paying visits in Kent and London) joined the others at the beginning of June; and from that date till September 1804 there is little that can be said definitely about Jane's life.

We know, however, that it was the intention of the Austens to spend the summer of 1801 by the sea—perhaps at Sidmouth; and a letter of Eliza Austen informs us that this plan was duly carried out. She writes to Phila Walter on October 29:—

I conclude that you know of our uncle and aunt Austen and their daughters having spent the summer in Devonshire. They are now returned to Bath, where they are superintending the fitting up of their new house.

So the house had at last been fixed on; and we learn in the *Memoir* that it was No. 4 Sydney Terrace, in the parish of Bathwick. The houses here face the Sydney Gardens, and it is a part of Bath that Jane seems to have fancied. Her residence there is now commemorated by a marble tablet. How long the Austens resided in this house cannot definitely be stated; perhaps they took it for three years—at any rate, by the beginning of 1805 they had moved to 27 Green Park Buildings. Possibly Mr. Austen, as he grew older, had found the distance to the centre of the town too great for his powers of walking.

One of the few facts we know concerning their stay in Sydney Place is that at one time Mrs. Austen was extremely ill, but the skill of her medical adviser, a certain Mr. Bowen, and the affectionate care of her daughters pulled her through and enabled her to live for another twenty-five years. Mrs. Austen has recorded the fact of her illness in some humorous verses, entitled 'Dialogue between Death and Mrs. A.'

>   Says Death, 'I've been trying these three weeks and more
>
>   To seize on old Madam here at Number Four,
>
>   Yet I still try in vain, tho' she's turned of three score;
>
>   To what is my ill-success owing?'

> 'I'll tell you, old Fellow, if you cannot guess,
>
> To what you're indebted for your ill success—
>
> To the prayers of my husband, whose love I possess,
>
> To the care of my daughters, whom Heaven will bless,
>
> To the skill and attention of Bowen.'

In 1802, in addition to the visit to Steventon with its distressing incidents, Jane was at Dawlish; for, in a letter written in 1814, she says of the library at Dawlish that it 'was pitiful and wretched twelve years ago and not likely to have anybody's publications.' A writer, too, in *Temple Bar* for February 1879, states that about this time the Austens went to Teignmouth (which would be very easily combined with a stay at Dawlish), and that they resided there some weeks.

This was the year of the short cessation of hostilities brought about by the Peace of Amiens. During its continuance, we are told that the Henry Austens went to France in the vain hope of recovering some of her first husband's property, and narrowly escaped being included amongst the *détenus*. 'Orders had been given by Bonaparte's Government to detain all English travellers; but at the post-houses Mrs. Henry Austen gave the necessary orders herself, and her French was so perfect that she passed everywhere for a native, and her husband escaped under this protection.'

Our only evidence of Jane's having been absent from Bath in 1803 is that Sir Egerton Brydges, in speaking of her, says: 'The last time I think that I saw her was at Ramsgate in 1803.'

On Francis Austen's promotion (already mentioned), Admiral Gambier seems rather to have gone out of his way to choose him as his flag-captain on the *Neptune;* but on the Peace of Amiens, he, like many others, went on half-pay. His first employment when war broke out again, in 1803, was the raising from among the Kent fishermen of a corps of 'sea fencibles,' to protect the coast from invasion. His head-quarters were at Ramsgate, and it was quite likely that Jane would visit him there, especially if she could combine this visit with one to Godmersham. We shall see later that the 'sea fencibles' did not take up the whole of Frank's time.

She must now have begun to turn her mind again to her neglected MSS., and especially to *Northanger Abbey*. This, no doubt, underwent a thorough revision (*Belinda*, mentioned in the famous dissertation on novels, was not published till 1801); and there is evidence that she sold the MS., under the title of *Susan*, in the spring of 1803: not, indeed, to a Bath publisher—as has been often stated—but to Messrs. Crosby & Son of London, for ten pounds, stipulating for an early publication. Distrustful of appearing under her own name in the transaction, Jane seems to have employed a certain Mr. Seymour—probably her brother Henry's man of business—a fact which suggests that the sale was effected while Jane was staying in London with Henry. For reasons best known to himself, Mr. Crosby did not proceed with the publication.

Besides *Northanger Abbey*, Jane seems to have written at this time the beginning of a tale which was published in the second edition of the Memoir as *The Watsons*, although the author had not given that, or any other name, to it. The setting of the story was very like that of the novels with which we are so familiar, and the characters were sketched in with a firm hand. One of these creations in particular might have been expected to re-appear in another book (if this work was to be laid aside); but such a procedure was contrary to Jane Austen's invariable practice. It is the character of a young man—Tom Musgrave by name—a clever and good-natured toady, with rather more attractive qualities than usually fall to the lot of the members of that fraternity. But why was it laid aside? The writer of the *Memoir* suggests that the author may have become aware 'of the evil of having placed her heroine too low, in a position of poverty and obscurity, which, though not necessarily connected with vulgarity, has a sad tendency to degenerate into it; and therefore, like a singer who has begun on too low a note, she discontinued the strain.'

To this we may add that circumstances soon occurred to divert her mind from original composition for a considerable period; and when at last she returned to it, she was much more likely to think of the two completed stories that were lying in her desk than of one that was only begun. She did, however, retain in her recollection the outline of the intended story. The MS. of *The Watsons*, still existing, is written on the small sheets of paper described in the *Memoir:* sheets which could be easily covered with a piece of blotting-paper in case of the arrival of unexpected visitors, and which would thus fit in with her desire for secrecy. All the pages are written in her beautifully neat handwriting; but some seem to flow on without doubt or difficulty, while others are subject to copious corrections. As all the MSS. of her six published novels have perished, it is worth our while to notice her methods where we can.

The first interruption that occurred to her writing in 1804 was of a pleasant nature, and none of her admirers need regret it: she went to Lyme with her family. They had been joined in their summer rambles by the Henry Austens, who afterwards proceeded with Cassandra to Weymouth, leaving Jane with her parents at Lyme. We have it on record that Jane loved the sight of the beauties of nature so much that she would sometimes say she thought it must form one of the joys of heaven; but she had few opportunities of visiting any scenes of especial beauty. We need not therefore be surprised that the impression produced by Lyme was so great that she retained a vivid and accurate memory of the details eleven years afterwards. In *Persuasion*, she allowed herself to dwell on them with greater fullness and greater enthusiasm than she had ever displayed on similar occasions before. Readers of that book who visit Lyme—especially if they have the valuable help of the Miss Hills' descriptions and sketches—will feel no difficulty in recognising the exact spot on the Cobb which was pointed out to Tennyson as the scene of the fall of Louisa Musgrove, or the well-placed but minute house at the corner of the pier, past which Captain Benwick was seen rushing for the doctor, and in which the Harvilles managed to entertain a large party; they may note the point on the steps leading down to the sea where Mr. Elliot first saw Anne; and if they go to the 'Royal Lion' Hotel and engage a private sitting-room, they can look from the window, as Mary Musgrove looked at her cousin's carriage, when she recognised the Elliot countenance, but failed to see the Elliot arms, because the great-coat was folded over the panels.

The letter which follows was written when Cassandra was just leaving Weymouth to go to Ibthorp where old Mrs. Lloyd lay very ill.

Lyme: Friday [September 14, 1804].

MY DEAR CASSANDRA,—I take the first sheet of fine striped paper to thank you for your letter from Weymouth, and express my hopes of your being at Ibthorp before this time. I expect to hear that you reached it yesterday evening, being able to get as far as Blandford on Wednesday. Your account of Weymouth contains nothing which strikes me so forcibly as there being no ice in the town. For every other vexation I was in some measure prepared, and particularly for your disappointment in not seeing the Royal Family go on board on Tuesday, having already heard from Mr. Crawford that he had seen you in the very act of being too late. But for there being no ice, what could prepare me? . . . You found my letter at Andover, I hope, yesterday, and have now for many hours been satisfied that your kind anxiety on my behalf was as much thrown away as kind anxiety usually is. I continue quite well; in proof of which I have bathed again this morning. It was absolutely necessary that I should have the little fever and indisposition which I had: it has been all the fashion this week in Lyme. . . . We are quite settled in our lodgings by this time, as you may suppose, and everything goes on in the usual order. The servants behave very well, and make no difficulties, though nothing certainly can exceed the inconvenience of the offices, except the general dirtiness of the house and furniture, and all its inhabitants. I endeavour, as far as I can, to supply your place, and be useful, and keep things in order. I detect dirt in the water decanters, as fast as I can, and keep everything as it was under your administration. . . . James is the delight of our lives, he is quite an Uncle Toby's annuity to us. My Mother's shoes were never so well blacked before, and our plate never looked so clean. He waits extremely well, is attentive, handy, quick and quiet, and in short has a great many more than all the cardinal virtues (for the cardinal virtues in themselves have been so often possessed that they are no longer worth having), and amongst the rest, that of wishing to go to Bath, as I understand from Jenny. He has the laudable thirst I fancy for travelling, which in poor James Selby was so much reprobated; and part of his disappointment in not going with his master arose from his wish of seeing London.

The ball last night was pleasant, but not full for Thursday. My father staid very contentedly till half-past nine (we went a little after eight), and then walked home with James and a lanthorn, though I believe the lanthorn was not lit, as the moon was up; but this lanthorn may sometimes be a great convenience to him. My mother and I staid about an hour later. Nobody asked me the two first dances; the two next I danced with Mr. Crawford, and had I chosen to stay longer might have danced with Mr. Granville, Mrs. Granville's son, whom my dear friend Miss A. offered to introduce to me, or with a new odd-looking man who had been eyeing me for some time, and at last, without any introduction, asked me if I meant to dance again. I think he must be Irish by his ease, and because I imagine him to belong to the hon^{ble} B.'s, who are the son, and son's wife of an Irish viscount, bold queer-looking people, just fit to be quality at Lyme.

I called yesterday morning (ought it not in strict propriety to be termed yester-morning?) on Miss A. and was introduced to her father and mother. Like other young ladies she is considerably genteeler than her parents. Mrs. A. sat darning a pair of stockings the whole of my visit. But do not mention this at home, lest a warning should act as an example. We afterwards walked together for an hour on the Cobb; she is very converseable in a common way; I do not perceive wit or genius, but she has sense and some degree of taste, and her manners are very engaging. She seems to like people rather too easily. She thought the D.'s pleasant, &c., &c.

Friday Evening.—The bathing was so delightful this morning and Molly so pressing with me to enjoy myself that I believe I staid in rather too long, as since the middle of the day I have felt unreasonably tired. I shall be more careful another time, and shall not bathe to-morrow as I had before intended. Jenny and James are walked to Charmouth this afternoon. I am glad to have such an amusement for him, as I am very anxious for his being at once quiet and happy. He can read, and I must get him some books. Unfortunately he has read the first Vol. of *Robinson Crusoe*. We have the Pinckards' newspaper however which I shall take care to lend him.

As the autumn of 1804 was succeeded by winter, Jane's thoughts were to be taken up by more serious considerations. On her birthday, December 16, occurred the death (by a fall from her horse) of her great friend, Mrs. Lefroy, on which we have already dwelt.

But she was shortly to suffer an even greater loss, for on January 21, 1805, her father died, after an illness of only forty-eight hours. Jane's letter, or rather two letters—for, the first being wrongly directed, she had to write a second—to her brother Frank on this occasion have fortunately been kept.

Green Park Buildings:
Tuesday evening, January 22, 1805.

MY DEAREST FRANK,—I wrote to you yesterday, but your letter to Cassandra this morning, by which we learn the probability of your being by this time at Portsmouth, obliges me to write to you again, having unfortunately a communication as necessary as painful to make to you. Your affectionate heart will be greatly wounded, and I wish the shock could have been lessened by a better preparation; but the event has been sudden and so must be the information of it. We have lost an excellent father. An illness of only eight and forty hours carried him off yesterday morning between ten and eleven. He was seized on Saturday with a return of the feverish complaint which he had been subject to for the last three years. . . . A physician was called in yesterday morning, but he was at that time past all possibility of cure; and Dr. Gibbs and Mr. Bowen had scarcely left his room before he sunk into a sleep from which he never woke.

It has been very sudden. Within twenty-four hours of his death he was walking about with only the help of a stick—was even reading.

We had, however, some hours of preparation, and when we understood his recovery to be hopeless, most fervently did we pray for the speedy release which ensued. To have seen him languishing long, struggling for hours, would have been dreadful, and, thank God, we were all spared from it.

Except the restlessness and confusion of high fever, he did not suffer, and he was mercifully spared from knowing that he was about to quit objects so beloved, and so fondly cherished as his wife and children ever were. His tenderness as a father, who can do justice to?

The funeral is to be on Saturday at Walcot Church. The serenity of the corpse is most delightful. It preserves the sweet benevolent smile which always distinguished him. They kindly press my mother to remove to Steventon as soon as it is all over, but I do not believe she will leave Bath at present. We must have this house for three months longer, and here we shall probably stay till the end of that time. We all unite in love, and I am

Affectionately yours,
J. A.

The companion letter, sent to a different address, gives a similar account, and contains also these words:—

Heavy as is the blow, we can already feel that a thousand comforts remain to us to soften it. Next to that of the consciousness of his worth and constant preparation for another world, is the remembrance of his having suffered, comparatively speaking, nothing. Being quite insensible of his own state, he was spared all pain of separation, and he went off almost in his sleep. My mother bears the shock as well as possible; she was quite prepared for it and feels all the blessing of his being spared a long illness. My uncle and aunt have been with us and show us every imaginable kindness.

Adieu, my dearest Frank. The loss of such a parent must be felt, or we should be brutes. I wish I could give you a better preparation, but it has been impossible.

Yours ever affectionately,
J. A.

Mr. Austen's death placed his widow and daughters in straitened circumstances; for most of his income had been derived from the livings of Steventon and Deane. In fact the income of Mrs. Austen, together with that of Cassandra (who had inherited one thousand pounds from her intended husband, Thomas Fowle), was no more than two hundred and ten pounds. Fortunately, she had sons who were only too glad to be able to help her, and her income was raised to four hundred and sixty pounds a year by contributions of one hundred pounds from Edward, and fifty pounds from James, Henry, and Frank respectively. Frank, indeed, was ready to do more; for Henry wrote to him to say that their mother 'feels the magnificence of your offer and accepts of half.' Mrs. Austen's first idea was to remain in Bath so long as her brother, Mr. Leigh Perrot, lived there. Accordingly, she gave up her house at Lady Day, and moved, with her daughters and one maid, into furnished lodgings at 25 Gay Street.

Early in April, Cassandra was staying at Ibthorp, where it was her lot to attend another death-bed—that of old Mrs. Lloyd.

25 Gay Street: Monday [April 8, 1805].

MY DEAR CASSANDRA,—Here is a day for you! Did Bath or Ibthorp ever see a finer 8th of April? It is March and April together, the glare of one and the warmth of the other. We do nothing but walk about. As far as your means will admit, I hope you profit by such weather too. I dare say you are already the better for change of place. We were out again last night. Miss Irvine invited us, when I met her in the Crescent, to drink tea with them, but I rather declined it, having no idea that my mother would be disposed for another evening visit there so soon; but when I gave her the message, I found her very well inclined to go; and accordingly, on leaving Chapel, we walked to Lansdown. This morning we have been to see Miss Chamberlayne look hot on horseback. Seven years and four months ago we went to the same riding-house to see Miss Lefroy's performance! What a different set are we now moving in! But seven years, I suppose, are enough to change every pore of one's skin and every feeling of one's mind. We did not walk long in the Crescent yesterday. It was hot and not crowded enough; so we went into the field, and passed close by S. T. and Miss S. again. I have not yet seen her face, but neither her dress nor air have anything of the dash or stylishness which the Browns talked of; quite the contrary; indeed, her dress is not even smart, and her appearance very quiet. Miss Irvine says she is never speaking a word. Poor wretch; I am afraid she is *en pénitence*. Here has been that excellent Mrs. Coulthart calling, while my mother was out, and I was believed to be so. I always respected her, as a good-hearted friendly woman. And the Brownes have been here; I find their affidavits on the table. The *Ambuscade* reached Gibraltar on the 9th of March, and found all well; so say the papers. We have had no letters from anybody, but we expect to hear from Edward to-morrow, and from you soon afterwards. How happy they are at Godmersham now! I shall be very glad of a letter from Ibthorp, that I may know how you all are, but particularly yourself. This is nice weather for Mrs. J. Austen's going to Speen, and I hope she will have a pleasant visit there. I expect a prodigious account of the christening dinner; perhaps it brought you at last into the company of Miss Dundas again.

Tuesday.—I received your letter last night, and wish it may be soon followed by another to say that all is over; but I cannot help thinking that nature will struggle again, and produce a revival. Poor woman! May her end be peaceful and easy as the exit we have witnessed! And I dare say it will. If there is no revival, suffering must be all over; even the consciousness of existence, I suppose, was gone when you wrote. The nonsense I have been writing in this and in my last letter seems out of place at such a time, but I will not mind it; it will do you no harm, and nobody else will be attacked by it. I am heartily glad that you can speak so comfortably of your own health and looks, though I can scarcely comprehend the latter being really approved. Could travelling fifty miles produce such an immediate change? You were looking very poorly here, and everybody seemed sensible of it. Is there a charm in a hack post-chaise? But if there were, Mrs. Craven's carriage might have undone it all. I am much obliged to you for the time and trouble you have bestowed on Mary's cap, and am glad it pleases her; but it will prove a useless gift at present, I suppose. Will not she leave Ibthorp on her mother's death? As a companion you are all that Martha can be supposed to want, and in that light, under these circumstances, your visit will indeed have been well timed.

The Cookes want us to drink tea with them to-night, but I do not know whether my mother will have nerves for it. We are engaged to-morrow evening—what request we are in! Mrs. Chamberlayne expressed to her niece her wish of being intimate enough with us to ask us to drink tea with her in a quiet way. We have therefore offered her ourselves and our quietness through the same medium. Our tea and sugar will last a great while. I think we are just the kind of people and party to be treated about among our relations; we cannot be supposed to be very rich.

Thursday.—I was not able to go on yesterday; all my wit and leisure were bestowed on letters to Charles and Henry. To the former I wrote in consequence of my mother's having seen in the papers that the *Urania* was waiting at Portsmouth for the convoy for Halifax. This is nice, as it is only three weeks ago that you wrote by the *Camilla*. . . . I wrote to Henry because I had a letter from him in which he desired to hear from me very soon. His to me was most affectionate and kind, as well as entertaining; there is no merit to him in *that;* he cannot help being amusing. . . . He offers to meet us on the sea coast, if the plan of which Edward gave him some hint takes place. Will not this be making the execution of such a plan more desirable and delightful than ever? He talks of the rambles we took together last summer with pleasing affection.

Yours ever,
J. A.

From the Same to the Same.
Gay Street: Sunday Evening,
April 21 [1805].

MY DEAR CASSANDRA,—I am much obliged to you for writing to me again so soon; your letter yesterday was quite an unexpected pleasure. Poor Mrs. Stent! it has been her lot to be always in the way; but we must be merciful, for perhaps in time we may come to be Mrs. Stents ourselves, unequal to anything, and unwelcome to everybody. Your account of Martha is very comfortable indeed, and now we shall be in no fear of receiving a worse. This day, if she has gone to church, must have been a trial to her feelings, but it will be the last of any acuteness. . . . Yesterday was a busy day with me. I went to Sydney Gardens soon after one and did not return until four, and after dinner I walked to Weston. My morning engagement was with the Cookes, and our party consisted of George and Mary, a Mr. and Miss B. who had been with us at the concert, and the youngest Miss W. Not Julia; we have done with her; she is very ill; but Mary. Mary W.'s turn is actually come to be grown up, and have a fine complexion, and wear a great square muslin shawl. I have not expressly enumerated myself among the party, but there I was, and my cousin George was very kind, and talked sense to me every now and then, in the intervals of his more animated fooling with Miss B., who is very young, and rather handsome, and whose gracious manners, ready wit, and solid remarks, put me somewhat in mind of my old acquaintance L. L. There was a monstrous deal of stupid quizzing and common-place nonsense talked, but scarcely any wit; all that bordered on it or on sense came from my cousin George, whom altogether I like very well. Mr. B. seems nothing more than a tall young man. . . . My evening engagement and walk was with Miss A., who had called on me the day before, and gently upbraided me in her turn with a change of manners to her since she had been in Bath, or at least of late. Unlucky me! that my notice should be of such consequence, and my manners so bad! She was so well disposed, and so reasonable, that I soon forgave her, and made this engagement with her in proof of it. She is really an agreeable girl, so I think I may like her; and her great want of a companion at home, which may well make any tolerable acquaintance important to her, gives her another claim on my attention. I shall as much as possible endeavour to keep my intimacies in their proper place, and prevent their clashing. . . . Among so many friends, it will be well if I do not get into a scrape; and now here is Miss Blachford come. I should have gone distracted if the Bullers had staid. . . .

I am quite of your opinion as to the folly of concealing any longer our intended partnership with Martha, and wherever there has of late been an enquiry on the subject I have always been sincere, and I have sent word of it to the Mediterranean in a letter to Frank. None of *our* nearest connections I think will be unprepared for it, and I do not know how to suppose that Martha's have not foreseen it.

When I tell you we have been visiting a Countess this morning, you will immediately, with great justice, but no truth, guess it to be Lady Roden. No: it is Lady Leven, the mother of Lord Balgonie. On receiving a message from Lord and Lady Leven through the Mackays, declaring their intention of waiting on us, we thought it right to go to them. I hope we have not done too much, but the friends and admirers of Charles must be attended to. They seem very reasonable, good sort of people, very civil, and full of his praise. We were shewn at first into an empty drawing-room, and presently in came his lordship, not knowing who we were, to apologise for the servant's mistake, and tell a lie himself that Lady Leven was not within. He is a tall gentlemanlike-looking man, with spectacles, and rather deaf. After sitting with him ten minutes we walked away; but, Lady Leven coming out of the dining parlour as we passed the door, we were obliged to attend her back to it, and pay our visit over again. She is a stout woman, with a very handsome face. By this means we had the pleasure of hearing Charles's praises twice over. They think themselves excessively obliged to him, and estimate him so highly as to wish Lord Balgonie, when he is quite recovered, to go out to him. . . . There is a pretty little Lady Marianne of the party, to be shaken hands with, and asked if she remembered Mr. Austen. . . .

I shall write to Charles by the next packet, unless you tell me in the meantime of your intending to do it.

>Believe me, if you chuse,
>Y^r aff^{te} Sister.

'Cousin George' was the Rev. George Leigh Cooke, long known and respected at Oxford, where he held important offices, and had the privilege of helping to form the minds of men more eminent than himself. As tutor at Corpus Christi College, he had under his charge Arnold, Keble, and Sir J. T. Coleridge.

The 'intended partnership' with Martha was an arrangement by which Martha Lloyd joined the family party: an arrangement which was based on their affectionate friendship for her, and which succeeded so well that it lasted through Southampton and Chawton, and did not end until after the death of Mrs. Austen in 1827.

CHAPTER XII.

FROM BATH TO SOUTHAMPTON 1805-1808

THE addition of Martha to the family party made it easy for the two sisters to leave their mother in August and pay a visit to Godmersham; and owing to the fact that they, each in turn, varied their stay at Godmersham by paying a short visit to Lady Bridges at Goodnestone Farm, we have three brief letters from Jane at this date. She was spending her time in the usual way, seeing a good deal of her sister-in-law's neighbours and connexions, and playing with her nephews and nieces.

Godmersham Park: Saturday [August 24, 1805].

MY DEAR CASSANDRA,— . . . George is a fine boy, and well behaved, but Daniel chiefly delighted me; the good humour of his countenance is quite bewitching. After tea we had a cribbage-table, and he and I won two rubbers of his brother and Mrs. Mary. Mr. Brett was the only person there, besides our two families.

Yesterday was a very quiet day with us; my noisiest efforts were writing to Frank, and playing battledore and shuttlecock with William; he and I have practised together two mornings, and improve a little; we have frequently kept it up *three* times, and once or twice *six*.

The two Edwards went to Canterbury in the chaise, and found Mrs. Knight as you found her, I suppose, the day before, cheerful but weak.

I have been used very ill this morning: I have received a letter from Frank which I ought to have had when Elizabeth and Henry had theirs, and which in its way from Albany to Godmersham has been to Dover and Steventon. It was finished on the 16th, and tells what theirs told before as to his present situation; he is in a great hurry to be married, and I have encouraged him in it, in the letter which ought to have been an answer to his. He must think it very strange that I do not acknowledge the receipt of his, when I speak of those of the same date to Eliz. and Henry; and to add to my injuries, I forgot to number mine on the outside.

Elizabeth has this moment proposed a scheme which will be very much for my pleasure if equally convenient to the other party; it is that when you return on Monday, I should take your place at Goodnestone for a few days. Harriot cannot be insincere, let her try for it ever so much, and therefore I defy her to accept this self-invitation of mine, unless it be really what perfectly suits her. As there is no time for an answer, I shall go in the carriage on Monday, and can return with you, if my going to Goodnestone is at all inconvenient.

Goodnestone Farm: Tuesday [August 27, 1805].

There is no chance of tickets for the Mr. Bridgeses, as no gentlemen but of the garrison are invited.

With a civil note to be fabricated to Lady F., and an answer written to Miss H., you will easily believe that we could not begin dinner till six. We were agreeably surprised by Edward Bridges's company to it. He had been, strange to tell, too late for the cricket match, too late at least to play himself, and, not being asked to dine with the players, came home. It is impossible to do justice to the hospitality of his attentions towards me; he made a point of ordering toasted cheese for supper entirely on my account.

Goodnestone Farm: Friday [August 30, 1805].

Next week seems likely to be an unpleasant one to this family on the matter of game. The evil intentions of the Guards are certain, and the gentlemen of the neighbourhood seem unwilling to come forward in any decided or early support of their rights. Edward Bridges has been trying to rouse their spirits, but without success. Mr. Hammond, under the influence of daughters and an expected ball, declares he will do nothing. . . .

> Yours affectionately,
> J. A.

Cassandra and Jane had a scheme for going to Worthing with some of their young nephews and nieces; but we can say no more about the plan, for the letters now cease until January 1807. As for the events of 1806, there is every reason to believe that the Austens spent the first part of that year in Bath, dividing their time somewhat uncomfortably between different lodgings.

Meanwhile, Francis Austen had been helping to make history—though not always in so front a rank as he would have desired to occupy. We left him raising the 'sea fencibles' at Ramsgate, instructing the defenders of the coast, and considering the possibilities of a landing by the French in their flat-bottomed vessels. It was at Ramsgate that he was noted as '*the* officer who knelt in Church,' and it was there that he met and fell in love with his future wife, Mary Gibson. She became in time one of the best loved of the sisters-in-law; but we are told that at the time the engagement was a slight shock to Cassandra and Jane, because the lady chosen was *not* Martha Lloyd, as they had hoped she might be.

Immediate marriage was out of the question, and in May 1804 Frank was appointed to the *Leopard*, the flagship of Admiral Louis, who at this time held a command in the squadron blockading Napoleon's flotilla. Frank's removal from the *Leopard* to the *Canopus* brought him home, for a short time, just at the date of his father's death in January 1805. In March, Admiral Louis hoisted his flag in the *Canopus* and soon became second-in-command to Nelson. Frank, as his flag-captain, took part in the chase after Villeneuve to the West Indies and back. Thus far, fortune had favoured him: a state of things which seemed likely to continue, as he was personally known to Nelson and had reason to hope that he would soon give him the command of a frigate. But a sad reverse was in store for him. September was spent in blockading Cadiz; and, after Nelson's arrival from England in the *Victory* on September 28, the *Canopus* was ordered to 'complete supplies' at Gibraltar. After this, followed an order to Admiral Louis to give protection, as far as Cartagena, to a convoy proceeding to Malta. Shaking themselves free from this duty on the news that the enemy's fleet was coming out of Cadiz, they made haste to join the main fleet in spite of contrary winds, and with the dreadful apprehension of being too late for the imminent battle. 'I do not profess,' he writes to Mary Gibson, 'to like fighting for its own sake, but if there has been an action with the combined fleets I shall ever consider the day on which I sailed from the squadron as the most inauspicious one of my life.' Six days later (on October 27) he had to add: 'Alas! my dearest Mary, all my fears are but too fully justified. The fleets have met, and, after a very severe contest, a most decisive victory has been gained by the English. . . . To lose all share in the glory of a day which surpasses all that ever went before is what I cannot think of with any degree of patience.' But he soon turns from selfish regrets to speak of the death of Nelson, and adds: 'I never heard of his equal, nor do I expect again to see such a man. To the soundest judgment he united prompt decision and speedy execution of his plans; and he possessed in a superior degree the happy talent of making every class of persons pleased with their situation, and eager to exert themselves in forwarding the public service.'

For his personal disappointment, Frank was, to a certain extent, consoled by taking part in Sir John Duckworth's cruise to the West Indies and in the victory over the French at St. Domingo; the squadron returning home, with three prizes, to receive the thanks of Parliament on their arrival at the beginning of May 1806. In the following July, Francis Austen and Mary Gibson were married.

Meanwhile, the long residence at Bath of his mother and sisters had come to an end. On July 2, Mrs. Austen, her two daughters, and Martha Lloyd, left Bath. Cassandra and Jane were thoroughly tired of the place—so says Jane in a letter written two years afterwards to Cassandra, reminding her of their happy feelings of escape. The immediate destination of the party was Clifton, and here Martha Lloyd left them—perhaps for Harrogate in accordance with the lines quoted above. The Austens did not stay long at Clifton, and by the end of the month were at Adlestrop Rectory on a visit to Mr. Thomas Leigh; but neither did this prove more than a brief resting-place, for on August 5 they set out, in somewhat peculiar circumstances, together with Mr. Leigh, his sister (Miss Elizabeth Leigh), Mr. Hill (agent of Mr. Leigh), and all the house party, to stay at Stoneleigh Abbey in Warwickshire.

The circumstances were as follows. On July 2, 1806, occurred the death of the Hon. Mary Leigh, who had been for twenty years life-tenant of the Stoneleigh estates, under the will of her brother, the last Lord Leigh. The estates now passed—according to Lord Leigh's will—unto the first and nearest of his kindred, being male and of his blood and name, that should be alive at the time. All the Leighs of the Stoneleigh branch had died out, and an heir had to be sought among their remote cousins, the Adlestrop Leighs. In ordinary circumstances the heir would have been James Henry Leigh, who was the head of this branch; but by the peculiar wording of Lord Leigh's will, all those of an older generation who were thus 'the first and nearest of his blood and name' appeared to take precedence of the natural heir, although this does not seem to have been the intention of Lord Leigh.

The *eldest* Leigh was the Rev. Thomas Leigh, who therefore became the legal owner of Stoneleigh; but as it was thought possible that there might be other claimants, Mr. Leigh's solicitor advised his taking immediate possession; and accordingly Mr. Leigh and all his house party moved from Adlestrop to Stoneleigh.

This visit, and the whole question of the succession to Stoneleigh, must have been especially interesting to Jane's mother; for it seemed likely that Mrs. Austen's own brother, Mr. Leigh Perrot, would, under the terms of the will, have a life interest in the estate after Mr. Thomas Leigh, if he survived him. It was, however, obviously most in accordance with the desire of the testator, and with the general opinion of the family, that the estate should go according to the usual rules of succession by primogeniture in the Adlestrop branch; and as all the parties to the transaction were on excellent terms with each other, and as they believed it to be quite doubtful what interpretation a court of law would put upon the will, they settled the matter without any such intervention. Mr. Leigh Perrot resigned his claim to the estate and gained instead a capital sum of £24,000 and an annuity of £2000, which lasted until the death of his wife in 1835. This is no doubt the agreement with Adlestrop, mentioned below in the letter of February 20, 1807, and it must, one would think, have been considered satisfactory: indeed, the writer speaks of the negotiation as 'happily over.' The remaining clause in it which ensured to the Leigh Perrots two bucks, two does, and the game off one manor annually was less successful, for the bucks sometimes arrived in such a condition as to demand immediate burial. Yet it can hardly have been this which made Jane at a later date speak of the 'vile compromise': we should rather treat this expression as one of her *obiter dicta*, not meant to be taken seriously.

'And here,' writes Mrs. Austen on August 13, 1806, 'we found ourselves on Tuesday (that is, yesterday se'nnight), eating fish, venison, and all manner of good things, in a large and noble parlour hung round with family portraits.'

Mrs. Austen had expected to find Stoneleigh very grand, but the magnificence of the place surpassed her expectations. After describing its exterior, she adds:—

At nine in the morning we say our prayers in a handsome chapel of which the pulpit, &c., is now hung in black. Then follows breakfast, consisting of chocolate, coffee, and tea, plum cake, pound cake, hot rolls, cold rolls, bread and butter, and dry toast for me. The house steward, a fine large respectable-looking man, orders all these matters. Mr. Leigh and Mr. Hill are busy a great part of the morning. *We* walk a good deal, for the woods are impenetrable to the sun, even in the middle of an August day. I do not fail to spend some part of every day in the kitchen garden, where the quantity of small fruit exceeds anything you can form an idea of.

She concludes her letter by saying:—

Our visit has been a most pleasant one. We all seem in good humour, disposed to be pleased, and endeavouring to be agreeable, and I hope we succeed. Poor Lady Saye and Sele, to be sure, is rather tormenting, though sometimes amusing, and affords Jane many a good laugh, but she fatigues me sadly on the whole. To-morrow we depart. We have seen the remains of Kenilworth, which afforded us much entertainment, and I expect still more from the sight of Warwick Castle, which we are going to see to-day.

From Stoneleigh, we may imagine the Austens to have gone on to pay a promised visit to Hamstall-Ridware—Edward Cooper's living in Staffordshire; but the curtain drops on them once more, and is not raised again until Jane is writing from Southampton on January 7, 1807. Owing to the gap in the letters, we have no means of knowing why the Austens selected Southampton as a home; nor are we told what Jane herself thought of the place. At any rate, it was a change from Bath, and she preferred it to Canterbury, which, from its nearness to Godmersham, would have been another very suitable place of residence. Southampton was in her old county, and within fairly easy reach of her old home; and probably one reason for choosing the neighbourhood of a naval centre was, that it enabled them to join forces with Frank Austen and his newly married wife: but we should doubt whether Jane ever felt really at home during her two or three years' residence there, or took much to the society of the place. No doubt the partnership with the Frank Austens and with Martha made it possible for the party to command better quarters, and to live in greater comfort than would have been within reach of the slender means of the Austens by themselves; and when Jane's letters begin again it is pretty clear that the party, though still in lodgings, were getting ready to take possession in March of their house in Castle Square. They were living in a very quiet way, not caring to add to their acquaintance more than was necessary. Cassandra was at this time on a visit to Godmersham, and Martha Lloyd was also away. The Austens were near enough to Steventon to be visited occasionally by James Austen and his wife; and between their own acquaintance, and Frank's friends in the service, they had what they wanted in the way of society.

Southampton: Wednesday [January 7, 1807].

Of your visit there [to Canterbury] I must now speak 'incessantly'; it surprises, but pleases me more, and I consider it as a very just and honourable distinction of you, and not less to the credit of Mrs. Knight. I have no doubt of your spending your time with her most pleasantly in quiet and rational conversation, and am so far from thinking her expectations of you will be deceived, that my only fear is of your being so agreeable, so much to her taste, as to make her wish to keep you with her for ever. If that should be the case, we must remove to Canterbury, which I should not like so well as Southampton.

Alphonsine did not do. We were disgusted in twenty pages, as, independent of a bad translation, it has indelicacies which disgrace a pen hitherto so pure; and we changed it for *The Female Quixote* which now makes our evening amusement: to me a very high one, as I find the work quite equal to what I remembered it.

Our acquaintance increase too fast. He [Frank] was recognised lately by Admiral Bertie, and a few days since arrived the Admiral and his daughter Catherine to wait upon us. There was nothing to like or dislike in either. To the Berties are to be added the Lances, with whose cards we have been endowed, and whose visit Frank and I returned yesterday. They live about a mile and three-quarters from S[outhampton] to the right of the new road to Portsmouth, and I believe their house is one of those which are to be seen almost anywhere among the woods on the other side of the Itchen. It is a handsome building, stands high, and in a very beautiful situation.

We found only Mrs. Lance at home, and whether she boasts any offspring besides a grand pianoforte did not appear. She was civil and chatty enough, and offered to introduce us to some acquaintance in Southampton, which we gratefully declined.

I suppose they must be acting by the orders of Mr. Lance of Netherton in this civility, as there seems no other reason for their coming near us.

Southampton: [February 8, 1807].

Our garden is putting in order by a man who bears a remarkably good character, has a very fine complexion, and asks something less than the first. The shrubs which border the gravel walk, he says, are only sweetbriar and roses, and the latter of an indifferent sort; we mean to get a few of the better kind, therefore, and at my own particular desire he procures us some syringas. I could not do without a syringa, for the sake of Cowper's line. We talk also of a laburnum. The border under the terrace wall is clearing away to receive currants and gooseberry bushes, and a spot is found very proper for raspberries.

The alterations and improvements within doors, too, advance very properly, and the offices will be made very convenient indeed. Our dressing table is constructing on the spot, out of a large kitchen table belonging to the house, for doing which we have the permission of Mr. Husket, Lord Lansdown's painter—domestic painter, I should call him, for he lives in the castle. Domestic chaplains have given way to this more necessary office, and I suppose whenever the walls want no touching up he is employed about my lady's face.

The morning was so wet that I was afraid we should not be able to see our little visitor, but Frank, who alone could go to church, called for her after service, and she is now talking away at my side and examining the treasures of my writing-desk drawers—very happy, I believe. Not at all shy, of course. Her name is Catherine, and her sister's Caroline. She is something like her brother, and as short for her age, but not so well-looking.

What is become of all the shyness in the world? Moral as well as natural diseases disappear in the progress of time, and new ones take their place. Shyness and the sweating sickness have given way to confidence and paralytic complaints.

Evening.—Our little visitor has just left us, and left us highly pleased with her; she is a nice, natural, open-hearted, affectionate girl, with all the ready civility which one sees in the best children in the present day; so unlike anything that I was myself at her age, that I am often all astonishment and shame. Half her time was spent at spillikins, which I consider as a very valuable part of our household furniture, and as not the least important benefaction from the family of Knight to that of Austen.

There, I flatter myself I have constructed you a smartish letter, considering my want of materials, but, like my dear Dr. Johnson, I believe I have dealt more in notions than facts.

Southampton: [Friday, February 20, 1807].

We have at last heard something of Mr. Austen's will. It is believed at Tunbridge that he has left everything after the death of his widow to Mr. M. Austen's third son John; and, as the said John was the only one of the family who attended the funeral, it seems likely to be true.

My mother has heard this morning from Paragon. My aunt talks much of the violent colds prevailing in Bath, from which my uncle has suffered ever since their return, and she has herself a cough much worse than any she ever had before, subject as she has always been to bad ones. She writes in good humour and cheerful spirits, however. The negotiation between them and Adlestrop so happily over, indeed, what can have power to vex her materially?

Saturday.—I have received your letter, but I suppose you do not expect me to be gratified by its contents. I confess myself much disappointed by this repeated delay of your return, for though I had pretty well given up all idea of your being with us before our removal, I felt sure that March would not pass quite away without bringing you. Before April comes, of course something else will occur to detain you. But as *you* are happy, all this is selfishness, of which here is enough for one page.

Frank's going into Kent depends, of course, upon his being unemployed; but as the First Lord, after promising Lord Moira that Captain A. should have the first good frigate that was vacant, has since given away two or three fine ones, he has no particular reason to expect an appointment now. *He*, however, has scarcely spoken about the Kentish journey. I have my information chiefly from her, and she considers her own going thither as more certain if he should be at sea than if not.

Frank has got a very bad cough, for an Austen; but it does not disable him from making very nice fringe for the drawing-room curtains.

I recommend Mrs. Grant's letters, as a present to her [Martha]; what they are about, and how many volumes they form, I do not know, having never heard of them but from Miss Irvine, who speaks of them as a new and much-admired work, and as one which has pleased her highly. I have inquired for the book here, but find it quite unknown.

We are reading Baretti's other book, and find him dreadfully abusive of poor Mr. Sharpe. I can no longer take his part against you, as I did nine years ago.

Our knowledge of the house which was the Austens' home at Southampton for two years, and of its surroundings, is derived from the personal reminiscences of the author of the *Memoir*, who was now old enough to visit his relatives, and who tells us that at this time he began to know, and 'what was the same thing, to love' his Aunt Jane. 'They lived,' he says, 'in a commodious old-fashioned house in a corner of Castle Square . . . with a pleasant garden, bounded on one side by the old city walls; the top of this wall was sufficiently wide to afford a pleasant walk, with an extensive view easily accessible to ladies by steps.' Castle Square itself was occupied 'by a fantastic edifice, too large for the space in which it stood, though too small to accord well with its castellated style, erected by the second Marquis of Lansdowne.' The whole of this building disappeared after the death of its eccentric owner in November 1809. His half-brother and successor in the peerage—the well-known statesman—became in after life an ardent admirer of Jane Austen's novels, and told a friend that 'one of the circumstances of his life which he looked back upon with vexation was that Miss Austen should once have been living some weeks in his neighbourhood without his knowing it.' Had he known it, however, he would have had no reason—in the Southampton period—for imagining her to be an author.

On March 9, 1807, we may imagine the party taking possession of their new house; but Frank can have seen but little of it before he took command of the *St. Albans* in April, and went to the Cape of Good Hope on convoying duty. He was back by June 30.

On Cassandra's return, the two sisters must have been together for a considerable period; but till June 1808 we know little that is definite about them, except that in September 1807, together with their mother, they paid a visit to Chawton House—Edward Austen's Hampshire residence.

During these years, Charles Austen was long engaged in the unpleasant and unprofitable duty of enforcing the right of search on the Atlantic seaboard of America. Hardly anything is said in the extant letters of his marriage to Fanny Palmer, daughter of the Attorney-General of Bermuda, which took place in 1807.

The month of June 1808 found Jane staying with her brother Henry in Brompton; but we have no details of her stay beyond the fact that she watched some of her acquaintance going to Court on the King's birthday. On June 14 she left London with her brother James, his wife and two children, on a visit to Godmersham.

> Godmersham: Wednesday [June 15, 1808].
>
> MY DEAR CASSANDRA,—Where shall I begin? Which of all my important nothings shall I tell you first? At half after seven yesterday morning Henry saw us into our own carriage, and we drove away from the Bath Hotel; which, by-the-bye, had been found most uncomfortable quarters—very dirty, very noisy, and very ill-provided. James began his journey by the coach at five. Our first eight miles were hot; Deptford Hill brought to my mind our hot journey into Kent fourteen years ago; but after Blackheath we suffered nothing, and as the day advanced it grew quite cool. At Dartford, which we reached within the two hours and three-quarters, we went to the Bull, the same inn at which we breakfasted in that said journey, and on the present occasion had about the same bad butter.

At half-past ten we were again off, and, travelling on without any adventure reached Sittingbourne by three. Daniel was watching for us at the door of the 'George,' and I was acknowledged very kindly by Mr. and Mrs. Marshall, to the latter of whom I devoted my conversation, while Mary went out to buy some gloves. A few minutes, of course, did for Sittingbourne; and so off we drove, drove, drove, and by six o'clock were at Godmersham.

Our two brothers were walking before the house as we approached, as natural as life. Fanny and Lizzie met us in the Hall with a great deal of pleasant joy; we went for a few minutes into the breakfast parlour, and then proceeded to our rooms. Mary has the Hall chamber. I am in the Yellow room—very literally—for I am writing in it at this moment. It seems odd to me to have such a great place all to myself, and to be at Godmersham without you is also odd.

You are wished for, I assure you: Fanny, who came to me as soon as she had seen her Aunt James to her room, and stayed while I dressed, was as energetic as usual in her longings for you. She is grown both in height and size since last year, but not immoderately, looks very well, and seems as to conduct and manner just what she was and what one could wish her to continue.

Elizabeth, who was dressing when we arrived, came to me for a minute attended by Marianne, Charles, and Louisa, and, you will not doubt, gave me a very affectionate welcome. That I had received such from Edward also I need not mention; but I do, you see, because it is a pleasure. I never saw him look in better health, and Fanny says he is perfectly well. I cannot praise Elizabeth's looks, but they are probably affected by a cold. Her little namesake has gained in beauty in the last three years, though not all that Marianne has lost. Charles is not quite so lovely as he was. Louisa is much as I expected, and Cassandra I find handsomer than I expected, though at present disguised by such a violent breaking-out that she does not come down after dinner. She has charming eyes and a nice open countenance, and seems likely to be very lovable. Her size is magnificent.

Thursday.—. . . I feel rather languid and solitary—perhaps because I have a cold; but three years ago we were more animated with you and Harriot and Miss Sharpe. We shall improve, I dare say, as we go on.

Friday.—Edward and Caroline seem very happy here; he has nice play-fellows in Lizzie and Charles. They and their attendant have the boys' attic. Anna will not be surprised that the cutting off her hair is very much regretted by several of the party in this house; I am tolerably reconciled to it by considering that two or three years may restore it again.

Godmersham: Monday [June 20, 1808].

This morning brought me a letter from Mrs. Knight, containing the usual fee, and all the usual kindness. She asks me to spend a day or two with her this week, to meet Mrs. C. Knatchbull, who, with her husband, comes to the White Friars to-day, and I believe I shall go. I have consulted Edward, and think it will be arranged for Mrs. J. A.'s going with me one morning, my staying the night, and Edward driving me home the next evening. Her very agreeable present will make my circumstances quite easy. I shall reserve half for my pelisse.

Wednesday.—I sent my answer by them [the Moores] to Mrs. Knight; my double acceptance of her note and her invitation, which I wrote without effort, for I am rich, and the rich are always respectable, whatever be their style of writing.

Ought I to be very much pleased with *Marmion?* As yet I am not. James reads it aloud every evening—the short evening, beginning at about ten, and broken by supper.

Godmersham: Sunday [June 26, 1808].

I am very much obliged to you for writing to me on Thursday, and very glad that I owe the pleasure of hearing from you again so soon to such an agreeable cause; but you will not be surprised, nor perhaps so angry as I should be, to find that Frank's history had reached me before in a letter from Henry. We are all very happy to hear of his health and safety; he wants nothing but a good prize to be a perfect character.

They [the Knatchbulls] return into Somersetshire by way of Sussex and Hants, and are to be at Fareham, and, perhaps, may be in Southampton, on which possibility I said all that I thought right, and, if they are in the place M$^{rs.}$ K. has promised to call in Castle Square; it will be about the end of July. . . . You and I need not tell each other how glad we shall be to receive attention from, or pay it to anyone connected with Mrs. Knight. I cannot help regretting that now, when I feel enough her equal to relish her society, I see so little of the latter.

Godmersham: Thursday [June 30, 1808].

You are very kind in mentioning old Mrs. Williams so often. Poor creature! I cannot help hoping that each letter may tell of her suffering being over. If she wants sugar I should like to supply her with it.

I give you all joy of Frank's return, which happens in the true sailor way, just after our being told not to expect him for some weeks. The wind has been very much against him, but I suppose he must be in our neighbourhood by this time. Fanny is in hourly expectation of him here. Mary's visit in the island is probably shortened by this event. Make our kind love and congratulations to her.

James and Edward are gone to Sandling to-day—a nice scheme for James, as it will show him a new and fine country. Edward certainly excels in doing the honours to his visitors, and providing for their amusement. They come back this evening.

It is pleasant to be among people who know one's connections and care about them, and it amuses me to hear John Bridges talk of 'Frank.' I have thought a little of writing to the Downs, but I shall not, it is so very certain that he would be somewhere else when my letter got there.

Friday, July 1.—It will be two years to-morrow since we left Bath for Clifton, with what happy feelings of escape!

In another week I shall be at home, and there, my having been at Godmersham will seem like a dream, as my visit to Brompton seems already.

The orange wine will want our care soon. But in the meantime, for elegance and ease and luxury, the Hattons and the Milles' dine here to-day, and I shall eat ice and drink French wine, and be above vulgar economy. Luckily the pleasures of friendship, of unreserved conversation, of similarity of taste and opinions, will make good amends for orange wine.

Little Edward is quite well again.

Yours affectionately, with love from all,
J. A.

CHAPTER XIII.

FROM SOUTHAMPTON TO CHAWTON 1808-1809

WE do not doubt that the orange wine was duly made, and the pleasure of unreserved conversation enjoyed during the remainder of the summer. Before the end of September, Cassandra had gone to Godmersham on what was to prove a long and a sad visit. She arrived just at the time of the birth of her sister-in-law's sixth son and eleventh child, John. For a time all went well with mother and child; but on October 8 Elizabeth Austen was suddenly seized with sickness, and died before the serious nature of her attack had been fully realised. This sad event occurred, as the reader will see, between the second and third of the following letters. Edward Austen's two eldest boys, Edward and George, were now at Winchester School, but were taken away for a time on their mother's death. They went at first to the James Austens, at Steventon, no one appearing to think a journey to so distant a county as Kent feasible; and Jane, whose immediate impulse seems to have been to do what she could for her nephews, resigned them rather unwillingly for the time. On October 22 they went on to their grandmother and aunt at Southampton; and then their Aunt Jane was able to devote herself entirely to them, as her own Jane Bennet once did to her small cousins, and to show how her 'steady sense and sweetness of temper exactly adapted her for attending to them in every way: teaching them, playing with them, and loving them'—words which she probably intended as a description of what Cassandra would have done in a similar position.

Castle Square: Saturday [October 1, 1808].

MY DEAR CASSANDRA,—Your letter this morning was quite unexpected, and it is well that it brings such good news to counterbalance the disappointment to me of losing my first sentence, which I had arranged full of proper hopes about your journey, intending to commit them to paper to-day, and not looking for certainty till to-morrow.

We are extremely glad to hear of the birth of the child, and trust everything will proceed as well as it begins. His mamma has our best wishes, and he our second best for health and comfort—though I suppose, unless he has our best too, we do nothing for *her*. We are glad it was all over before your arrival, and I am most happy to find who the godmother is to be. My mother was some time guessing the names.

About an hour and a half after your toils on Wednesday ended, ours began. At seven o'clock Mrs. Harrison, her two daughters and two visitors, with Mr. Debary and his eldest sister, walked in.

A second pool of commerce, and all the longer by the addition of the two girls, who during the first had one corner of the table and spillikins to themselves, was the ruin of us; it completed the prosperity of Mr. Debary, however, for he won them both.

Mr. Harrison came in late, and sat by the fire, for which I envied him, as we had our usual luck of having a very cold evening. It rained when our company came, but was dry again before they left us.

The Miss Ballards are said to be remarkably well-informed; their manners are unaffected and pleasing, but they do not talk quite freely enough to be agreeable, nor can I discover any right they had by taste or feeling to go their late tour.

We have got the second volume of *Espriella's Letters*, and I read it aloud by candlelight. The man describes well, but is horribly anti-English. He deserves to be the foreigner he assumes.

The Marquis has put off being cured for another year; after waiting some weeks in vain for the return of the vessel he had agreed for, he is gone into Cornwall to order a vessel built for himself by a famous man in that country, in which he means to go abroad a twelvemonth hence.

With love to all,

Yours affectionately,
J. A.

Fanny Austen (afterwards Lady Knatchbull), Edward's eldest daughter, had nearly completed her sixteenth year. She was admirably adapted for the difficult position into which she was about to be thrown: that of companion to her father, mistress of a large household, and adviser to her younger brothers and sisters. She was sensible, even-tempered, affectionate, and conscientious. She did indeed prove 'almost another sister' to Jane, who, as Cassandra said afterwards, was perhaps better known to her than to any other human being, except Cassandra herself. Though this niece did not profess any special literary ability, her Aunt always valued her sound judgment on each new book: and in return she gave her, without fear of offending, advice on the most delicate subjects. The short extracts from Fanny's diary, which her son, Lord Brabourne, gives us, show how constantly 'Aunt Jane' was the object of her thoughts.

Castle Square: Friday [October 7, 1808].

MY DEAR CASSANDRA,—Your letter on Tuesday gave us great pleasure, and we congratulate you all upon Elizabeth's hitherto happy recovery; to-morrow, or Sunday, I hope to hear of its advancing in the same style. We are also very glad to know that you are so well yourself, and pray you to continue so.

We found ourselves tricked into a thorough party at Mrs. M.'s, a quadrille and a commerce table, and music in the other room. There were two pools at commerce, but I would not play more than one, for the stake was three shillings, and I cannot afford to lose that twice in an evening. The Miss M.'s were as civil and as silly as usual.

Saturday.—Thank you for your letter, which found me at the breakfast table with my two companions.

I am greatly pleased with your account of Fanny; I found her in the summer just what you describe, almost another sister; and could not have supposed that a niece would ever have been so much to me. She is quite after one's own heart; give her my best love, and tell her that I always think of her with pleasure.

Martha was an hour and a half in Winchester, walking about with the three boys and at the pastry-cook's. She thought Edward grown, and speaks with the same admiration as before of his manners; she saw in George a little likeness to his uncle Henry.

[October 13.]

I have received your letter, and with most melancholy anxiety was it expected, for the sad news reached us last night, but without any particulars. It came in a short letter to Martha from her sister, begun at Steventon and finished in Winchester.

We have felt—we do feel—for you all, as you will not need to be told: for you, for Fanny, for Henry, for Lady Bridges, and for dearest Edward, whose loss and whose sufferings seem to make those of every other person nothing. God be praised that you can say what you do of him: that he has a religious mind to bear him up, and a disposition that will gradually lead him to comfort.

My dear, dear Fanny, I am so thankful that she has you with her! You will be everything to her; you will give her all the consolation that human aid can give. May the Almighty sustain you all, and keep you, my dearest Cassandra, well; but for the present I dare say you are equal to everything.

You will know that the poor boys are at Steventon. Perhaps it is best for them, as they will have more means of exercise and amusement there than they could have with us, but I own myself disappointed by the arrangement. I should have loved to have them with me at such a time. I shall write to Edward by this post.

With what true sympathy our feelings are shared by Martha you need not be told; she is the friend and sister under every circumstance.

We need not enter into a panegyric on the departed, but it is sweet to think of her great worth, of her solid principles, of her true devotion, her excellence in every relation of life. It is also consolatory to reflect on the shortness of the sufferings which led her from this world to a better.

Farewell for the present, my dearest sister. Tell Edward that we feel for him and pray for him.

Saturday night [October 15, 1808].

Your accounts make us as comfortable as we can expect to be at such a time. Edward's loss is terrible, and must be felt as such, and these are too early days indeed to think of moderation in grief, either in him or his afflicted daughter, but soon we may hope that our dear Fanny's sense of duty to that beloved father will rouse her to exertion. For his sake, and as the most acceptable proof of love to the spirit of her departed mother, she will try to be tranquil and resigned. Does she feel you to be a comfort to her, or is she too much overpowered for anything but solitude?

Your account of Lizzy is very interesting. Poor child! One must hope the impression *will* be strong, and yet one's heart aches for a dejected mind of eight years old.

We are anxious to be assured that Edward will not attend the funeral, but when it comes to the point I think he must feel it impossible.

I am glad you can say what you do of Mrs. Knight and of Goodnestone in general; it is a great relief to me to know that the shock did not make any of them ill. But what a task was yours to announce it! *Now* I hope you are not overpowered with letter-writing, as Henry and John can ease you of many of your correspondents.

Upon your letter to Dr. Goddard's being forwarded to them, Mary wrote to ask whether my mother wished to have her grandsons sent to her. We decided on their remaining where they were, which I hope my brother will approve of. I am sure he will do us the justice of believing that in such a decision we sacrificed inclination to what we thought best.

I shall write by the coach to-morrow to Mrs. J. A., and to Edward, about their mourning, though this day's post will probably bring directions to them on that subject from yourselves. I shall certainly make use of the opportunity of addressing our nephew on the most serious of all concerns, as I naturally did in my letter to him before. The poor boys are, perhaps, more comfortable at Steventon than they could be here, but you will understand *my feelings* with respect to it.

To-morrow will be a dreadful day for you all. Mr. Whitfield's will be a severe duty. Glad shall I be to hear that it is over.

That you are for ever in our thoughts you will not doubt. I see your mournful party in my mind's eye under every varying circumstance of the day; and in the evening especially figure to myself its sad gloom: the efforts to talk, the frequent summons to melancholy orders and cares, and poor Edward, restless in misery, going from one room to another, and perhaps not seldom upstairs, to see all that remains of his Elizabeth.

There must be a letter missing between October 15 and October 24, containing Jane's first comment on the offer of a cottage at Chawton, made by Edward Austen to his mother. In the midst of his grief—perhaps, in consequence of his loss—he wished to bind his mother and sisters more closely to himself. He gave them a choice between a house near Godmersham, and one at Chawton; but the mother and sisters were what Jane afterwards called 'Hampshire-born Austens,' and clung to their county. The offer was particularly opportune, for Mrs. Austen was already hesitating between Kent and Hampshire as a place of residence. The attractions of a home at Chawton became greater the more they were considered; and though it was held to be necessary to consult the Frank Austens, whom they would be leaving, no doubt was entertained as to their answer.

Castle Square: Monday [October 24, 1808].

MY DEAR CASSANDRA,—Edward and George came to us soon after seven on Saturday, very well, but very cold, having by choice travelled on the outside, and with no great coat but what Mr. Wise, the coachman, good-naturedly spared them of his, as they sat by his side. They were so much chilled when they arrived, that I was afraid they must have taken cold; but it does not seem at all the case; I never saw them looking better.

They behave extremely well in every respect, showing quite as much feeling as one wishes to see, and on every occasion speaking of their father with the liveliest affection. His letter was read over by each of them yesterday, and with many tears; George sobbed aloud, Edward's tears do not flow so easily; but as far as I can judge they are both very properly impressed by what has happened. Miss Lloyd, who is a more impartial judge than I can be, is exceedingly pleased with them.

George is almost a new acquaintance to me, and I find him in a different way as *engaging as Edward*.

We do not want amusement: bilbocatch, at which George is indefatigable, spillikins, paper ships, riddles, conundrums, and cards, with watching the flow and ebb of the river, and now and then a stroll out, keep us well employed; and we mean to avail ourselves of our kind papa's consideration, by not returning to Winchester till quite the evening of Wednesday.

The *St. Albans*, I find, sailed on the very day of my letters reaching Yarmouth, so that we must not expect an answer at present; we scarcely feel, however, to be in suspense, or only enough to keep our plans to ourselves. We have been obliged to explain them to our young visitors, in consequence of Fanny's letter, but we have not yet mentioned them to Steventon. We are all quite familiarised to the idea ourselves; my mother only wants Mrs. Seward to go out at Midsummer.

What sort of a kitchen garden is there? Mrs. J. A. expresses her fear of our settling in Kent, and, till this proposal was made, we began to look forward to it here; my mother was actually talking of a house at Wye. It will be best, however, as it is.

I hope your sorrowing party were at church yesterday, and have no longer *that* to dread. Martha was kept at home by a *cold, but I went with my two nephews, and I saw Edward was much affected by the sermon, which, indeed, I could have supposed purposely addressed* to the afflicted, if the text had not naturally come in the course of Dr. Mant's observations on the Litany: 'All that are in danger, necessity, or tribulation,' was the subject of it. The weather did not allow us afterwards to get farther than the quay, where George was very happy as long as we could stay, flying about from one side to the other, and skipping on board a collier immediately.

In the evening we had the Psalms and Lessons, and a sermon at home, to which they were very attentive; but you will not expect to hear that they did not return to conundrums the moment it *was over*.

While I write now, George is most industriously making and naming paper ships, at which he afterwards shoots with horse-chestnuts, brought from Steventon on purpose; and Edward equally intent over the *Lake of Killarney*, twisting himself about in one of our great chairs.

Tuesday.—The day began cheerfully, but it is not likely to continue what it should, for them or for us. *We had a little water party* yesterday; I and my two nephews went from the Itchen Ferry up to Northam, where we landed, looked into the 74, and walked home, and it was so much enjoyed that I had intended to take them to Netley to-day; the tide is just right for our going immediately after moonshine, but I am afraid there will be rain; if we cannot get so far, however, we may perhaps go round from the ferry to the quay.

I had not proposed doing more than cross the Itchen yesterday, but it proved so pleasant, and so much to the satisfaction of all, that when we reached the middle of the stream we agreed to be rowed up the river; both the boys rowed great part of the way, and their questions and remarks, as well as their enjoyment, were very amusing; George's enquiries were endless, and his eagerness in everything reminds me often *of his Uncle Henry*.

Our evening was equally agreeable in its way: I introduced *speculation*, and it was so much approved that we hardly knew how to leave off.

Of Chawton I think I can have nothing more to say, but that everything you say about it in the letter now before me will, I am sure, as soon as I am able to read it to her, make my mother consider the plan with more and more pleasure.

Sunday [November 21, 1808].

Your letter, my dear Cassandra, obliges me to write immediately, that you may have the earliest notice of Frank's intending, if possible, to go to Godmersham exactly at the time now fixed for your visit to Goodnestone.

Your news of Edward Bridges was *quite* news, for I have had no letter from Wrotham. I wish him happy with all my heart, and hope his choice may turn out according to his own expectations, and beyond those of his family; and I dare say it will. Marriage is a great improver, and in a similar situation Harriet may be as amiable as Eleanor. As to money, that will come, you may be sure, because they cannot do without it. When you see him again, pray give him our congratulations and best wishes. This match will certainly set John and Lucy going.

There are six bedchambers at Chawton; Henry wrote to my mother the other day, and luckily mentioned the number, which is just what we wanted to be assured of. He speaks also of garrets for store places, one of which she immediately planned fitting up for Edward's man servant; and now perhaps it must be for our own; for she is already quite reconciled to our keeping one. The difficulty of doing without one had been thought of before. His name shall be Robert, if you please.

Yes, the Stoneleigh business is concluded, but it was not till yesterday that my mother was regularly informed of it, though the news had reached us on Monday evening by way of Steventon.

Our brother we may perhaps see in the course of a few days, and we mean to take the opportunity of his help to go one night to the play. Martha ought to see the inside of the theatre once while she lives in Southampton, and I think she will hardly wish to take a second view.

How could you have a wet day on Thursday? With us it was a prince of days, the most delightful we have had for weeks; soft, bright, with a brisk wind from the south-west; everybody was out and talking of spring, and Martha and I did not know how to turn back. On Friday evening we had some very blowing weather—from 6 to 9, I think we never heard it worse, even here. And one night we had so much rain that it forced its way again into the store closet, and though the evil was comparatively slight and the mischief nothing, I had some employment the next day in drying parcels, &c. I have now moved still more out of the way.

Adieu! remember me affectionately to everybody, and believe me,

Ever yours,
J. A.

The home at Chawton was now looked upon as a certainty; though none of its future inhabitants inspected it until February 1809, when Cassandra visited it on her way back from Godmersham.

It was some years since they had lived in the country, and their future home was likely to be very quiet; so, as Jane recovered her spirits, she determined to crowd into her remaining months at Southampton as much society and amusement as possible. She went to two of the Southampton assemblies—her last recorded appearances as an active ball-goer.

Castle Square: Friday [December 9, 1808].

MY DEAR CASSANDRA,—Soon after I had closed my last letter to you we were visited by Mrs. Dickens and her sister-in-law, Mrs. Bertie, the wife of a lately-made Admiral. Mrs. F. A., I believe, was their first object, but they put up with us very kindly, and Mrs. D. finding in Miss Lloyd a friend of Mrs. Dundas, had another motive for the acquaintance. She seems a really agreeable woman—that is, her manners are gentle, and she knows a great many of our connections in West Kent. Mrs. Bertie lives in the Polygon, and was out when we returned her visit, which are *her* two virtues.

A larger circle of acquaintance, and an increase of amusement, is quite in character with our approaching removal. Yes, I mean to go to as many balls as possible, that I may have a good bargain. Everybody is very much concerned at our going away, and everybody is acquainted with Chawton, and speaks of it as a remarkably pretty village, and everybody knows the house we describe, but nobody fixes on the right.

I am very much obliged to Mrs. Knight for such a proof of the interest she takes in me, and she may depend upon it that I *will* marry Mr. Papillon, whatever may be his reluctance or my own. I owe her much more than such a trifling sacrifice.

Our ball was rather more amusing than I expected. Martha liked it very much, and I did not gape till the last quarter of an hour. It was past nine before we were sent for, and not twelve when we returned. The room was tolerably full, and there were, perhaps, thirty couple of dancers. The melancholy part was, to see so many dozen young women standing by without partners, and each of them with two ugly naked shoulders.

It was the same room in which we danced fifteen years ago. I thought it all over, and in spite of the shame of being so much older, felt with thankfulness that I was quite as happy now as then. We paid an additional shilling for our tea, which we took as we chose in an adjoining and very comfortable room.

There were only four dances, and it went to my heart that the Miss Lances (one of them, too, named Emma) should have partners only for two. You will not expect to hear that *I* was asked to dance, but I was—by the gentleman whom we met *that Sunday* with Captain D'Auvergne. We have always kept up a bowing acquaintance since, and, being pleased with his black eyes, I spoke to him at the ball, which brought on me this civility; but I do not know his name, and he seems so little at home in the English language, that I believe his black eyes may be the best of him. Captain D'Auvergne has got a ship.

Having now cleared away my smaller articles of news, I come to a communication of some weight: no less than that my uncle and aunt are going to allow James £100 a year. We hear of it through Steventon. Mary sent us the other day an extract from my aunt's letter on the subject, in which the donation is made with the greatest kindness, and intended as a compensation for his loss in the conscientious refusal of Hampstead living; £100 a year being all that he had at the time called its worth, as I find it was always intended at Steventon to divide the real income with Kintbury.

I am glad you are to have Henry with you again; with him and the boys you cannot but have a cheerful, and at times even a merry, Christmas.

We want to be settled at Chawton in time for Henry to come to us for some shooting in October, at least, or a little earlier, and Edward may visit us after taking his boys back to Winchester. Suppose we name the 4th of September. Will not that do?

Distribute the affectionate love of a heart not so tired as the right hand belonging to it.

Tuesday [December 27, 1808].

. . . Lady Sondes' match surprises, but does not offend me; had her first marriage been of affection, or had there been a grown-up single daughter, I should not have forgiven her; but I consider everybody as having a right to marry *once* in their lives for love, if they can, and provided she will now leave off having bad headaches and being pathetic, I can allow her, I can *wish* her, to be happy.

Do not imagine that your picture of your *tête-à-tête* with Sir B. makes any change in our expectations here; he could not be really reading, though he held the newspaper in his hand; he was making up his mind to the deed, and the manner of it. I think you will have a letter from him soon.

We have now pretty well ascertained James's income to be eleven hundred pounds, curate paid, which makes us very happy—the ascertainment as well as the income.

Wednesday.—I must write to Charles next week. You may guess in what extravagant terms of praise Earle Harwood speaks of him. He is looked up to by everybody in all America.

Yes, yes, we *will* have a pianoforte, as good a one as can be got for thirty guineas, and I will practise country dances, that we may have some amusement for our nephews and nieces, when we have the pleasure of their company.

Tuesday [January 10, 1809].

I am not surprised, my dear Cassandra, that you did not find my last letter very full of matter, and I wish this may not have the same deficiency; but we are doing nothing ourselves to write about, and I am therefore quite dependent upon the communications of our friends, or my own wits.

The *St. Albans* perhaps may soon be off to help bring home what may remain by this time of our poor army, whose state seems dreadfully critical. The Regency seems to have been heard of only here; my most political correspondents make no mention of it. Unlucky that I should have wasted so much reflection on the subject.

I can now answer your question to my mother more at large, and likewise more at small—with equal perspicuity and minuteness; for the very day of our leaving Southampton is fixed; and if the knowledge is of no *use* to Edward, I am sure it will give him pleasure. Easter Monday, April 3, is the day; we are to sleep that night at Alton, and be with our friends at Bookham the next, if they are then at home; there we remain till the following Monday, and on Tuesday, April 11, hope to be at Godmersham.

William will be quite recovered, I trust, by the time you receive this. What a comfort his cross-stitch must have been! Pray tell him that I should like to see his work very much. I hope our answers this morning have given satisfaction; we had great pleasure in Uncle Deedes' packet; and pray let Marianne know, in private, that I think she is quite right to work a rug for Uncle John's coffee urn, and that I am sure it must give great pleasure to herself now, and to him when he receives it.

The preference of Brag over Speculation does not greatly surprise me, I believe, because I feel the same myself; but it mortifies me deeply, because Speculation was under my patronage; and, after all, what is there so delightful in a pair royal of Braggers? It is but three nines or three knaves, or a mixture of them. When one comes to reason upon it, it cannot stand its ground against Speculation—of which I hope Edward is now convinced. Give my love to him if he is.

We are now in *Margiana*, and like it very well indeed. We are just going to set off for Northumberland to be shut up in Widdrington Tower, where there must be two or three sets of victims already immured under a very fine villain.

Wednesday.—Charles's rug will be finished to-day, and sent to-morrow to Frank, to be consigned by him to Mr. Turner's care; and I am going to send *Marmion* out with it—very generous in me, I think.

Have you nothing to say of your little namesake? We join in love and many happy returns.

                                        Yours affectionately,
                                              J. AUSTEN.

The Manydown ball was a smaller thing than I expected, but it seems to have made Anna very happy. At *her* age it would not have done for *me*.

Tuesday [January 17, 1809].

I hope you have had no more illness among you, and that William will be soon as well as ever. His working a footstool for Chawton is a most agreeable surprise to me, and I am sure his grandmamma will value it very much as a proof of his affection and industry, but we shall never have the heart to put our feet upon it. I believe I must work a muslin cover in satin stitch to keep it from the dirt. I long to know what his colours are. I guess greens and purples.

To set against your new novel, of which nobody ever heard before, and perhaps never may again, we have got *Ida of Athens*, by Miss Owenson, which must be very clever, because it was written, as the authoress says, in three months. We have only read the preface yet, but her *Irish Girl* does not make me expect much. If the warmth of her language could affect the body it might be worth reading in this weather.

Adieu! I must leave off to stir the fire and call on Miss Murden.

Evening.—I have done them both, the first very often. We found our friend as comfortable as she can ever allow herself to be in cold weather. There is a very neat parlour behind the shop for her to sit in, not very light indeed, being *à la* Southampton, the middle of three deep, but very lively from the frequent sound of the pestle and mortar.

Tuesday [January 24, 1809].

I had the happiness yesterday of a letter from Charles, but I shall say as little about it as possible, because I know *that* excruciating Henry will have had a letter likewise, to make all my intelligence valueless. It was written at Bermuda on the 7th and 10th of December. All well, and Fanny still only in expectation of being otherwise. He had taken a small prize in his late cruise—a French schooner, laden with sugar; but bad weather parted them, and she had not yet been heard of. His cruise ended December 1st. My September letter was the latest he had received.

You rejoice me by what you say of Fanny. I hope she will not turn good-for-nothing this ever so long. We thought of and talked of her yesterday with sincere affection, and wished her a long enjoyment of all the happiness to which she seems born. While she gives happiness to those about her she is pretty sure of her own share.

I am gratified by her having pleasure in what I write, but I wish the knowledge of my being exposed to her discerning criticism may not hurt my style, by inducing too great a solicitude. I begin already to weigh my words and sentences more than I did, and am looking about for a sentiment, an illustration, or a metaphor in every corner of the room. Could my ideas flow as fast as the rain in the store closet it would be charming.

We have been in two or three dreadful states within the last week, from the melting of the snow, &c., and the contest between us and the closet has now ended in our defeat. I have been obliged to move almost everything out of it, and leave it to splash itself as it likes.

You have by no means raised my curiosity after Caleb. My disinclination for it before was affected, but now it is real. I do not like the evangelicals. Of course I shall be delighted when I read it, like other people, but till I do I dislike it.

Your silence on the subject of our ball makes me suppose your curiosity too great for words. We were very well entertained, and could have stayed longer but for the arrival of my list shoes to convey me home, and I did not like to keep them waiting in the cold. The room was tolerably full, and the ball opened by Miss Glyn. The Miss Lances had partners, Captain D'Auvergne's friend appeared in regimentals, Caroline Maitland had an officer to flirt with, and Mr. John Harrison was deputed by Captain Smith, being himself absent, to ask me to dance. Everything went well, you see, especially after we had tucked Mrs. Lance's neckerchief in behind and fastened it with a pin.

Adieu, sweet You. This is grievous news from Spain. It is well that Dr. Moore was spared the knowledge of such a son's death.

Monday [January 30].

I am not at all ashamed about the name of the novel, having been guilty of no insult towards your handwriting; the diphthong I always saw, but knowing how fond you were of adding a vowel wherever you could, I attributed it to that alone, and the knowledge of the truth does the book no service; the only merit it could have was in the name of Caleb, which has an honest, unpretending sound, but in Cœlebs there is pedantry and affectation. Is it written only to classical scholars?

I am sorry to find that Sir J. Moore has a mother living, but though a very heroic son he might not be a very necessary one to her happiness. Deacon Morrell may be more to Mrs. Morrell.

I wish Sir John had united something of the Christian with the hero in his death. Thank heaven! we have had no one to care for particularly among the troops—no one, in fact, nearer to us than Sir John himself.

The store closet, I hope, will never do so again, for much of the evil is proved to have proceeded from the gutter being choked up, and we have had it cleared. We had reason to rejoice in the child's absence at the time of the thaw, for the nursery was not habitable. We hear of similar disasters from almost everybody.

Yours very affectionately,
J. AUSTEN.

Miss Austen, Edward Austen's, Esq.
Godmersham Park, Faversham, Kent.

This letter brings the Southampton series to an end. The party were not to take up their residence at Chawton till the beginning of September; but they left Southampton in April, and we may presume that they carried out the programme mentioned in Jane's letter of January 10, and went by way of Alton to Bookham, and on to Godmersham.

In the whole series of letters written from Southampton, there is not a single allusion to Jane's being engaged upon any novel; and it has been inferred—probably correctly—that her pen was idle during these years. The fact that she had already written three novels, but had not succeeded in publishing a single one, can hardly have encouraged her to write more. But it seems almost certain that, a few days before she left Southampton, she made an effort to secure the publication of the novel which we know as *Northanger Abbey*, by the publisher to whom she had sold it as far back as 1803.

The circumstances are somewhat involved, but appear to be as follows: Among the letters preserved by Cassandra, is one said not to be in Jane's hand, addressed to Messrs. Crosbie [*sic*] & Co., of which these are the contents:—

GENTLEMEN,—In the spring of the year 1803 a MS. novel in two vols., entitled *Susan*, was sold to you by a gentleman of the name of Seymour, and the purchase money £10 rec$^{d.}$ at the same time. Six years have since passed, and this work, of which I am myself the Authoress, has never to the best of my knowledge appeared in print, tho' an early publication was stipulated for at the time of sale. I can only account for such an extraordinary circumstance by supposing the MS. by some carelessness to have been lost, and if that was the case am willing to supply you with another copy, if you are disposed to avail yourselves of it, and will engage for no farther delay when it comes into your hands. It will not be in my power from particular circumstances to command this copy before the month of August, but then if you accept my proposal you may depend on receiving it. Be so good as to send me a line in answer as soon as possible as my stay in this place will not exceed a few days. Should no notice be taken of this address, I shall feel myself at liberty to secure the publication of my work by applying elsewhere.

I am, Gentlemen, etc., etc.,
M. A. D.

Direct to Mrs. Ashton Dennis,
Post Office, Southampton
April 5, 1809.

With this letter was preserved the following reply:—

MADAM,—We have to acknowledge the receipt of your letter of the 5th inst. It is true that at the time mentioned we purchased of Mr. Seymour a MS. novel entitled *Susan*, and paid him for it the sum of £10, for which we have his stamped receipt, as a full consideration, but there was not any time stipulated for its publication, neither are we bound to publish it. Should you or anyone else [publish it] we shall take proceedings to stop the sale. The MS. shall be yours for the same as we paid for it.

For CROSBY & CO.
I am yours, etc.
RICHARD CROSBY.

From the fact that this letter was carefully preserved among Jane's correspondence, from the almost exact coincidence of the dates at which the writer was to leave Southampton, &c., and from the fact that a Mr. Seymour was Henry Austen's man of business, there can be no reasonable doubt that the letter refers to one of Jane Austen's works. It need cause no surprise that she should have written under an assumed name, or that she should have got some one else to write for her in view of the secrecy which she long maintained regarding the authorship of her novels. If we assume, then, that the letter concerns one of Jane Austen's novels—which novel is it? At first sight it might naturally seem to be the story called *Lady Susan*, which was published in the second edition of the *Memoir;* but there are two objections to this: one, that so far from making two volumes, *Lady Susan* could hardly have made more than one very thin volume; secondly, that *Lady Susan* is generally looked upon as an early and immature production; and Jane's judgment should have been too good to allow her to desire the publication of an inferior work at a time when she had already completed, in one form or another, three such novels as *Sense and Sensibility*, *Pride and Prejudice*, and *Northanger Abbey*. If, therefore, it was not *Lady Susan*—What was it? We cannot doubt that it was the novel we now know as *Northanger Abbey*. When that book was prepared for the press in 1816, it contained the following 'advertisement' or prefatory note:—

This little work was finished in the year 1803, and intended for immediate publication. It was disposed of to a bookseller, it was even advertised, and why the business proceeded no further, the author has never been able to learn.

So far, this accords closely enough with the history of the MS. *Susan* as related in the letter to Messrs. Crosby. For other details we must go to the *Memoir*, where we read:—

It [*Northanger Abbey*] was sold in 1803 to a publisher in Bath for ten pounds; but it found so little favour in his eyes that he chose to abide by his first loss rather than risk further expense by publishing such a work. . . . But when four novels of steadily increasing success had given the writer some confidence in herself, she wished to recover the copyright of this early work. One of her brothers undertook the negotiation. He found the purchaser very willing to receive back his money and to resign all claim to the copyright.

This, too, accords closely enough with the history of the MS. *Susan*, with the exception of one expression—namely, 'publisher in Bath'; but probably the writer of the *Memoir* here made a slip, acting on the very natural inference that a book in the main written about Bath, by a writer at that time living in Bath, would naturally have been offered to a publisher in that town.

We are, indeed, confronted by two alternatives: either that Jane Austen, in the year 1803, sold two MSS. for the sum of ten pounds each—one named *Susan*, to a London publisher, which has disappeared altogether, unless it is the same as the sketch *Lady Susan* (which, as we have seen, is improbable), and the other

198

(*Northanger Abbey*) to a Bath publisher; or that the publisher was really a London and not a Bath publisher, and that the original Christian name of Catherine Morland was Susan.

CHAPTER XIV.

SENSE AND SENSIBILITY 1809-1811

WE are now bringing Jane Austen to the home which she was to occupy through all the remaining eight years of her life—the home from which she went to lie on her deathbed at Winchester. Into this period were to be crowded a large proportion of her most important literary work, and all the contemporary recognition which she was destined to enjoy. The first six of these years must have been singularly happy. So far as we know, she was in good health, she was a member of a cheerful family party, and she was under the protection of brothers who would see that she and her mother and sister suffered no discomfort. The eldest, James, Rector of Steventon, could reach his mother's house in a morning's ride through pleasant country lanes; Edward, the Squire, occasionally occupied the 'Great House' at Chawton, and often lent it to one of his naval brothers; while Henry in London was only too happy to receive his sisters, show them the sights of the metropolis, and transact Jane's literary business. At home were her mother, her life-long friend Martha, and above all her 'other self'—Cassandra—from whom she had no secrets, and with whom disagreement was impossible. But besides all these living objects of interest, Jane also had her own separate and peculiar world, peopled by the creations of her own bright imagination, which by degrees became more and more real to her as she found others accepting and admiring them. She must have resumed the habit of writing with diffidence, after her previous experience; but the sense of progress, and the success which attended her venture in publishing *Sense and Sensibility* would by degrees make ample amends for past disappointments. She was no doubt aided by the quiet of her home and its friendly surroundings. In this tranquil spot, where the past and present even now join peaceful hands, she found happy leisure, repose of mind, and absence of distraction, such as any sustained creative effort demands.

Chawton was a charming village, about a mile from Alton, and deep in the country; although two main roads from Gosport and Winchester respectively joined on their way towards London just in front of the Austens' cottage. Indeed, the place still refuses to be modernised, in spite of three converging railways, and a necessary but civil notice in the corner requesting motorists to 'drive slowly through the village.' The venerable manor-house (then always called the 'Great House') is on the slope of a hill above the Church, surrounded by garden, meadows, and trees, and commanding a view over the intervening valley to a hill opposite, crowned with a beech wood and known as 'Chawton Park.' The cottage is in the centre of the village, and, as it actually abuts on the road, the Austens could easily see or be seen by travellers. It is supposed to have been built as a posting inn, but it had lately been occupied by Edward Austen's steward. The author of the *Memoir* describes his uncle's improvements to the place in the following words:—

A good-sized entrance and two sitting-rooms made the length of the house, all intended originally to look upon the road; but the large drawing-room window was blocked up and turned into a book-case, and another opened at the side which gave to view only turf and trees, as a high wooden fence and hornbeam hedge shut out the Winchester road, which skirted the whole length of the little domain.

He goes on to speak of the garden laid out at the same time, which proved a great interest to the party of ladies, and in which old Mrs. Austen worked vigorously, almost to the end of her days, often attired in a green round smock like a labourer's: a costume which must have been nearly as remarkable as the red habit of her early married life.

Jane Austen was now between thirty-three and thirty-four years old. She was absolutely free from any artistic self-consciousness, from any eccentricity of either temper or manner. 'Hers was a mind well balanced on a basis of good sense, sweetened by an affectionate heart, and regulated by fixed principles; so that she was to be distinguished from many other amiable and sensible women only by that peculiar genius which shines out clearly . . . in her works.' Her tastes were as normal as her nature. She read English literature with eagerness, attracted by the eighteenth-century perfection of style—and still more by the return to nature in Cowper and the introduction of romance in Scott—but repelled by coarseness, which she found even in the *Spectator*, and the presence of which in Fielding made her rank him below Richardson. As for the latter, 'Every circumstance narrated in *Sir Charles Grandison*, all that was ever said or done in the "Cedar Parlour," was familiar to her; and the wedding days of Lady L. and Lady G. were as well remembered as if they had been living friends.' Her 'dear Dr. Johnson' was a constant companion; and a younger friend was found in Crabbe, whom—as she used to pretend—she was quite prepared to marry: not knowing at the time whether he had a wife living or not. As to her other tastes, she greatly delighted in the beauties of nature, and no doubt would have enjoyed foreign travel, had not that pleasure been quite out of her reach. Her attitude to music, as an art, is more doubtful. She learnt to play the piano in her youth, and after spending many years without an instrument, took it up again on settling at

Chawton; but she says herself that she did this in order to be able to play country-dances for her nephews and nieces; and when she goes to a concert she sometimes remarks on her inability to enjoy it. A concert in Sydney Gardens, however, was not perhaps likely to offer to the hearer many examples of high art; and we have no means of knowing whether, if she had had a chance of being introduced to classical music, it would have appealed to her, as it sometimes does to intellectual people who have been previously quite ignorant that they possessed any musical faculty. We are told that she had a sweet voice, and sang with feeling. 'The Soldier's Adieu' and 'The Yellow-haired Laddie' survive as the names of two of her songs.

She was extraordinarily neat-handed in anything which she attempted. Her hand-writing was both strong and pretty; her hemming and stitching, over which she spent much time, 'might have put a sewing-machine to shame'; and at games, like spillikins or cup-and-ball, she was invincible.

If this description does not seem to imply so wide a mental outlook as we wish to see in a distinguished author, we must remember that Jane Austen (as her nephew tells us) 'lived in entire seclusion from the literary world,' and probably 'never was in company with any person whose talents or whose celebrity equalled her own.' She was in the middle of a small family circle, the members of which were well-educated according to the fashion of the times, intelligent, and refined; but not especially remarkable for learning or original thought. They accepted the standards and views of their generation, interpreting them in a reasonable and healthy manner. She had therefore no inducement, such as might come from the influence of superior intellects, to dive into difficult problems. Her mental efforts were purely her own, and they led her in another direction; but she saw what she did see so very clearly, that she would probably have been capable of looking more deeply into the heart of things, had any impulse from outside induced her to try. Her vision, however, might not have remained so admirably adapted for the delicate operations nearer to the surface which were her real work in life.

Jane's person is thus described for us by her niece Anna, now becoming a grown-up girl and a keen observer: 'The figure tall and slight, but not drooping; well balanced, as was proved by her quick firm step. Her complexion of that rare sort which seems the particular property of light brunettes; a mottled skin, not fair, but perfectly clear and healthy; the fine naturally curling hair, neither light nor dark; the bright hazel eyes to match, and the rather small, but well-shaped, nose.' This is a delightful description; but she adds that in spite of all this, her aunt was not regularly handsome, though most attractive. As to her charm and lovableness there is absolute unanimity among all those who were near enough to her to know what she really was. Jane had by this time seen a good deal of society, and enjoyed it, though with a certain critical aloofness which belonged to her family, and which was hardly to be avoided by so clever a person as herself. This critical spirit was evidently a quality of which she endeavoured to rid herself as of a fault; and one of her nieces, who was too young to know her aunt intimately, until almost the end of her life, was able then to say: 'She was in fact one of the last people in society to be afraid of. I do not suppose she ever in her life said a sharp thing. She was naturally shy and not given to talk much in company, and people fancied, knowing that she was clever, that she was on the watch for good material for books from their conversation. Her intimate friends knew how groundless was the apprehension and that it wronged her.' She was not only shy: she was also at times very grave. Her niece Anna is inclined to think that Cassandra was the more equably cheerful of the two sisters. There was, undoubtedly, a quiet intensity of nature in Jane for which some critics have not given her credit. Yet at other times she and this same niece could joke so heartily over their needlework and talk such nonsense together that Cassandra would beg them to stop out of mercy to her, and not keep her in such fits of laughing. Sometimes the laughter would be provoked by the composition of extempore verses, such as those given in the *Memoir* celebrating the charm of the 'lovely Anna'; sometimes the niece would skim over new novels at the Alton Library, and reproduce them with wilful exaggeration. On one occasion she threw down a novel on the counter with contempt, saying she knew it must be rubbish from its name. The name was *Sense and Sensibility*—the secret of which had been strictly kept, even from her.

The niece who shared these hearty laughs with her aunts—James's eldest daughter, Anna—differed widely from her cousin, Edward's daughter, Fanny. She was more brilliant both in looks and in intelligence, but also more mercurial and excitable. Both occupied a good deal of Jane's thoughts and affections; but Anna must have been the one who caused her the most amusement and also the most anxiety. The interest in her was heightened when she became engaged to the son of Jane's old friend, Mrs. Lefroy. Anna's giddiness was merely that of youth; she settled down into a steady married life as the careful mother of a large family. She cherished an ardent affection for her Aunt Jane, who evidently exercised a great influence on her character.

Jane Austen's literary work was done mainly in the general sitting-room: liable at any moment to be interrupted by servants, children, or visitors—to none of whom had been entrusted the secret of her authorship. Her small sheets of paper could easily be put away or covered with blotting-paper, whenever the creaking swing-door (which she valued for that reason) gave notice that anyone was coming.

Her needlework was nearly always a garment for the poor; though she had also by her some satin stitch ready to take up in case of the appearance of company. The nature of the work will help to contradict an extraordinary misconception—namely, that she was indifferent to the needs and claims of the poor: an idea probably based on the fact that she never used them as 'copy.' Nothing could be further from the truth. She was of course quite ignorant of the conditions of life in the great towns, and she had but little money to give, but work, teaching, and sympathy were freely bestowed on rustic neighbours. A very good criterion of her attitude towards her own characters is often furnished by their relations with the poor around them. Instances of this may be found in Darcy's care of his tenants and servants, in Anne Elliot's farewell visits to nearly all the inhabitants of Kellynch, and in Emma's benevolence and good sense when assisting her poorer neighbours.

So began the Austens' life at Chawton—probably a quieter life than any they had yet led; their nearest neighbours being the Middletons (who rented the 'Great House' for five years and were still its inmates), the Benns at Faringdon, the Harry Digweeds, Mr. Papillon the Rector (a bachelor living with his sister), and the Clements and Prowting families.

The ladies took possession of their cottage on July 7, and the first news that we have of them is in a letter from Mrs. Knight, dated October 26, 1809: 'I heard of the Chawton party looking very comfortable at breakfast from a gentleman who was travelling by their door in a post-chaise about ten days ago.'

After this the curtain falls again, and we have no letters and no information for a year and a half from this time. We are sure, however, that Jane settled down to her writing very soon, for by April 1811 *Sense and Sensibility* was in the printers' hands, and *Pride and Prejudice* far advanced.

Since her fit of youthful enthusiasm, when she had composed three stories in little more than three years, she had had much experience of life to sober and strengthen her. Three changes of residence, the loss of her father, the friendship of Mrs. Lefroy and the shock of her death, her own and her sister's sad love stories, the crisis in the Leigh Perrot history, and her literary disappointments—all these must have made her take up her two old works with a chastened spirit, and a more mature judgment. We cannot doubt that extensive alterations were made: in fact, we know that this was the case with *Pride and Prejudice*. We feel equally certain that, of the two works, *Sense and Sensibility* was essentially the earlier, both in conception and in composition, and that no one could have sat down to write that work who had already written *Pride and Prejudice*. There is, indeed, no lack of humour in the earlier work—the names of Mrs. Jennings, John Dashwood, and the Palmers are enough to assure us of this; but the humorous parts are not nearly so essential to the story as they become in her later novels: the plot is desultory, and the principal characters lack interest. We feel, in the presence of the virtue and sense of Elinor, a rebuke which never affects us in the same way with Jane Bennet, Fanny Price, or Anne Elliot; while Marianne is often exasperating. Edward Ferrars is rather stiff; and Colonel Brandon is so far removed from us that we never even learn his Christian name.

Mr. Helm makes some acute remarks on the freedom which Elinor shows in talking of embarrassing subjects with Willoughby, and on her readiness to attribute his fall to the world rather than to himself. We are to imagine, however, that Elinor had been attracted by him before, and felt his personal charm again while she was under its spell: all the more, because she was herself in a special state of excitement, from the rapid changes in Marianne's condition, and the expectation of seeing her mother. Her excuses for Willoughby were so far from representing any opinion of the author's, that they did not even represent her own after a few hours of reflection. It is one of the many instances which we have of Jane Austen's subtle dramatic instinct.

On the whole, there is great merit in the book, and much amusement to be got from it; but it seems natural to look upon it as an experiment on the part of the author, before she put forth her full powers in *Pride and Prejudice*. We are glad, by the way, to hear from Jane herself that Miss Steele never caught the Doctor after all.

We must now accompany the author to London, whither she went in April 1811 to stay with her brother Henry and his wife (who had moved from Brompton to 64 Sloane Street), having been preceded by her novel, then in the hands of the printers.

Cassandra had in the meanwhile gone to Godmersham.

Sloane Street: Thursday [April 18, 1811].

MY DEAR CASSANDRA,— . . . The badness of the weather disconcerted an excellent plan of mine—that of calling on Miss Beckford again; but from the middle of the day it rained incessantly. Mary and I, after disposing of her father and mother, went to the Liverpool Museum and the British Gallery, and I had some amusement at each, though my preference for men and women always inclines me to attend more to the company than the sight.

I did not see Theo. till late on Tuesday; he was gone to Ilford, but he came back in time to show his usual nothing-meaning, harmless, heartless civility. Henry, who had been confined the whole day to the bank, took me in his way home, and, after putting life and wit into the party for a quarter of an hour, put himself and his sister into a hackney coach.

Eliza is walking out by herself. She has plenty of business on her hands just now, for the day of the party is settled, and drawing near. Above 80 people are invited for next Tuesday evening, and there is to be some very good music—five professionals, three of them glee singers, besides amateurs. Fanny will listen to this. One of the hirelings is a Capital on the harp, from which I expect great pleasure. The foundation of the party was a dinner to Henry Egerton and Henry Walter, but the latter leaves town the day before. I am sorry, as I wished *her* prejudice to be done away, but should have been more sorry if there had been no invitation.

I am a wretch, to be so occupied with all these things as to seem to have no thoughts to give to people and circumstances which really supply a far more lasting interest—the society in which you are; but I do think of you all, I assure you, and want to know all about everybody, and especially about your visit to the W. Friars; 'mais le moyen' not to be occupied by one's own concerns?

Saturday.—Frank is superseded in the *Caledonia.* Henry brought us this news yesterday from Mr. Daysh, and he heard at the same time that Charles may be in England in the course of a month. Sir Edward Pollen succeeds Lord Gambier in his command, and some captain of his succeeds Frank; and I believe the order is already gone out. Henry means to enquire farther to-day. He wrote to Mary on the occasion. This is something to think of. Henry is convinced that he will have the offer of something else, but does not think it will be at all incumbent on him to accept it; and then follows, what will he do? and where will he live?

The D'Antraigues and Comte Julien cannot come to the party, which was at first a grief, but she has since supplied herself so well with performers that it is of no consequence; their not coming has produced our going to them to-morrow evening, which I like the idea of. It will be amusing to see the ways of a French circle.

Our first object to-day was Henrietta St., to consult with Henry in consequence of a very unlucky change of the play for this very night—*Hamlet* instead of *King John*—and we are to go on Monday to *Macbeth* instead; but it is a disappointment to us both.

Love to all.

Thursday [April 25, 1811].

No, indeed, I am never too busy to think of *S. and S.* I can no more forget it than a mother can forget her sucking child; and I am much obliged to you for your enquiries. I have had two sheets to correct, but the last only brings us to Willoughby's first appearance. Mrs. K. regrets in the most flattering manner that she must wait *till* May, but I have scarcely a hope of its being out in June. Henry does not neglect it; he *has* hurried the printer, and says he will see him again to-day. It will not stand still during his absence, it will be sent to Eliza.

The *Incomes* remain as they were, but I will get them altered if I can. I am very much gratified by Mrs. K.'s interest in it; and whatever may be the event of it as to my credit with her, sincerely wish her curiosity could be satisfied sooner than is now probable. I think she will like my Elinor, but cannot build on anything else.

Our party went off extremely well. There were many solicitudes, alarms, and vexations, beforehand, of course, but at last everything was quite right. The rooms were dressed up with flowers, &c., and looked very pretty. A glass for the mantelpiece was lent by the man who is making their own. Mr. Egerton and Mr. Walter came at half-past five, and the festivities began with a pair of very fine soles.

Yes, Mr. Walter—for he postponed his leaving London on purpose—which did not give much pleasure at the time, any more than the circumstance from which it rose—his calling on Sunday and being asked by Henry to take the family dinner on that day, which he did; but it is all smoothed over now, and she likes him very well.

At half-past seven arrived the musicians in two hackney coaches, and by eight the lordly company began to appear. Among the earliest were George and Mary Cooke, and I spent the greatest part of the evening very pleasantly with them. The drawing-room being soon hotter than we liked, we placed ourselves in the connecting passage, which was comparatively cool, and gave us all the advantage of the music at a pleasant distance, as well as that of the first view of every new comer.

I was quite surrounded by acquaintance, especially gentlemen; and what with Mr. Hampson, Mr. Seymour, Mr. W. Knatchbull, Mr. Guillemarde, Mr. Cure, a Captain Simpson, brother to *the* Captain Simpson, besides Mr. Walter and Mr. Egerton, in addition to the Cookes, and Miss Beckford, and Miss Middleton, I had quite as much upon my hands as I could do.

Including everybody we were sixty-six—which was considerably more than Eliza had expected, and quite enough to fill the back drawing-room and leave a few to be scattered about in the other and in the passage.

The music was extremely good. It opened (tell Fanny) with 'Poike de Parp pin praise pof Prapela;' and of the other glees I remember, 'In peace love tunes,' 'Rosabelle,' 'The Red Cross Knight,' and 'Poor Insect.' Between the songs were lessons on the harp, or harp and pianoforte together; and the harp-player was Wiepart, whose name seems famous, though new to me. There was one female singer, a short Miss Davis, all in blue, bringing up for the public line, whose voice was said to be very fine indeed; and all the performers gave great satisfaction by doing what they were paid for, and giving themselves no airs. No amateur could be persuaded to do anything.

This said Captain Simpson told us, on the authority of some other Captain just arrived from Halifax, that Charles was bringing the *Cleopatra* home, and that she was probably by this time in the Channel; but, as Captain S. was certainly in liquor, we must not quite depend on it. It must give one a sort of expectation, however, and will prevent my writing to him any more. I would rather he should not reach England till I am at home, and the Steventon party gone.

My mother and Martha both write with great satisfaction of Anna's behaviour. She is quite an Anna with variations, but she cannot have reached her last, for that is always the most flourishing and showy; she is at about her third or fourth, which are generally simple and pretty.

We *did* go to the play after all on Saturday. We went to the Lyceum, and saw the *Hypocrite*, an old play taken from Molière's *Tartuffe*, and were well entertained. Dowton and Mathews were the good actors; Mrs. Edwin was the heroine, and her performance is just what it used to be. I have no chance of seeing Mrs. Siddons; she *did* act on Monday, but, as Henry was told by the box-keeper that he did not think she would, the plans, and all thought of it, were given up. I should particularly have liked seeing her in *Constance*, and could swear at her with little effort for disappointing me.

Eliza caught her cold on Sunday in our way to the D'Antraigues. The horses actually gibbed on this side of Hyde Park Gate: a load of fresh gravel made it a formidable hill to them, and they refused the collar; I believe there was a sore shoulder to irritate. Eliza was frightened and we got out, and were detained in the evening air several minutes. The cold is in her chest, but she takes care of herself, and I hope it may not last long.

This engagement prevented Mr. Walter's staying late—he had his coffee and went away. Eliza enjoyed her evening very much, and means to cultivate the acquaintance; and I see nothing to dislike in them but their taking quantities of snuff. Monsieur, the old Count, is a very fine-looking man, with quiet manners, good enough for an Englishman, and, I believe, is a man of great information and taste. He has some fine paintings, which delighted Henry as much as the son's music gratified Eliza; and among them a miniature of Philip V. of Spain, Louis XIV.'s grandson, which exactly suited *my* capacity. Count Julien's performance is very wonderful.

We met only Mrs. Latouche and Miss East, and we are just now engaged to spend next Sunday evening at Mrs. L.'s, and to meet the D'Antraigues, but M. le Comte must do without Henry. If he would but speak English, *I* would take to him.

Sloane Street: [Tuesday, April 30, 1811].

My head-dress was a bugle-band like the border to my gown, and a flower of Mrs. Tilson's. I depended upon hearing something of the evening from Mr. W. K[natchbull], and am very well satisfied with his notice of me—'A pleasing-looking young woman'—that must do; one cannot pretend to anything better now; thankful to have it continued a few years longer!

We have tried to get *Self-Control*, but in vain. I *should* like to know what her estimate is, but am always half afraid of finding a clever novel *too clever*, and of finding my own story and my own people all forestalled.

I forgot to tell you in my last that our cousin, Miss Payne, called in on Saturday, and was persuaded to stay dinner. She told us a great deal about her friend Lady Cath. Brecknell, who is most happily married, and Mr. Brecknell is very religious, and has got black whiskers.

Yours very affectionately,
JANE.

Early in May, Jane left London; and, after paying a short visit to Mrs. Hill (*née* Catherine Bigg) at Streatham, returned home to Chawton, where she found only her mother and her niece Anna.

Chawton: Wednesday [May 29, 1811].

MY DEAR CASSANDRA,— . . . You certainly must have heard before I can tell you that Col. Orde has married our cousin, Margt. Beckford, the Marchess. of Douglas's sister. The papers say that her father disinherits her, but I think too well of an Orde to suppose that she has not a handsome independence of her own.

We sat upstairs [at the Digweeds'] and had thunder and lightning as usual. I never knew such a spring for thunderstorms as it has been. Thank God! we have had no bad ones here. I thought myself in luck to have my uncomfortable feelings shared by the mistress of the house, as that procured blinds and candles. It had been excessively hot the whole day. Mrs. Harding is a good-looking woman, but not much like Mrs. Toke, inasmuch as she is very brown and has scarcely any teeth; she seems to have some of Mrs. Toke's civility. Miss H. is an elegant, pleasing, pretty-looking girl, about nineteen, I suppose, or nineteen and a half, or nineteen and a quarter, with flowers in her head and music at her finger ends. She plays very well indeed. I have seldom heard anybody with more pleasure.

Friday [May 31].

I have taken your hint, slight as it was, and have written to Mrs. Knight, and most sincerely do I hope it will not be in vain. I cannot endure the idea of her giving away her own wheel, and have told her no more than the truth, in saying that I could never use it with comfort. I had a great mind to add that, if she persisted in giving it, I would spin nothing with it but a rope to hang myself, but I was afraid of making it appear a less serious matter of feeling than it really is.

From Monday to Wednesday Anna is to be engaged at Faringdon, in order that she may come in for the gaieties of Tuesday (the 4th), on Selborne Common, where there are to be volunteers and felicities of all kinds. Harriet B[enn] is invited to spend the day with the John Whites, and her father and mother have very kindly undertaken to get Anna invited also.

Poor Anna is suffering from *her* cold, which is worse to-day, but as she has no sore throat I hope it may spend itself by Tuesday. She had a delightful evening with the Miss Middletons—syllabub, tea, coffee, singing, dancing, a hot supper, eleven o'clock, everything that can be imagined agreeable. She desires her best love to Fanny, and will answer her letter before she leaves

Chawton, and engages to send her a particular account of the Selborne day.

How horrible it is to have so many people killed! And what a blessing that one cares for none of them!

I return to my letter-writing from calling on Miss Harriot Webb, who is short and not quite straight and cannot pronounce an R any better than her sisters; but she has dark hair, a complexion to suit, and, I think, has the pleasantest countenance and manner of the three—the most natural. She appears very well pleased with her new home, and they are all reading with delight Mrs. H. More's recent publication.

You cannot imagine—it is not in human nature to imagine—what a nice walk we have round the orchard. The row of beech look very well indeed, and so does the young quickset hedge in the garden. I hear to-day that an apricot has been detected on one of the trees. My mother is perfectly convinced *now* that she shall not be overpowered by her cleftwood, and I believe would rather have more than less.

God bless you, and I hope June will find you well, and bring us together.

Thursday [June 6].

[Anna] does not return from Faringdon till this evening, and I doubt not has had plenty of the miscellaneous, unsettled sort of happiness which seems to suit her best. We hear from Miss Benn, who was on the Common with the Prowtings, that she was very much admired by the gentlemen in general.

We began pease on Sunday, but our gatherings are very small, not at all like the gathering in the *Lady of the Lake*. Yesterday I had the agreeable surprise of finding several scarlet strawberries quite ripe; had *you* been at home, this would have been a pleasure lost. There are more gooseberries and fewer currants than I thought at first. We must buy currants for our wine.

I had just left off writing and put on my things for walking to Alton, when Anna and her friend Harriot called in their way thither, so we went together. Their business was to provide mourning against the King's death, and my mother has had a bombasin bought for her. I am not sorry to be back again, for the young ladies had a great deal to do, and without much method in doing it.

Yours affectionately,
J. A.

The printing of *Sense and Sensibility* cannot have been very rapid, for in September 28 there is the following entry in Fanny Austen's diary: 'Letter from At. Cass to beg we would not mention that Aunt Jane wrote *Sense and Sensibility*.' This looks as if it were still on the eve of publication, and it was not in fact advertised until October 31.

CHAPTER XV.

PRIDE AND PREJUDICE 1812-1814

THE title-page of *Sense and Sensibility* describes the book as being 'by a Lady.' This ascription satisfied the author's desire for concealment, but it puzzled the advertisers. The first advertisement—that in the *Morning Chronicle* on October 31, 1811—merely describes it as 'a novel, called *Sense and Sensibility*, by Lady ——.' In the same paper, on November 7, it is styled an 'extraordinary novel by Lady ——'; while on November 28 it sinks to being an 'interesting novel,' but is ascribed to 'Lady A.'

Jane's expectations were so modest that she laid by a sum out of her very slender resources to meet the expected loss. She must have been delighted at the result. By July 1813 every copy of the first edition had been sold; and not only had her expenses been cleared but she was one hundred and forty pounds to the good. If we compare this with the thirty pounds that Fanny Burney received for *Evelina*, the one hundred pounds that Maria Edgeworth got for *Castle Rackrent*, or the hundred and forty pounds gained by Miss Ferrier for her first novel, we shall see that Jane Austen had no reason to complain.

The money was no doubt very welcome; but still more important from another point of view was the favourable reception of the work. Had it been a failure and an expense to its author, she would hardly have dared, nor could she have afforded, to make a second venture. On the success of *Sense and Sensibility*, we may say, depended the existence of *Pride and Prejudice*. Now she could return with renewed spirit to the preparation of the more famous work which was to follow, and on which she had already been engaged for some time, concurrently with her first-published novel.

We have no letters and little news for 1812; but we know that in April Edward Austen and his daughter Fanny came to Chawton House for three weeks. It was their last visit as Austens; for on the death of Mrs. Knight—his kind and generous patron and friend—in October of that year, Edward and all his family took the name of Knight: a name which had been borne by every successive owner of the Chawton Estate since the sixteenth century. In June, Jane went with her mother to stay for a fortnight at Steventon Rectory—the last visit ever paid by Mrs. Austen to any place. When she determined never to leave home again, she said that her latest visit should be to her eldest son. Accordingly she went, and took a final farewell of the place where nearly the whole of her married life had been spent. She was then seventy-two years old, and lived on for sixteen more; but she kept her resolution and never again left Chawton Cottage for a single night. Her long survival can hardly have been expected by those who had to nurse her through frequent fits of illness; but these ailments do not seem to have been of the sort that kills. She was, however, always ready to contemplate the near approach of death both for herself and others;

for in July 1811, after buying some bombazine in which to mourn for the poor King, she said: 'If I outlive him it will answer my purpose; if I do not, somebody may mourn for me in it: it will be wanted for one or the other, I dare say, before the moths have eaten it up.' As it happened, the King lived nine more years, and Mrs. Austen sixteen; and it was the lot of the latter to lose two children before her own time came. When Jane died in 1817, the health of her eldest brother, James, was failing, and two years and a half later he died. His mother lived on; but during the last years of her life she endured continual pain not only patiently but with characteristic cheerfulness. She once said to her grandson, Edward Austen: 'Ah, my dear, you find me just where you left me—on the sofa. I sometimes think that God Almighty must have forgotten me; but I dare say He will come for me in His own good time.'

Our letters recommence in January 1813—almost at the exact date of the publication of *Pride and Prejudice*—a date which will seem to many people the central point in Jane Austen's life. She appeared, indeed, to be rather of that opinion herself, so far as her modest, unassuming nature would allow her to attribute importance to one of her own works. She calls it her 'darling child,' and does not know how she can tolerate people who will not care at least for Elizabeth. But we had better let her speak for herself. The first of the following letters was written before the publication took place; but the others deal largely with *Pride and Prejudice*, while there is an under-current of allusions to *Mansfield Park*— now approaching completion.

Chawton: Sunday evening [January 24, 1813].

MY DEAR CASSANDRA,—This is exactly the weather we could wish for, if you are but well enough to enjoy it. I shall be glad to hear that you are not confined to the house by an increase of cold.

We quite run over with books. My mother has got Sir John Carr's *Travels in Spain* from Miss B. and *I* am reading a Society octavo, *An Essay on the Military Police and Institutions of the British Empire* by Capt. Pasley of the Engineers: a book which I protested against at first, but which upon trial I find delightfully written and highly entertaining. I am as much in love with the author as ever I was with Clarkson or Buchanan, or even the two Mr. Smiths of the City—the first soldier I ever sighed for—but he does write with extraordinary force and spirit. Yesterday, moreover, brought us Mrs. Grant's *Letters* with Mr. White's compliments; but I have disposed of them, compliments and all, for the first fortnight to Miss Papillon, and among so many readers or retainers of books as we have in Chawton I dare say there will be no difficulty in getting rid of them for another fortnight if necessary. I learn from Sir J. Carr that there is no Government House at Gibraltar; I must alter it to the Commissioner's.

Our party on Wednesday was not unagreeable. . . . We were eleven altogether, as you will find on computation, adding Miss Benn and two strange gentlemen, a Mr. Twyford, curate of Great Worldham, who is living in Alton, and his friend Mr. Wilkes. I don't know that Mr. T. is anything except very dark-complexioned, but Mr. W. was a useful addition, being an easy, talking, pleasantish young man—a *very* young man, hardly twenty, perhaps. He is of St. John's, Cambridge, and spoke very highly of H. Walter as a scholar. He said he was considered as the best classic in the University. How such a report would have interested my father!

Upon Mrs. D.'s mentioning that she had sent the *Rejected Addresses* to Mr. H., I began talking to her a little about them, and expressed my hope of their having amused her. Her answer was 'Oh dear, yes, very much, very droll indeed—the opening of the House and the striking up of the fiddles!' What she meant, poor woman, who shall say? I sought no farther. The P.'s have now got the book, and like it very much; their niece Eleanor has recommended it most warmly to them—*She* looks like a rejected addresser. As soon as a whist party was formed, and a round table threatened, I made my mother an excuse and came away, leaving just as many for *their* round table as there were at Mrs. Grant's. I wish they might be as agreeable a set.

The Miss Sibleys want to establish a Book Society in their side of the country like ours. What can be a stronger proof of that superiority in ours over the Manydown and Steventon society, which I have always foreseen and felt? No emulation of the kind was ever inspired by *their* proceedings; no such wish of the Miss Sibleys was ever heard in the course of the many years of that Society's existence. And what are their Biglands and their Barrows, their Macartneys and Mackenzies to Captain Pasley's *Essay on the Military Police of the British Empire* and the *Rejected Addresses?*

I have walked once to Alton, and yesterday Miss Papillon and I walked together to call on the Garnets. . . . *I* had a very agreeable walk, and if *she* had not, more shame for her, for I was quite as entertaining as she was. Dame G. is pretty well, and we found her surrounded by her well-behaved, healthy, large-eyed children. I took her an old shift, and promised her a set of our linen, and my companion left some of her Bank Stock with her.

Tell Martha that I hunt away the rogues every night from under her bed; they feel the difference of her being gone.

Friday [January 29, 1813].

I hope you received my little parcel by J. Bond on Wednesday evening, my dear Cassandra, and that you will be ready to hear from me again on Sunday, for I feel that I must write to you to-day. . . . I want to tell you that I have got my own darling child from London. On Wednesday I received one copy sent down by Falkener, with three lines from Henry to say that he had given another to Charles and sent a third by the coach to Godmersham.

The advertisement is in our paper to-day for the first time: 18*s*. He shall ask 1*l*. 1*s*. for my two next, and 1*l*. 8*s*. for my stupidest of all. Miss Benn dined with us on the very day of the book's coming, and in the evening we set fairly at it, and read half the first vol. to her, prefacing that, having intelligence from Henry that such a work would soon appear, we had desired him to send it whenever it came out, and I believe it passed with her unsuspected. She was amused, poor soul! *That* she could not help, you know, with two such people to lead the way, but she really does seem to admire Elizabeth. I must confess that I think her as delightful a creature as ever appeared in print, and how I shall be able to tolerate those who do not like *her* at least I do not know. There are a few typical errors; and a 'said he,' or a 'said she,' would sometimes make the dialogue more immediately clear; but—

I do not write for such dull elves

As have not a great deal of ingenuity themselves.

The second volume is shorter than I could wish, but the difference is not so much in reality as in look, there being a larger proportion of narrative in that part. I have lop't and crop't so successfully, however, that I imagine it must be rather shorter than *Sense and Sensibility* altogether. Now I will try and write of something else; and it shall be a complete change of subject—ordination. I am glad to find your enquiries have ended so well. If you could discover whether Northamptonshire is a country of hedgerows, I should be glad again.

Thursday [February 4, 1813].

Your letter was truly welcome, and I am much obliged to you for all your praise; it came at a right time, for I had had some fits of disgust. Our second evening's reading to Miss Benn had not pleased me so well, but I believe something must be attributed to my mother's too rapid way of getting on: though she perfectly understands the characters herself, she cannot speak as they ought. Upon the whole, however, I am quite vain enough and well-satisfied enough. The work is rather too light, and bright, and sparkling; it wants shade; it wants to be stretched out here and there with a long chapter of sense, if it could be had; if not, of solemn specious nonsense, about something unconnected with the story; an essay on writing, a critique on Walter Scott, or the history of Buonaparte, or anything that would form a contrast, and bring the reader with increased delight to the playfulness and epigrammatism of the general style. I doubt your quite agreeing with me here. I know your starched notions. The caution observed at Steventon with regard to the possession of the book is an agreeable surprise to me, and I heartily wish it may be the means of saving you from anything unpleasant—but you must be prepared for the neighbourhood being perhaps already informed of there being such a work in the world and in the Chawton world. . . . The greatest blunder in the printing that I have met with is in page 220, l. 3, where two speeches are made into one. There might as well have been no supper at Longbourn; but I suppose it was the remains of Mrs. Bennet's old Meryton habits.

Tuesday [February 9, 1813].

This will be a quick return for yours, my dear Cassandra; I doubt its having much else to recommend it; but there is no saying; it may turn out to be a very long and delightful letter.

I am exceedingly pleased that you can say what you do, after having gone through the whole work, and Fanny's praise is very gratifying. My hopes were tolerably strong of *her*, but nothing like a certainty. Her liking Darcy and Elizabeth is enough. She might hate all the others if she would. I have her opinion under her own hand this morning, but your transcript of it, which I read first, was not, and is not, the less acceptable. To *me* it is of course all praise, but the more exact truth which she sends *you* is good enough. . . .

I have been applied to for information as to the oath taken in former times of Bell, Book, and Candle, but have none to give. Perhaps you may be able to learn something of its origin and meaning at Manydown. Ladies who read those enormous great stupid thick quarto volumes which one always sees in the breakfast parlour there must be acquainted with everything in the world. I detest a quarto. Capt. Pasley's book is too good for their Society. They will not understand a man who condenses his thoughts into an octavo.

Miss Benn dined here on Friday. I have not seen her since—there is still work for one evening more. I know nothing of the P.'s.

The C.'s are at home, and are reduced to read. They have got Miss Edgeworth. I have disposed of Mrs. Grant for the second fortnight to Mrs. D. It can make no difference to *her* which of the twenty-six fortnights in the year the three volumes lay in her house.

Yours very affectionately,
J. AUSTEN.

Miss Austen, Manydown—by favour of Mr. Gray.

As she read and re-read *Pride and Prejudice*, Jane must have become aware (if she did not know it before) that she had advanced far beyond *Sense and Sensibility*. Indeed, the earlier work seems to fade out of her mind, so far as allusions to its principal characters are concerned; while those of the later novel remain vivid and attractive to their creator. Even the minor characters were real to her; and she forgot nothing—down to the marriage of Kitty to a clergyman near Pemberley, and that of Mary to one of Uncle Philips's clerks.

In this work there seemed to be hardly anything for which she need apologise. Here everything is complete; the humour, though brilliant, is yet always subordinate to the progress of the story; the plot is inevitable, and its turning-point (the first proposal of Darcy) occurs exactly when it ought; while all fear of a commonplace ending is avoided by the insertion of the celebrated interview between Lady Catherine and Elizabeth. It gives us also an excellent example of the way in which Jane Austen composed her stories. We are always in the confidence of the heroine, who is hardly off the stage throughout the whole novel; we see the other characters with her eyes, even when they are persons—like Jane Bennet—with whom we believe ourselves to be intimately acquainted. At the same time, such is the subtle irony of the author that we are quite aware of her intention to make us understand more of the heroine's state of mind than the heroine herself does, and to distinguish between her conscious and unconscious thoughts. Elizabeth has to change from hatred to love—real hatred and real love—in a volume and a half. But it would wound her self-respect if she acknowledged to herself that the pace at which she moved was so rapid; and the change is constantly only half admitted. Even near the end—when she says that, if Darcy is prevented from seeking her hand by the representations of Lady Catherine, she shall soon cease to regret him—we know that this is far from the truth: that her affection is really steadfast, and that she is only trying to disguise from herself her own anxiety. Other examples might easily be found.

On April 25, 1813, occurred the death of Eliza, Henry Austen's wife. She had suffered from a long and painful illness, and the end was 'a release at last.' These circumstances would diminish the grief felt at her loss; but the event must have carried their minds back to early days at Steventon; and Jane was sure to remember with gratitude the affection and attention which Eliza had bestowed upon her much younger cousin.

Soon afterwards, Henry went down to Chawton; and on May 20 he drove Jane up to London in his curricle. This was a short visit, and, owing to Henry's being in deep mourning, no theatres were visited. Jane went, however, to three picture-galleries—her mind still full of Bennets and Darcys.

Sloane Street: [Thursday, May 20, 1813].

MY DEAR CASSANDRA,—Before I say anything else, I claim a paper full of halfpence on the drawing-room mantelpiece; I put them there myself, and forgot to bring them with me. I cannot say that I have yet been in any distress for money, but I chuse to have my due, as well as the Devil. How lucky we were in our weather yesterday! This wet morning makes one more sensible of it. We had no rain of any consequence. The head of the curricle was put half up three or four times, but our share of the showers was very trifling, though they seemed to be heavy all round us, when we were on the Hog's-back, and I fancied it might then be raining so hard at Chawton as to make you feel for us much more than we deserved. Three hours and a quarter took us to Guildford, where we staid barely two hours, and had only just time enough for all we had to do there; that is, eating a long, comfortable breakfast, watching the carriages, paying Mr. Herington, and taking a little stroll afterwards. From some views which that stroll gave us, I think most highly of the situation of Guildford. We wanted all our brothers and sisters to be standing with us in the bowling-green, and looking towards Horsham. . . . I was very lucky in my gloves—got them at the first shop I went to, though I went into it rather because it was near than because it looked at all like a glove shop, and gave only four shillings for them; upon hearing which everybody at Chawton will be hoping and predicting that they cannot be good for anything, and their worth certainly remains to be proved; but I think they look very well. We left Guildford at twenty minutes before twelve (I hope somebody cares for these minutiæ), and were at Esher in about two hours more. I was very much pleased with the country in general. Between Guildford and Ripley I thought it particularly pretty, also about Painshill and everywhere else; and from a Mr. Spicer's grounds at Esher, which we walked into before our dinner, the views were beautiful. I cannot say what we did *not* see, but I should think that there could not be a wood, or a meadow, or palace, or a remarkable spot in England that was not spread out before us on one side or the other. Claremont is going to be sold: a Mr. Ellis has it now. It is a house that seems never to have prospered. . . . After dinner we walked forward to be overtaken at the coachman's time, and before he did overtake us we were very near Kingston. I fancy it was about half-past six when we reached this house—a twelve hours' business, and the horses did not appear more than reasonably tired. I was very tired too, and very glad to get to bed early, but am quite well to-day. I am very snug with the front drawing-room all to myself, and would not say 'thank you' for any company but you. The quietness of it does me good. I have contrived to pay my two visits, though the weather made me a great while about it, and left me only a few minutes to sit with Charlotte Craven. She looks very well, and her hair is done up with an elegance to do credit to any education. Her manners are as unaffected and pleasing as ever. She had heard from her mother to-day. Mrs. Craven spends another fortnight at Chilton. I saw nobody but Charlotte, which pleased me best. I was shewn upstairs into a drawing-room, where she came to me, and the appearance of the room, so totally unschool-like, amused me very much; it was full of all the modern elegancies.

Monday [May 24, 1813].

I am very much obliged to you for writing to me. You must have hated it after a worrying morning.

I went the day before to Layton's, as I proposed, and got my mother's gown—seven yards at 6*s*. 6*d*. I then walked into No. 10, which is all dirt and confusion, but in a very promising way, and after being present at the opening of a new account, to my great amusement, Henry and I went to the exhibition in Spring Gardens. It is not thought a good collection, but I was very well pleased, particularly (pray tell Fanny) with a small portrait of Mrs. Bingley, excessively like her.

I went in hopes of seeing one of her sister, but there was no Mrs. Darcy. Perhaps, however, I may find her in the great exhibition, which we shall go to if we have time. I have no chance of her in the collection of Sir Joshua Reynolds's paintings, which is now showing in Pall Mall, and which we are also to visit.

Mrs. Bingley's is exactly herself—size, shaped face, features, and sweetness; there never was a greater likeness. She is dressed in a white gown, with green ornaments, which convinces me of what I had always supposed, that green was a favourite colour with her. I dare say Mrs. D. will be in yellow.

The events of yesterday were, our going to Belgrave Chapel in the morning, our being prevented by the rain from going to evening service at St. James, Mr. Hampson's calling, Messrs. Barlow and Phillips dining here, and Mr. and Mrs. Tilson's coming in the evening *à l'ordinaire. She* drank tea with us both Thursday and Saturday; *he* dined out each day, and on Friday we were with them, and they wish us to go to them to-morrow evening to meet Miss Burdett, but I do not know how it will end. Henry talks of a drive to Hampstead, which may interfere with it.

I should like to see Miss Burdett very well, but that I am rather frightened by hearing that she wishes to be introduced to *me*. If I *am* a wild beast I cannot help it. It is not my own fault.

Get us the best weather you can for Wednesday, Thursday, and Friday. We are to go to Windsor in our way to Henley, which will be a great delight. We shall be leaving Sloane Street about 12, two or three hours after Charles's party have begun their journey. You will miss them, but the comfort of getting back into your own room will be great. And then the tea and sugar!

I am very much obliged to Fanny for her letter; it made me laugh heartily, but I cannot pretend to answer it. Even had I more time, I should not feel at all sure of the sort of letter that Miss D. would write. I hope Miss Benn is got well again, and will have a comfortable dinner with you to-day.

Monday Evening.—We have been both to the exhibition and Sir J. Reynolds's, and I am disappointed, for there was nothing like Mrs. D. at either. I can only imagine that Mr. D. prizes any picture of her too much to like it should be exposed to the public eye. I can imagine he would have that sort of feeling—that mixture of love, pride, and delicacy.

Setting aside this disappointment, I had great amusement among the pictures; and the driving about, the carriage being open, was very pleasant. I liked my solitary elegance very much, and was ready to laugh all the time at my being where I was. I could not but feel that I had naturally small right to be parading about London in a barouche.

I should not wonder if we got no farther than Reading on Thursday evening, and so reach Steventon only to a reasonable dinner hour the next day; but whatever I may write or you may imagine we know it will be something different. I shall be quiet to-morrow morning; all my business is done, and I shall only call again upon Mrs. Hoblyn, &c.

Yours affectionately,
J. AUSTEN.

Miss Austen, Chawton.

A very happy summer awaited the cottage party. Godmersham wanted painting, and its owner moved his family for some months to Chawton. There were almost daily meetings between the two houses, and the friendship between Fanny Knight and her Aunt Jane became still closer as they spent 'delicious mornings' together.

Meanwhile, Frank, in command of the *Elephant*, was stationed in the Baltic, and engaged sometimes in convoying small vessels backwards and forwards, sometimes in protecting the transports which took Bernadotte's Swedish troops to the seat of war.

The following letter from his sister Jane reached him no doubt in due course.

Chawton: [July 3, 1813].

MY DEAREST FRANK,—Behold me going to write you as handsome a letter as I can! Wish me good luck. We have had the pleasure of hearing from you lately through Mary, who sent us some of the particulars of yours of June 18 (I think), written off Rugen, and we enter into the delight of your having so good a pilot. Why are you like Queen Elizabeth? Because you know how to chuse wise ministers. Does not this prove you as great a Captain as she was a Queen? This may serve as a riddle for you to put forth among your officers, by way of increasing your proper consequence. It must be a real enjoyment to you, since you are obliged to leave England, to be where you are, seeing something of a new country and one which has been so distinguished as Sweden. You must have great pleasure in it. I hope you may have gone to Carlscroon. Your profession has its *douceurs* to recompense for some of its privations; to an enquiring and observing mind like yours such *douceurs* must be considerable. Gustavus Vasa, and Charles XII., and Cristina and Linneus. Do their ghosts rise up before you? I have a great respect for former Sweden, so zealous as it was for Protestantism. And I have always fancied it more like England than other countries; and, according to the map, many of the names have a strong resemblance to the English. July begins unpleasantly with us, cold and showery, but it is often a baddish month. We had some fine dry weather preceding it, which was very acceptable to the Holders of Hay, and the Masters of Meadows. In general it must have been a good hay-making season.

Edward has got in all his in excellent order; I speak only of Chawton, but here he has better luck than Mr. Middleton ever had in the five years that he was tenant. Good encouragement for him to come again, and I really hope he will do so another year. The pleasure to us of having them here is so great that if we were not the best creatures in the world we should not deserve it. We go on in the most comfortable way, very frequently dining together, and always meeting in some part of every day. Edward is very well, and enjoys himself as thoroughly as any Hampshire-born Austen can desire. Chawton is not thrown away upon him.

He will soon have all his children about him. Edward, George and Charles are collected already, and another week brings Henry and William.

We are in hopes of another visit from our true lawful Henry very soon; he is to be our guest this time. He is quite well, I am happy to say, and does not leave it to my pen, I am sure, to communicate to you the joyful news of his being Deputy Receiver no longer. It is a promotion which he thoroughly enjoys, as well he may; the work of his own mind. He sends you all his own plans of course. The scheme for Scotland we think an excellent one both for himself and his nephew. Upon the whole his spirits are very much recovered. If I may so express myself his mind is not a mind for affliction; he is too busy, too active, too sanguine. Sincerely as he was attached to poor Eliza moreover, and excellently as he behaved to her, he was always so used to be away from her at times, that her loss is not felt as that of many a beloved wife might be, especially when all the circumstances of her long and dreadful illness are taken into the account. He very long knew that she must die, and it was indeed a release at last. Our mourning for her is not over, or we should be putting it on again for Mr. Thomas Leigh, who has just closed a good life at the age of seventy-nine.

Poor Mrs. L. P. [Leigh Perrot] would now have been mistress of Stoneleigh had there been none of the vile compromise, which in good truth has never been allowed to be of much use to them. It will be a hard trial.

You will be glad to hear that every copy of *S. and S.* is sold, and that it has brought me £140, besides the copyright, if that should ever be of any value. I have now, therefore, written myself into £250, which only makes me long for more. I have something in hand which I hope the credit of *P. and P.* will sell well, though not half so entertaining, and by the bye shall you object to my mentioning the *Elephant* in it, and two or three other old ships? I *have* done it, but it shall not stay to make you angry. They are only just mentioned.

I hope you continue well and brush your hair, but not all off.

Yours very affectionately,
J. A.

On September 14, Jane left Chawton for London and Godmersham, travelling as one of her brother Edward's large family party.

CHAPTER XVI.

MANSFIELD PARK 1812-1814

JANE was now about to pay what proved to be her last visit to Godmersham. On the way thither she, with one division of the Knight family party, halted for a couple of days in London, to stay with Henry at 10 Henrietta Street.

Henrietta Street: Wednesday [September 15, 1813, 1/2 past 8].

Here I am, my dearest Cassandra, seated in the breakfast-, dining-, sitting-room, beginning with all my might. Fanny will join me as soon as she is dressed and begin her letter.

We arrived at a quarter-past four, and were kindly welcomed by the coachman, and then by his master, and then by William, and then by Mrs. Perigord, who all met us before we reached the foot of the stairs. Mde. Bigeon was below dressing us a most comfortable dinner of soup, fish, bouillée, partridges, and an apple tart, which we sat down to soon after five, after cleaning and dressing ourselves, and feeling that we were most commodiously disposed of. The little adjoining dressing-room to our apartment makes Fanny and myself very well off indeed, and as we have poor Eliza's bed our space is ample every way.

Lady Robert is delighted with *P. and P.*, and really *was* so, as I understand, before she knew who wrote it, for, of course, she knows now. He told her with as much satisfaction as if it were my wish. He did not tell *me* this, but he told Fanny. And Mr. Hastings! I am quite delighted with what such a man writes about it. Henry sent him the books after his return from Daylesford, but you will hear the letter too.

Fanny and the two little girls are gone to take places for to-night at Covent Garden; *Clandestine Marriage* and *Midas*. The latter will be a fine show for L. and M. They revelled last night in *Don Juan*, whom we left in hell at half-past eleven. We had scaramouch and a ghost, and were delighted. I speak of *them; my* delight was very tranquil, and the rest of us were sober-minded. *Don Juan* was the last of three musical things. *Five Hours at Brighton*, in three acts—of which one was over before we arrived, none the worse—and the *Beehive*, rather less flat and trumpery.

Miss Hare had some pretty caps, and is to make me one like one of them, only *white* satin instead of blue. It will be white satin and lace, and a little white flower perking out of the left ear, like Harriot Byron's feather. I have allowed her to go as far as £1 16*s*. My gown is to be trimmed everywhere with white ribbon plaited on somehow or other. She says it will look well. I am not sanguine. They trim with white very much.

Mr. Hall was very punctual yesterday, and curled me out at a great rate. I thought it looked hideous, and longed for a snug cap instead, but my companions silenced me by their admiration.

We had very good places in the box next the stage-box, front and second row; the three old ones behind of course. I was particularly disappointed at seeing nothing of Mr. Crabbe. I felt sure of him when I saw that the boxes were fitted up with crimson velvet.

It was not possible for me to get the worsteds yesterday. I heard Edward last night pressing Henry to come to [? Godmersham], and I think Henry engaged to go there after his November collection. Nothing has been done as to *S. and S.* The books came to hand too late for him to have time for it before he went.

I long to have you hear Mr. H.'s opinion of *P. and P.* His admiring my Elizabeth so much is particularly welcome to me.

Miss Austen, Chawton.

Her delight at the appreciation of her book by Warren Hastings may be compared with a passage from Madame d'Arblay's diary, which forms a curious link between the two writers.

Mrs. Cooke [Jane Austen's cousin], my excellent neighbour, came in just now to read me a paragraph of a letter from Mrs. Leigh of Oxfordshire, her sister. . . . After much civility about the new work [*Camilla*] and its author, it finishes thus: 'Mr. Hastings I saw just now; I told him what was going forward; he gave a great jump and exclaimed: "Well, then, now I can serve her, thank heaven, and I will! I will write to Anderson to engage Scotland, and I will attack the East Indies myself."'

Henrietta Street: Thursday [September 16, 1813, after dinner].

Thank you, my dearest Cassandra, for the nice long letter I sent off this morning.

We are now all four of us young ladies sitting round the circular table in the inner room writing our letters, while the two brothers are having a comfortable coze in the room adjoining. It is to be a quiet evening, much to the satisfaction of four of the six. My eyes are quite tired of dust and lamps.

We . . . went to Wedgwood's, where my brother and Fanny chose a dinner set. I believe the pattern is a small lozenge in purple, between lines of narrow gold, and it is to have the crest.

With love to you all, including Triggs, I remain,

Yours very affectionately,
J. AUSTEN.

The journey from London to Godmersham was no doubt duly narrated in a letter now missing. Those from Godmersham are filled with the ordinary comings and goings of a large family party, and allusions to Kent neighbours—of whom Cassandra would know just enough to be interested in their proceedings.

Godmersham Park: Thursday [September 23, 1813].

MY DEAREST CASSANDRA,—Thank you five hundred and forty times for the exquisite piece of workmanship which was brought into the room this morning, while we were at breakfast, with some very inferior works of art in the same way, and which I read with high glee, much delighted with everything it told, whether good or bad. It is so rich in striking intelligence that I hardly know what to reply to first. I believe finery must have it.

I am extremely glad that you like the poplin. I thought it would have my mother's approbation, but was not so confident of yours. Remember that it is a present. Do not refuse me. I am very rich.

Let me know when you begin the new tea, and the new white wine. My present elegancies have not yet made me indifferent to such matters. I am still a cat if I see a mouse.

"Tis night, and the landscape is lovely no more,' but to make amends for that, our visit to the Tyldens is over. My brother, Fanny, Edwd., and I went; Geo. stayed at home with W. K. There was nothing entertaining, or out of the common way. We met only Tyldens and double Tyldens. A whist-table for the gentlemen, a grown-up musical young lady to play backgammon with Fanny, and engravings of the Colleges at Cambridge for me. In the morning we returned Mrs. Sherer's visit. I like *Mr.* S. very much.

Poor Dr. Isham is obliged to admire *P. and P.*, and to send me word that he is sure he shall not like Madame D'Arblay's new novel half so well. Mrs. C[ooke] invented it all, of course. He desires his compliments to you and my mother.

I am now alone in the library, mistress of all I survey; at least I may say so, and repeat the whole poem if I like it, without offence to anybody.

I have *this* moment seen Mrs. Driver driven up to the kitchen door. I cannot close with a grander circumstance or greater wit.

Yours affectionately,
J. A.

Miss Austen, Chawton.

The next of Jane's surviving letters was addressed to her brother Frank.

Godmersham Park [September 25, 1813].

MY DEAREST FRANK,—The 11th of this month brought me your letter, and I assure you I thought it very well worth its two and three-pence. I am very much obliged to you for filling me so long a sheet of paper; you are a good one to traffic with in that way, you pay most liberally; my letter was a scratch of a note compared to yours, and then you write so even, so clear, both in style and penmanship, so much to the point, and give so much intelligence, that it is enough to kill one. I am sorry Sweden is so poor, and my riddle so bad. The idea of a fashionable bathing-place in Mecklenberg! How can people pretend to be fashionable or to bathe out of England? Rostock market makes one's mouth water; our cheapest butcher's meat is double the price of theirs; nothing under nine-pence all this summer, and I believe upon recollection nothing under ten-pence. Bread has sunk and is likely to sink more, which we hope may make meat sink too. But I have no occasion to think of the price of bread or of meat where I am now; let me shake off vulgar cares and conform to the happy indifference of East Kent wealth. I wonder whether you and the King of Sweden knew that I was come to Godmersham with my brother. Yes, I suppose you have received due notice of it by some means or other. I have not been here these four years, so I am sure the event deserves to be talked of before and behind, as well as in the middle. We left Chawton on the 14th, spent two entire days in town, and arrived here on the 17th. My brother, Fanny, Lizzie, Marianne and I composed this division of the family, and filled his carriage inside and out. Two post-chaises, under the escort of George, conveyed eight more across the country, the chair brought two, two others came on horseback, and the rest by coach, and so by one means or another, we all are removed. It puts me in remind of St. Paul's shipwreck, when all are said, by different means, to reach the shore in safety. I left my mother, Cassandra, and Martha well, and have had good accounts of them since. At present they are quite alone, but they are going to be visited by Mrs. Heathcote and Miss Bigg, and to have a few days of Henry's company likewise.

Of our three evenings in town, one was spent at the Lyceum, and another at Covent Garden. *The Clandestine Marriage* was the most respectable of the performances, the rest were sing-song and trumpery; but it did very well for Lizzie and Marianne, who were indeed delighted, but I wanted better acting. There was no actor worth naming. I believe the theatres are thought at a very low ebb at present. Henry has probably sent you his own account of his visit in Scotland. I wish he had had more time, and could have gone further north, and deviated to the lakes on his way back; but what he was able to do seems to have afforded him great enjoyment, and he met with scenes of higher beauty in Roxburghshire than I had supposed the South of Scotland possessed. Our nephew's gratification was less keen than our brother's. Edward is no enthusiast in the beauties of nature. His enthusiasm is for the sports of the field only. He is a very promising and pleasing young man, however, behaves with great propriety to his father, and great kindness to his brothers and sisters, and we must forgive his thinking more of grouse and partridges than lakes and mountains.

In this house there is a constant succession of small events, somebody is always going or coming; this morning we had Edward Bridges unexpectedly to breakfast with us, on his way from Ramsgate, where is his wife, to Lenham, where is his church, and to-morrow he dines and sleeps here on his return. They have been all the summer at Ramsgate for her health; she is a poor honey—the sort of woman who gives me the idea of being determined never to be well and who likes her spasms and nervousness, and the consequence they give her, better than anything else. This is an ill-natured statement to send all over the Baltic. The Mr. Knatchbulls, dear Mrs. Knight's brothers, dined here the other day. They came from the Friars, which is still on their hands. The elder made many inquiries after you. Mr. Sherer is quite a new Mr. Sherer to me; I heard him for the first time last Sunday, and he gave us an excellent sermon, a little too eager sometimes in his delivery, but that is to me a better extreme than the want of animation, especially when it evidently comes from the heart, as in him. The clerk is as much like you as ever. I am always glad to see him on that account. But the Sherers are going away.

He has a bad curate at Westwell, whom he can eject only by residing there himself. He goes nominally for three years, and a Mr. Paget is to have the curacy of Godmersham; a married man, with a very musical wife, which I hope may make her a desirable acquaintance to Fanny.

I thank you very warmly for your kind consent to my application, and the kind hint which followed it. I was previously aware of what I should be laying myself open to; but the truth is that the secret has spread so far as to be scarcely the shadow of a secret now, and that, I believe, whenever the third appears, I shall not even attempt to tell lies about it. I shall rather try to make all the money than all the mystery I can of it. People shall pay for their knowledge if I can make them. Henry heard *P. and P.* warmly praised in Scotland by Lady Robert Kerr and another lady; and what does he do, in the warmth of his brotherly vanity and love, but immediately tell them who wrote it? A thing once set going in that way—one knows how it spreads, and he, dear creature, has set it going so much more than once. I know it is all done from affection and partiality, but at the same time let me here again express to you and Mary my sense of the *superior* kindness which you have shown on the occasion in doing what I wished. I am trying to harden myself. After all, what a trifle it is, in all its bearings, to the really important points of one's existence, even in this world.

Your very affectionate sister,
J. A.

There is to be a second edition of *S. and S.* Egerton advises it.

The last paragraph of this letter sets two things plainly before us: a strong preference for remaining unknown if she could, and the invariable sweetness of temper which forbade her to blame a brother whom she loved because he had made such concealment impossible. That this acquiescence, however, was not reached without a struggle the last few words of the paragraph show.

Next follows a letter to Cassandra, dated Monday (October 11):—

We had our dinner party on Wednesday, with the addition of Mrs. and Miss Milles. . . . Both mother and daughter are much as I have always found them. I like the mother—first, because she reminds me of Mrs. Birch; and, secondly, because she is cheerful and grateful for what she is at the age of ninety and upwards. The day was pleasant enough. I sat by Mr. Chisholme, and we talked away at a great rate about nothing worth hearing.

Lizzie is very much obliged to you for your letter and will answer it soon, but has so many things to do that it may be four or five days before she can. This is quite her own message, spoken in rather a desponding tone. Your letter gave pleasure to all of us; we had all the reading of it of course, I *three times*, as I undertook, to the great relief of Lizzie, to read it to Sackree, and afterwards to Louisa.

Mrs. —— called here on Saturday. I never saw her before. She is a large, ungenteel woman, with self-satisfied and would-be elegant manners.

On Thursday, Mr. Lushington, M.P. for Canterbury, and manager of the Lodge Hounds, dines here, and stays the night. He is chiefly young Edward's acquaintance. If I can I will get a frank from him, and write to you all the sooner. I suppose the Ashford ball will furnish something.

I am looking over *Self-Control* again, and my opinion is confirmed of its being an excellently-meant, elegantly-written work, without anything of nature or probability in it. I declare I do not know whether Laura's passage down the American river is not the most natural, possible, everyday thing she ever does.

Tuesday.—I admire the sagacity and taste of Charlotte Williams. Those large dark eyes always judge well. I will compliment her by naming a heroine after her.

Southey's *Life of Nelson:* I am tired of *Lives of Nelson*, being that I never read any. I will read this, however, if Frank is mentioned in it.

[October 14, 1813.]

Now I will prepare for Mr. Lushington, and as it will be wisest also to prepare for his not coming, or my not getting a frank, I shall write very close from the first, and even leave room for the seal in the proper place. When I have followed up my last with this I shall feel somewhat less unworthy of you than the state of our correspondence now requires.

Mr. W. is about five- or six-and-twenty, not ill-looking, and not agreeable. He is certainly no addition. A sort of cool, gentlemanlike manner, but very silent. They say his name is Henry, a proof how unequally the gifts of fortune are bestowed. I have seen many a John and Thomas much more agreeable.

We did not go to the ball. It was left to her to decide, and at last she determined against it. She knew that it would be a sacrifice on the part of her father and brothers if they went, and I hope it will prove that *she* has not sacrificed much. It is not likely that there should have been anybody there whom she would care for. *I* was very glad to be spared the trouble of dressing and going, and being weary before it was half over, so my gown and my cap are still unworn. It will appear at last, perhaps, that I might have done without either. I produced my brown bombazine yesterday, and it was very much admired indeed, and I like it better than ever.

The comfort of the billiard-table here is very great; it draws all the gentlemen to it whenever they are within, especially after dinner, so that my brother, Fanny, and I have the library to ourselves in delightful quiet.

Friday.—They came last night at about seven. We had given them up, but *I still* expected them to come. Dessert was nearly over; a better time for arriving than an hour and a half earlier. They were late because they did not set out earlier, and did not allow time enough. Charles did not *aim* at more than reaching Sittingbourne by three, which could not have brought them here by dinner time. They had a very rough passage; he would not have ventured if he had known how bad it would be.

However, here they are, safe and well, just like their own nice selves, Fanny looking as neat and white this morning as possible, and dear Charles all affectionate, placid, quiet, cheerful good humour. They are both looking very well, but poor little Cassy is grown extremely thin, and looks poorly. I hope a week's country air and exercise may do her good. I am sorry to say it can be but a week. The baby does not appear so large in proportion as she was, nor quite so pretty, but I have seen very little of her. Cassy was too tired and bewildered just at first to seem to know anybody. We met them in the hall—the women and girl part of us—but before we reached the library she kissed me very affectionately, and has since seemed to recollect me in the same way.

It was quite an evening of confusion, as you may suppose. At first we were all walking about from one part of the house to the other; then came a fresh dinner in the breakfast-room for Charles and his wife, which Fanny and I attended; then we moved into the library, were joined by the dining-room people, were introduced, and so forth; and then we had tea and coffee, which was not over till past 10. Billiards again drew all the odd ones away, and Edward, Charles, the two Fannies, and I sat snugly talking. I shall be glad to have our numbers a little reduced, and by the time you receive this we shall be only a family, though a large family, party. Mr. Lushington goes to-morrow.

Now I must speak of *him*, and I like him very much. I am sure he is clever, and a man of taste. He got a volume of Milton last night, and spoke of it with warmth. He is quite an M.P., very smiling, with an exceeding good address and readiness of language. I am rather in love with him. I dare say he is ambitious and insincere. He puts me in mind of Mr. Dundas. He has a wide smiling mouth, and very good teeth, and something the same complexion and nose.

[October 18, 1813.]

No; I have never seen the death of Mrs. Crabbe. I have only just been making out from one of his prefaces that he probably was married. It is almost ridiculous. Poor woman! I will comfort *him* as well as I can, but I do not undertake to be good to her children. She had better not leave any.

October 26.

Our Canterbury scheme took place as proposed, and very pleasant it was—Harriot and I and little George within, my brother on the box with the master coachman.

Our chief business was to call on Mrs. Milles, and we had, indeed, so little else to do that we were obliged to saunter about anywhere and go backwards and forwards as much as possible to make out the time and keep ourselves from having two hours to sit with the good lady—a most extraordinary circumstance in a Canterbury morning.

Old Toke came in while we were paying our visit. I thought of Louisa. Miss Milles was queer as usual, and provided us with plenty to laugh at. She undertook in *three words* to give us the history of Mrs. Scudamore's reconciliation, and then talked on about it for half an hour, using such odd expressions, and so foolishly minute, that I could hardly keep my countenance.

Owing to a difference of clocks the coachman did not bring the carriage so soon as he ought by half an hour; anything like a breach of punctuality was a great offence, and Mr. Moore was very angry, which I was rather glad of. I wanted to see him angry; and, though he spoke to his servant in a very loud voice and with a good deal of heat, I was happy to perceive that he did not scold Harriot at all. Indeed, there is nothing to object to in his manners to her, and I do believe that he makes her—or she makes herself—very happy. They do not spoil their boy.

George Hatton called yesterday, and I saw him, saw him for ten minutes; sat in the same room with him, heard him talk, saw him bow, and was not in raptures. I discerned nothing extraordinary. I should speak of him as a gentlemanlike young man—*eh bien! tout est dit.* We are expecting the ladies of the family this morning.

[November 3, 1813.]

I will keep this celebrated birthday by writing to you, and as my pen seems inclined to write large, I will put my lines very close together. I had but just time to enjoy your letter yesterday before Edward and I set off in the chair for Canty., and I allowed him to hear the chief of it as we went along.

But now I cannot be quite easy without staying a little while with Henry, unless he wishes it otherwise; his illness and the dull time of year together make me feel that it would be horrible of me not to offer to remain with him, and therefore unless you know of any objection, I wish you would tell him with my best love that I shall be most happy to spend ten days or a fortnight in Henrietta St., if he will accept me. I do not offer more than a fortnight, because I shall then have been some time from home; but it will be a great pleasure to be with him, as it always is.

Edward and I had a delightful morning for our drive *there* [to Canterbury], I enjoyed it thoroughly; but the day turned off before we were ready, and we came home in some rain and the apprehension of a great deal. It has not done us any harm, however. He went to inspect the gaol, as a visiting magistrate, and took me with him. I was gratified, and went through all the feelings which people must go through, I think, in visiting such a building. We paid no other visits, only walked about snugly together and shopped. I bought a concert ticket and a sprig of flowers for my old age.

What a convenient carriage Henry's is, to his friends in general! Who has it next? I am glad William's going is voluntary, and on no worse grounds. An inclination for the country is a venial fault. He has more of Cowper than of Johnson in him—fonder of tame hares and blank verse than of the full tide of human existence at Charing Cross.

Oh! I have more of such sweet flattery from Miss Sharp. She is an excellent kind friend. I am read and admired in Ireland, too. There is a Mrs. Fletcher, the wife of a judge, an old lady, and very good and very clever, who is all curiosity to know about me—what

I am like, and so forth. I am not known to her by *name*, however. This comes through Mrs. Carrick, not through Mrs. Gore. You are quite out there.

I do not despair of having my picture in the Exhibition at last—all white and red, with my head on one side; or perhaps I may marry young Mr. D'Arblay. I suppose in the meantime I shall owe dear Henry a great deal of money for printing, &c.

I hope Mrs. Fletcher will indulge herself with *S. and S.*

November 6.

Having half an hour before breakfast (very snug in my own room, lovely morning, excellent fire—fancy me!) I will give you some account of the last two days. And yet, what is there to be told? I shall get foolishly minute unless I cut the matter short.

We met only the Bretons at Chilham Castle, besides a Mr. and Mrs. Osborne and a Miss Lee staying in the house, and were only fourteen altogether. My brother and Fanny thought it the pleasantest party they had ever known there, and I was very well entertained by bits and scraps.

By-the-bye, as I must leave off being young, I find many *douceurs* in being a sort of *chaperon*, for I am put on the sofa near the fire, and can drink as much wine as I like. We had music in the evening: Fanny and Miss Wildman played, and Mr. James Wildman sat close by and listened, or pretended to listen.

. . . Mrs. Harrison and I found each other out, and had a very comfortable little complimentary friendly chat. She is a sweet woman—still quite a sweet woman in herself, and so like her sister! I could almost have thought I was speaking to Mrs. Lefroy. She introduced me to her daughter, whom I think pretty, but most dutifully inferior to *la Mère Beauté*.

I was just introduced at last to Mary Plumptre, but should hardly know her again. She was delighted with *me*, however, good enthusiastic soul! And Lady B. found me handsomer than she expected, so you see I am not so very bad as you might think for.

Since I wrote last, my 2nd edit. has stared me in the face. Mary tells me that Eliza means to buy it. I wish she may. It can hardly depend upon any more Fyfield Estates. I cannot help hoping that *many* will feel themselves obliged to buy it. I shall not mind imagining it a disagreeable duty to them, so as they do it. Mary heard before she left home that it was very much admired at Cheltenham, and that it was given to Miss Hamilton. It is pleasant to have such a respectable writer named. I cannot tire *you*, I am sure, on this subject, or I would apologise.

What weather, and what news! We have enough to do to admire them both. I hope you derive your full share of enjoyment from each.

Lady Eliz. Hatton and Annamaria called here this morning. Yes, they called; but I do not think I can say anything more about them. They came, and they sat, and they went.

Sunday.—Excellent sweetness of you to send me such a nice long letter; it made its appearance, with one from my mother, soon after I and my impatient feelings walked in. How glad I am that I did what I did! I was only afraid that *you* might think the offer superfluous, but you have set my heart at ease. Tell Henry that I *will* stay with him, let it be ever so disagreeable to him.

You shall hear from me once more, some day or other.

Yours very affectionately,
J. A.

Miss Austen, 10 Henrietta Street.

Even in the middle of this large family party, Jane was not likely to forget the literary profession which she had now seriously adopted. Indeed, it was just at this time that the second edition of *Sense and Sensibility*, on which she had ventured under the advice of her publisher Egerton, appeared. According to our dates, she was not now actually engaged in regular composition—for *Mansfield Park* was completed 'soon after June 1813,' and *Emma* was not begun till January 21, 1814. We may guess, however, that she was either putting a few humorous touches to Mrs. Norris and

Lady Bertram, or else giving herself hints in advance for Miss Bates or Mr. Woodhouse; for we learn something of her process from an eyewitness, her niece Marianne Knight, who related her childish remembrances of her aunt not very many years ago. 'Aunt Jane,' she said, 'would sit very quietly at work beside the fire in the Godmersham library, then suddenly burst out laughing, jump up, cross the room to a distant table with papers lying upon it, write something down, returning presently and sitting down quietly to her work again.' She also remembered how her aunt would take the elder girls into an upstairs room and read to them something that produced peals of laughter, to which the little ones on the wrong side of the door listened, thinking it very hard that they should be shut out from hearing what was so delightful! The laughter may have been the result of the second novel then published, for there is an entry in Fanny Knight's diary: 'We finished *Pride and Prejudice*'; or it may have been caused by a first introduction to Aunt Norris and Lady Bertram. Happy indeed were those who could hear their creator make her characters 'speak as they ought.' The dramatic element in her works is so strong that for complete enjoyment on a first acquaintance it is almost indispensable that they should be read aloud by some person capable of doing them justice. She had this power herself, according to the concurrent testimony of those who heard her, and she handed it on to her nephew, the author of the *Memoir*.

On November 13 Jane left Godmersham with Edward, spent two days with some connexions of his at Wrotham, and reached London on the 15th, in time to dine with Henry in Henrietta Street.

After that she had various plans; but we do not know which she adopted; and there is nothing further to tell of her movements until March 1814. We know, however, that *Emma* was begun in January; and that on March 2, when Henry drove his sister up to London, spending a night at Cobham on the way, he was engaged in reading *Mansfield Park* for the first time. Jane was of course eager to communicate Henry's impressions to Cassandra.

Henrietta Street: Wednesday [March 2, 1814].

MY DEAR CASSANDRA,—You were wrong in thinking of us at Guildford last night: we were at Cobham. On reaching G. we found that John and his horses were gone on. We therefore did no more there than we did at Farnham—sit in the carriage while fresh horses were put in—and proceeded directly to Cobham, which we reached by seven, and about eight were sitting down to a very nice roast fowl, &c. We had altogether a very good journey, and everything at Cobham was comfortable. I could not pay Mr. Herington! That was the only alas! of the business. I shall therefore return his bill, and my mother's £2, that you may try your luck. We did not begin reading till Bentley Green. Henry's approbation is hitherto even equal to my wishes. He says it is very different from the other two, but does not appear to think it at all inferior. He has only married Mrs. R. I am afraid he has gone through the most entertaining part. He took to Lady B. and Mrs. N. most kindly, and gives great praise to the drawing of the characters. He understands them all, likes Fanny, and, I think, foresees how it will all be. I finished the *Heroine* last night, and was very much amused by it. I wonder James did not like it better. It diverted me exceedingly. We went to bed at ten. I was very tired, but slept to a miracle, and am lovely to-day, and at present Henry seems to have no complaint. We left Cobham at half-past eight, stopped to bait and breakfast at Kingston, and were in this house considerably before two, quite in the style of Mr. Knight. Nice smiling Mr. Barlowe met us at the door and, in reply to enquiries after news, said that peace was generally expected. I have taken possession of my bedroom, unpacked my bandbox, sent Miss P.'s two letters to the twopenny post, been visited by M^{de} Bigeon and am now writing by myself at the new table in the front room. It is snowing. We had some snowstorms yesterday, and a smart frost at night, which gave us a hard road from Cobham to Kingston; but as it was then getting dirty and heavy, Henry had a pair of leaders put on from the latter place to the bottom of Sloane St. His own horses, therefore, cannot have had hard work. I watched for *veils* as we drove through the streets, and had the pleasure of seeing several upon vulgar heads. And now, how do you all do?—you in particular, after the worry of yesterday and the day before. I hope Martha had a pleasant visit again, and that you and my mother could eat your beef-pudding.

Depend upon my thinking of the chimney-sweeper as soon as I wake to-morrow. Places are secured at Drury Lane for Saturday, but so great is the rage for seeing Kean that only a third and fourth row could be got; as it is in a front box, however, I hope we shall do pretty well—*Shylock*, a good play for Fanny—she cannot be much affected, I think.

Mrs. Perigord has just been here. She tells me that we owe her master for the silk-dyeing. My poor old muslin has never been dyed yet. It has been promised to be done several times. What wicked people dyers are. They begin with dipping their own souls in scarlet sin. . . . It is evening. We have drank tea, and I have torn through the third vol. of the *Heroine*. I do not think it falls off. It is a delightful burlesque, particularly on the Radcliffe style. Henry is going on with *Mansfield Park*. He admires H. Crawford: I mean properly, as a clever, pleasant man. I tell you all the good I can, as I know how much you will enjoy it. . . . We hear that Mr. Kean is more admired than ever. . . . There are no good places to be got in Drury Lane for the next fortnight, but Henry means to secure some for Saturday fortnight, when you are reckoned upon. Give my love to little Cass. I hope she found my bed comfortable last night. I have seen nobody in London yet with such a long chin as Dr. Syntax, nor anybody quite so large as Gogmagoglicus.

Saturday [March 5, 1814].

Do not be angry with me for beginning another letter to you. I have read the *Corsair*, mended my petticoat, and have nothing else to do. Getting out is impossible. It is a nasty day for everybody. Edward's spirits will be wanting sunshine, and here is nothing but thickness and sleet; and though these two rooms are delightfully warm, I fancy it is very cold abroad.

Sunday.—We were quite satisfied with Kean. I cannot imagine better acting, but the part was too short; and, excepting him and Miss Smith, and *she* did not quite answer my expectation, the parts were ill filled and the play heavy. We were too much tired to stay for the whole of *Illusion* ('Nour-jahad'), which has three acts; there is a great deal of finery and dancing in it, but I think little merit.

Elliston was 'Nour-jahad,' but it is a solemn sort of part, not at all calculated for his powers. There was nothing of the *best* Elliston about him. I might not have known him but for his voice.

Henry has this moment said that he likes my *M. P.* better and better; he is in the third volume. I believe *now* he has changed his mind as to foreseeing the end; he said yesterday, at least, that he defied anybody to say whether H. C. would be reformed, or would forget Fanny in a fortnight.

I shall like to see Kean again excessively, and to see him with you too. It appeared to me as if there were no fault in him anywhere; and in his scene with 'Tubal' there was exquisite acting.

Monday.—You cannot think how much my ermine tippet is admired both by father and daughter. It was a noble gift.

Perhaps you have not heard that Edward has a good chance of escaping his lawsuit. His opponent 'knocks under.' The terms of agreement are not quite settled.

We are to see *The Devil to Pay* to-night. I expect to be very much amused. Excepting Miss Stephens, I daresay *Artaxerxes* will be very tiresome.

Tuesday.—Well, Mr. Hampson dined here, and all that. I was very tired of *Artaxerxes*, highly amused with the farce, and, in an inferior way, with the pantomime that followed. Mr. J. Plumptre joined in the latter part of the evening, walked home with us, ate some soup, and is very earnest for our going to Covent Garden again to-night to see Miss Stephens in the *Farmer's Wife*. He is to try for a box. I do not particularly wish him to succeed. I have had enough for the present. Henry dines to-day with Mr. Spencer.

Wednesday [March 9, 1814].

Well, we went to the play again last night, and as we were out a great part of the morning too, shopping, and seeing the Indian jugglers, I am very glad to be quiet now till dressing time. We are to dine at the Tilsons', and to-morrow at Mr. Spencer's.

We had not done breakfast yesterday when Mr. J. Plumptre appeared to say that he had secured a box. Henry asked him to dine here, which I fancy he was very happy to do, and so at five o'clock we four sat down to table together while the master of the house was preparing for going out himself. The *Farmer's Wife* is a musical thing in three acts, and, as Edward was steady in not staying for anything more, we were at home before ten.

Fanny and Mr. J. P. are delighted with Miss S[tephens], and her merit in singing is, I dare say, very great; that she gave *me* no pleasure is no reflection upon her, nor, I hope, upon myself, being what Nature made me on that article. All that I am sensible of in Miss S. is a pleasing person and no skill in acting. We had Mathews, Liston, and Emery; of course, some amusement.

Our friends were off before half-past eight this morning, and had the prospect of a heavy cold journey before them. I think they both liked their visit very much. I am sure Fanny did. Henry sees decided attachment between her and his new acquaintance.

Henry has finished *Mansfield Park*, and his approbation has not lessened. He found the last half of the last volume *extremely interesting*.

On Friday we are to be snug with only Mr. Barlowe and an evening of business. I am so pleased that the mead is brewed. Love to all. I have written to Mrs. Hill, and care for nobody.

Yours affectionately,
J. AUSTEN.

Henry must have read from a proof copy; for *Mansfield Park* was not yet published, though on the eve of being so. It was announced in the *Morning Chronicle* on May 23, and we shall see from the first letter in the next chapter that the Cookes had already been reading it before June 13. It was probably a small issue; but whatever the size may have been, it was entirely sold out in the autumn.

The author broke new ground in this work, which (it should be remembered) was the first dating wholly from her more mature

Chawton period. Though her novels were all of one type she had a remarkable faculty for creating an atmosphere—differing more or less in each book; and an excellent instance of this faculty is afforded by the decorous, though somewhat cold, dignity of Sir Thomas Bertram's household. In this household Fanny Price grows up, thoroughly appreciating its orderliness, but saved by Edmund's affection and her own warmhearted simplicity from catching the infection of its coldness. She required, however, an experience of the discomforts and vulgarity of Portsmouth to enable her to value to the full the home which she had left. In the first volume she had been too much of a Cinderella to take her proper position in the family party, and it was a real stroke of art to enhance the dignity of the heroine through the courtship of a rich and clever man of the world. A small point worth noticing in the third volume is the manner in which, when the horrible truth breaks in upon Fanny—and upon the reader—the tension is relaxed by Mrs. Price's commonplace remarks about the carpet.

Probably, most readers will look upon the theatricals and the Portsmouth episode as the most brilliant parts of the book; but the writing throughout is full of point, and the three sisters—Lady Bertram, Mrs. Norris, and Mrs. Price—are all productions of the author's most delicately barbed satire. Mrs. Norris, indeed, is an instance of her complex characters so justly praised by Macaulay. One thinks of her mainly as parsimonious; but her parsimony would be worth much less than it is, if it were not set off by her servility to Sir Thomas, her brutality to Fanny, and her undisciplined fondness for her other nieces. Lady Bertram is formed for the enjoyment of all her readers; and a pale example of what she might have become under less propitious circumstances is given by Mrs. Price. Mrs. Norris, we are told, would have done much better than Mrs. Price in her position. It must have given Jane Austen great pleasure to make this remark. None of her bad characters (except possibly Elizabeth Elliot) were quite inhuman to her, and to have found a situation in which Mrs. Norris might have shone would be a real satisfaction.

One more remark may be made on *Mansfield Park*. It affords what perhaps is the only probable instance in these books of a portrait drawn from life. She must, one would think, have had in her mind her brother Charles—as he had been twelve or fourteen years earlier—when she drew so charming a sketch of a young sailor in William Price.

We must not forget, however, the author's strong denial of depicting individuals, and her declaration that she was too proud of her gentlemen 'to admit that they were only Mr. A. or Colonel B.'; nor yet her modest confession, when speaking of two of her favourites—Edmund Bertram and Mr. Knightley—that she was aware they were 'very far from what I know English gentlemen often are.'

Jane Austen may perhaps enjoy the distinction of having added words or expressions to colloquial English. The name 'Collins' is almost established as the description of a letter of thanks after a visit; and we have heard of a highly intelligent family among whom a guinea is always alluded to as 'something considerable' in memory of the sum believed (on the authority of the *Memoir*) to have been given to William Price by Aunt Norris.

CHAPTER XVII.

EMMA 1814-1815

THE last letter but one of the foregoing chapter contains two sentences mentioning the writer's brother, Mr. Knight, which will help us to carry on our story.

Writing on March 5, 1814, Jane says: 'It is a nasty day for everybody. Edward's spirits will be wanting sunshine, and here is nothing but thickness and sleet'; and towards the conclusion of the same letter we find the following: 'Perhaps you have not heard that Edward has a good chance of escaping his lawsuit. His opponent "knocks under." The terms of agreement are not quite settled.'

There can, we think, be little doubt that both passages—the depressed and the hopeful—refer to a claim over Edward's Hampshire property made by some of the heirs-at-law of the former Knight family whom the Brodnaxes of Godmersham had succeeded. Unfortunately, the cheerful forecast contained in the second passage did not prove to be in accordance with the facts. The lawsuit hung on for three years and was then compromised by Mr. Knight's paying a large sum of money.

Perhaps the claim also had its influence in producing the one unflattering estimate of Jane which we shall have to lay before the reader.

Miss Mitford was a convinced—but apparently a reluctant—admirer of her genius; and she dwells without disguise on what she considers the want of taste in *Pride and Prejudice*, though even here she adds that Miss Austen 'wants nothing but the *beau idéal* of the female character to be a perfect novel writer.'

In another letter she refers to her mother's unfavourable reminiscences of Jane Austen as a husband-hunter; although Mrs.

Mitford's remark must (as we have already pointed out) have been based on an entire misrepresentation, owing to Jane's youthful age at the time when that lady could have known her.

She proceeds thus:—

A friend of mine who visits her now, says that she has stiffened into the most perpendicular, precise, taciturn piece of 'single blessedness' that ever existed, and that, till *Pride and Prejudice* showed what a precious gem was hidden in that unbending case, she was no more regarded in society than a poker or a fire-screen, or any other thin, upright piece of wood or iron that fills the corner in peace and quietness. The case is very different now: she is still a poker—but a poker of whom every one is afraid. It must be confessed that this silent observation from such an observer is rather formidable. Most writers are good-humoured chatterers—neither very wise nor very witty; but nine times out of ten (at least in the few that I have known) unaffected and pleasant, and quite removing by their conversation any fear that may have been excited by their works. But a wit, a delineator of character, who does not talk, is terrific indeed!

Miss Mitford has, however, the candour to add a qualification which diminishes the force of her earlier remarks, and bears upon our present subject. She says:—

After all, I do not know that I can quite vouch for this account, though the friend from whom I received it is truth itself; but her family connexions must render her disagreeable to Miss Austen, since she is the sister-in-law of a gentleman who is at law with Miss A.'s brother for the greater part of his fortune. You must have remarked how much her stories hinge upon entailed estates—doubtless she has learnt to dislike entails. Her brother was adopted by a Mr. Knight, who left him his name and two much better legacies in an estate of five thousand a year in Kent, and another of nearly double the value in Hampshire; but it seems he forgot some ceremony—passing a fine, I think they call it—with regard to the Hampshire property, which Mr. Baverstock has claimed in right of his mother, together with the mesne rents, and is likely to be successful.

Miss Mitford, indeed, could hardly have done less, after repeating this somewhat spiteful gossip, than mention the hostile quarter from which it arose. We have considered it right to quote part of it, as the writer is an author of some note: but we venture to think that those readers who have accompanied us so far will believe that Jane was guilty of nothing worse than being shy, and talking but little among strangers; and that such strangers as knew something of her literary ability believed, but were quite wrong in believing, that she was taking stock of their peculiarities with a view to introducing them into her next novel.

Jane had now completed the first of three visits which she was to pay to Henry this year, and Cassandra was in London in her place; while the Godmersham party were spending two months at Chawton. The two following letters were written by Jane from Chawton in anticipation of a visit to the Cookes at Bookham. Incidentally, Mr. Cooke's remark (quoted in the first) shows that *Mansfield Park* was already published. We must not forget, however, that its author had been, since January 1814, deep in the composition of *Emma*, and she would be sure to use a visit to the neighbourhood of Leatherhead and Box Hill to verify geographical and other details for her new work. Since her fame was fully established, there have been many attempts to identify the locality of Highbury. 'There is a school of serious students who place it at Esher; another band of enthusiasts support Dorking'; but Mr. E. V. Lucas, in his introduction to a recent edition of the novel, prefers the claim of Leatherhead, which, he says, is rightly placed as regards London and Kingston, and not far wrong as regards Box Hill. Near Leatherhead is a house called 'Randalls'; and in 1761 the vestry of the parish paid their thanks 'in the most respectful manner to Mr. Knightley,' who had remodelled the pulpit and reading-desk of the church.

Cobham should be mentioned as another possible alternative, as the distances from London, Richmond, Kingston, and Box Hill suit well. But the most probable supposition of all is that the author purposely avoided identifying it with any one village, while sufficiently defining its position in the county of Surrey.

Chawton: Tuesday [June 14, 1814].

MY DEAREST CASSANDRA,—Fanny takes my mother to Alton this morning, which gives me an opportunity of sending you a few lines without any other trouble than that of writing them.

This is a delightful day in the country, and I hope not much too hot for town. Well, you had a good journey, I trust, and all that, and not rain enough to spoil your bonnet. It appeared so likely to be a wet evening that I went up to the Gt. House between three and four, and dawdled away an hour very comfortably, though Edwd. was not very brisk. The air was clearer in the evening and he was better. We all five walked together into the kitchen garden and along the Gosport road, and they drank tea with us.

The only letter to-day is from Mrs. Cooke to me. They do not leave home till July, and want me to come to them, according to my promise. And, after considering everything, I have resolved on going.

In addition to their standing claims on me they admire *Mansfield Park* exceedingly. Mr. Cooke says 'it is the most sensible novel he ever read,' and the manner in which I treat the clergy delights them very much. Altogether, I must go, and I want you to join me there when your visit in Henrietta St. is over. Put this into your capacious head.

Take care of yourself, and do not be trampled to death in running after the Emperor. The report in Alton yesterday was that they would certainly travel this road either to or from Portsmouth. I long to know what this bow of the Prince's will produce.

Thursday [June 23].

I heard yesterday from Frank. When he began his letter he hoped to be here on Monday, but before it was ended he had been told that the naval review would not take place till Friday, which would probably occasion him some delay, as he cannot get some necessary business of his own attended to while Portsmouth is in such a bustle. I hope Fanny has seen the Emperor, and then I may fairly wish them all away. I go to-morrow, and hope for some delays and adventures.

Henry at White's! Oh, what a Henry! I do not know what to wish as to Miss B., so I will hold my tongue and my wishes.

We have called upon Miss Dusantoy and Miss Papillon, and been very pretty. Miss D. has a great idea of being Fanny Price—she and her youngest sister together, who is named Fanny.

Yours very affectionately,
J. AUSTEN.

Jane's visit to Bookham began on June 24, as soon as the Knights had left Chawton. She was to be away for more than a fortnight, and must have been at Chawton again for a month till the middle of August, when she once more went to join Henry in London. On this occasion she had no rich brother to take her in his carriage, and was forced to come by Yalden's somewhat crowded coach—four inside and fifteen on the top. Henry had moved between June and August, finding a house in his old neighbourhood at 23 Hans Place. Next to him (but separated from him by the entrance to the Pavilion, now the road leading to Pont Street), at No. 22, was the St. Quentins' celebrated school, at which Miss Mitford had been a pupil, as well as Miss Landon and Lady Caroline Lamb. Three doors off, at No. 26, lived Henry's partner, Mr. Tilson, with whom it was possible to converse across the intermediate gardens.

23 Hans Place: Tuesday morning [August, 1814].

MY DEAR CASSANDRA,—I had a very good journey, not crowded, two of the three taken up at Bentley being children, the others of a reasonable size; and they were all very quiet and civil. We were late in London, from being a great load, and from changing coaches at Farnham; it was nearly four, I believe, when we reached Sloane Street. Henry himself met me, and as soon as my trunk and basket could be routed out from all the other trunks and baskets in the world, we were on our way to Hans Place in the luxury of a nice, large, cool, dirty hackney coach.

There were four in the kitchen part of Yalden, and I was told fifteen at top, among them Percy Benn. We met in the same room at Egham, but poor Percy was not in his usual spirits. He would be more chatty, I dare say, in his way *from* Woolwich. We took up a young Gibson at Holybourn, and, in short, everybody either *did* come up by Yalden yesterday, or wanted to come up. It put me in mind of my own coach between Edinburgh and Stirling.

It is a delightful place—more than answers my expectation. Having got rid of my unreasonable ideas, I find more space and comfort in the rooms than I had supposed, and the garden is quite a love. I am in the front attic, which is the bedchamber to be preferred.

Wednesday.—I got the willow yesterday, as Henry was not quite ready when I reached Hen$^{a.}$ St. I saw Mr. Hampson there for a moment. He dines here to-morrow and proposed bringing his son; so I must submit to seeing George Hampson, though I had hoped to go through life without it. It was one of my vanities, like your not reading *Patronage*.

Is not this all that can have happened or been arranged? Not quite. Henry wants me to see more of his Hanwell favourite, and has written to invite her to spend a day or two here with me. His scheme is to fetch her on Saturday. I am more and more convinced that he will marry again soon, and like the idea of *her* better than of anybody else, at hand.

Yours very truly and affectionately,
JANE.

Miss Austen, Chawton.
By favour of Mr. Gray.

All through this year and the early part of the next, *Emma* (begun January 1814, finished March 29, 1815) was assiduously worked at. Although polished to the highest degree, it was more quickly composed than any previous work and gave evidence of a practised hand. It was also the most 'Austenish' of all her novels, carrying out most completely her idea of what was fitted to her tastes and capacities. She enjoyed having a heroine 'whom no one would like but herself,' and working on 'three or four families in a country village.' *Emma* appeals therefore more exclusively than any of the others to an inner circle of admirers: but such admirers may possibly place it at the head of her compositions. There are no stirring incidents; there is no change of scene. The heroine, whose society we enjoy throughout, never sleeps away from home, and even there sees only so much company as an invalid father can welcome. No character in the book is ill, no one is ruined, there is no villain, and no paragon. On the other hand, the plot is admirably contrived and never halts; while the mysteries—exclusively mysteries of courtship and love—are excellently maintained. Emma never expresses any opinion which is thoroughly sound, and seldom makes any forecast which is not belied by the event, yet we always recognise her acuteness, and she by degrees obtains our sympathy. The book also illustrates to the highest degree the author's power of drawing humorous characters; Miss Bates, Mr. Woodhouse, and Mrs. Elton in the first class, and Harriet Smith in the second. And the humour is always essential to the delineation of character—it is never an excrescence. It also depends more on what is said than on any tricks of speech; there are no catch-words, and every one speaks practically the same excellent English. Besides this, *Emma* also gives a very good instance of the author's habit of building up her characters almost entirely without formal description, and leaving analysis to her readers.

Her custom of following her creations outside the printed pages enables us to say that the word swept aside unread by Jane Fairfax was 'pardon'; and that the Knightleys' exclusion from Donwell was ended by the death of Mr. Woodhouse in two years' time. According to a less well-known tradition, Jane Fairfax survived her elevation only nine or ten years. Whether the John Knightleys afterwards settled at Hartfield, and whether Frank Churchill married again, may be legitimate subjects for speculation.

Meanwhile, *Mansfield Park* was selling well, and the idea of a second edition began to be mooted. Writing from Chawton to her niece Fanny on another subject (November 18, 1814), she tells her that the first edition is all sold, and adds:—

Your Uncle Henry is rather wanting me to come to town to settle about a second edition, but as I could not very conveniently leave home now, I have written him my will and pleasure, and, unless he still urges it, shall not go. I am very greedy, and want to make the most of it, but as you are much above caring about money I shall not plague you with any particulars. The pleasures of vanity are more within your comprehension, and you will enter into mine at receiving the *praise* which every now and then comes to me through some channel or other.

She did, however, leave home; and our next extract is from a letter written to Fanny from 23 Hans Place, and dated November 30:—

Thank you, but it is not yet settled whether I *do* hazard a second edition. We are to see Egerton to-day, when it will probably be determined. People are more ready to borrow and praise than to buy, which I cannot wonder at; but though I like praise as well as anybody, I like what Edward calls 'Pewter' too.

Apparently, Egerton did not fancy taking the risk; for there was no second edition until 1816, when it appeared from the publishing house of Murray.

Jane's stay in London was a short one; but it included a visit to her niece Anna, who had lately been married to Ben Lefroy, and who was living for the time at Hendon. Early in December, Jane returned home; and three weeks later she and Cassandra set out for a couple of visits: one for a week to Mrs. Heathcote and Miss Bigg in Winchester; the other of longer duration, to their brother at Steventon. Then the curtain is rung down once more, not to be raised till the end of September 1815. During this quiet time, *Emma* was prepared for the press, and it was no doubt in connexion with its publication that she went to Hans Place on October 4, 1815, for a visit which proved to be much longer and more eventful than the last. For some reason that we are unable to explain, Jane now forsook her former publisher, Mr. Egerton, and put her interests in the charge of the historic house of Murray. She travelled up once more in the company of Henry, who had been paying his mother and sisters a short visit at the cottage. The prolongation of Jane's stay in London to more than a couple of months was caused by Henry's dangerous illness. She gives the news in a letter written to Cassandra and dated Tuesday, October 17:—

... What weather we have! What shall we do about it? The 17th October and summer still! Henry is not quite well—a bilious attack with fever. He came back early from Henrietta Street yesterday and went to bed—the comical consequence of which was that Mr. Seymour and I dined together *tête-à-tête*. He is calomeling, and therefore in a way to be better, and I hope may be well to-morrow.

Wednesday.—Henry's illness is much more serious than I expected. He has been in bed since three o'clock on Monday. It is a fever—something bilious but chiefly inflammatory. I am not alarmed, but I have determined to send this letter to-day by the post, that you may know how things are going on. There is no chance of his being able to leave Town on Saturday. I asked Mr. Haden that question to-day. Mr. H. is the apothecary from the corner of Sloane Street, successor to Mr. Smith, a very young man, said to be clever, and he is certainly very attentive, and appears hitherto to have understood the complaint.

As for myself, you may be sure I shall return as soon as I can. Tuesday is in my brain, but you will feel the uncertainty of it.

You must fancy Henry in the backroom upstairs, and I am generally there also, working or writing.

Even in illness, the interests of *Emma* were not neglected; and a day or two later Henry was able to dictate the following letter to Mr. Murray:—

DEAR SIR,—Severe illness has confined me to my bed ever since I received yours of ye 15th. I cannot yet hold a pen, and employ an amanuensis. The politeness and perspicuity of your letter equally claim my earliest exertion. Your official opinion of the merits of *Emma* is very valuable and satisfactory. Though I venture to differ occasionally from your critique, yet I assure you the quantum of your commendation rather exceeds than falls short of the author's expectation and my own. The terms you offer are so very inferior to what we had expected that I am apprehensive of having made some great error in my arithmetical calculation. On the subject of the expence and profit of publishing you must be much better informed than I am, but documents in my possession appear to prove that the sum offered by you for the copyright of *Sense and Sensibility*, *Mansfield Park*, and *Emma* is not equal to the money which my sister has actually cleared by one very moderate edition of *Mansfield Park;*—(you yourself expressed astonishment that so small an edition of such a work should have been sent into the world)—and a still smaller one of *Sense and Sensibility*.

Henry, however, became so alarmingly ill that on October 22 Jane dispatched expresses to her brothers and sister, summoning them to London. Mr. Knight left Godmersham for town on the 23rd, but owing to a delay in the delivery of the letter, James Austen did not receive his till the 24th. He rode to Chawton that evening, and the next day he and Cassandra arrived in London. For a time Henry's life was in imminent danger, but after a week's anxiety he was so far on the road to recovery that his two brothers were able to return home, leaving Jane and Cassandra in charge.

It was owing to Jane's untiring exertions at this time that her health began to suffer. One other consequence too, but of a less tragical kind, was due to Henry's illness. The physician that attended him—supplementing, no doubt, Mr. Haden—was one of the Prince Regent's physicians, and he, either knowing or hearing (for it was now an open secret) that Jane Austen was the author of *Pride and Prejudice*, informed her that the Prince greatly admired her novels, 'that he read them often, and kept a set in every one of his residences; that he himself had thought it right to inform His Royal Highness that Miss Austen was staying in London.' The Prince did not so far condescend as to desire to see Miss Austen in person, but he instructed his librarian, Mr. Clarke, to wait upon her and show her any civility in his power. The result was that on November 13 Jane was shown over the library and other apartments at Carlton House, and in the course of the visit Mr.

Clarke announced that if Miss Austen had any other novel forthcoming, she was at liberty to dedicate it to the Prince. We cannot tell what may have been the exact amount of pleasure given to Jane by this piece of information, as Cassandra was at that time also in Hans Place, and there is therefore no letter of Jane to her on the subject. But, at any rate, Jane was loyal enough to wish to do what was right and proper in the circumstances. Consequently, on November 15, we find her writing to Mr. Clarke as follows:—

SIR,—I must take the liberty of asking you a question. Among the many flattering attentions which I received from you at Carlton House on Monday last, was the information of my being at liberty to dedicate any future work to His Royal Highness, the Prince Regent, without the necessity of any solicitation on my part. Such, at least, I believed to be your words; but as I am very anxious to be quite certain of what was intended, I entreat you to have the goodness to inform me how such a permission is to be understood, and whether it is incumbent on me to show my sense of the honour by inscribing the work now in the press to His Royal Highness; I should be equally concerned to appear either presumptuous or ungrateful.

To which Mr. Clarke replied:—

Carlton House: November 16, 1815.

DEAR MADAM,—It is certainly not *incumbent* on you to dedicate your work now in the press to His Royal Highness; but if you wish to do the Regent that honour either now or at any future period, I am happy to send you that permission, which need not require any more trouble or solicitation on your part.

Your late works, Madam, and in particular *Mansfield Park*, reflect the highest honour on your genius and your principles. In every new work your mind seems to increase its energy and power of discrimination. The Regent has read and admired all your publications.

Accept my sincere thanks for the pleasure your volumes have given me: in the perusal of them I felt a great inclination to write and say so. And I also, dear Madam, wished to be allowed to ask you to delineate in some future work the habits of life, and character, and enthusiasm of a clergyman, who should pass his time between the metropolis and the country, who should be something like Beattie's Minstrel:—

Silent when glad, affectionate tho' shy,

And now his look was most demurely sad;

And now he laughed aloud, yet none knew why.

Neither Goldsmith, nor La Fontaine in his *Tableau de Famille*, have in my mind quite delineated an English clergyman, at least of the present day, fond of and entirely engaged in literature, no man's enemy but his own. Pray, dear Madam, think of these things.

Believe me at all times with sincerity and respect,

Your faithful and obliged servant,
J. S. CLARKE, *Librarian*.

P.S.—I am going for about three weeks to Mr. Henry Streatfeild, Chiddingstone, Sevenoaks, but hope on my return to town to have the honour of seeing you again.

On November 17 Henry was sufficiently recovered to address a letter to Mr. John Murray on his sister's behalf. This was followed by a letter from herself on November 23.

Hans Place: Thursday [November 23, 1815].

SIR,—My brother's note last Monday has been so fruitless, that I am afraid there can be but little chance of my writing to any good effect; but yet I am so very much disappointed and vexed by the delays of the printers, that I cannot help begging to know whether there is no hope of their being quickened. Instead of the work being ready by the end of the present month, it will hardly, at the rate we now proceed, be finished by the end of the next; and as I expect to leave London early in December, it is of consequence that no more time should be lost. Is it likely that the printers will be influenced to greater dispatch and punctuality by knowing that the work is to be dedicated, by permission, to the Prince Regent? If you can make that circumstance operate, I shall be very glad. My brother returns *Waterloo* with many thanks for the loan of it. We have heard much of Scott's account of Paris. If it be not incompatible with other arrangements, would you favour us with it, supposing you have any set already opened? You may depend upon its being in careful hands.

> I remain, Sir, your ob.^{t.} humble Se.^{t.,}
> J. AUSTEN.

Meanwhile, as Henry was mending, his brother Edward, who had brought his daughter Fanny up to town, left her as a companion to her Aunt Jane, and escorted Cassandra to Chawton.

> Hans Place: Friday [November 24, 1815].

MY DEAREST CASSANDRA,—I have the pleasure of sending you a much better account of *my affairs*, which I know will be a great delight to you.

I wrote to Mr. Murray yesterday myself, and Henry wrote at the same time to Roworth. Before the notes were out of the house, I received three sheets and an apology from R. We sent the notes, however, and I had a most civil one in reply from Mr. M. He is so very polite, indeed, that it is quite overcoming. The printers have been waiting for paper—the blame is thrown upon the stationer; but he gives his word that I shall have no farther cause for dissatisfaction. He has lent us *Miss Williams* and *Scott*, and says that any book of his will always be at *my* service. In short, I am soothed and complimented into tolerable comfort.

To-morrow Mr. Haden is to dine with us. There is happiness! We really grow so fond of Mr. Haden that I do not know what to expect. He, and Mr. Tilson, and Mr. Philips made up our circle of wits last night; Fanny played, and he sat and listened and suggested improvements, till Richard came in to tell him that 'the doctor was waiting for him at Captn. Blake's'; and then he was off with a speed that you can imagine. He never does appear in the least above his profession, or out of humour with it, or I should think poor Captn. Blake, whoever he is, in a very bad way.

Yours very affectionately,
J. AUSTEN.

I have been listening to dreadful insanity. It is Mr. Haden's firm belief that a person *not* musical is fit for every sort of wickedness. I ventured to assert a little on the other side, but wished the cause in abler hands.

Hans Place: Sunday [November 26, 1815].

I *did* mention the P. R. in my note to Mr. Murray; it brought me a fine compliment in return. Whether it has done any other good I do not know, but Henry thought it worth trying.

The printers continue to supply me very well. I am advanced in Vol. III. to my *arra*-root, upon which peculiar style of spelling there is a modest query in the margin. I will not forget Anna's arrowroot. I hope you have told Martha of my first resolution of letting nobody know that I *might* dedicate, &c., for fear of being obliged to do it, and that she is thoroughly convinced of my being influenced now by nothing but the most mercenary motives.

Then came dinner and Mr. Haden, who brought good manners and clever conversation. From 7 to 8 the harp; at 8 Mrs. L. and Miss E. arrived, and for the rest of the evening the drawing-room was thus arranged: on the sofa side the two ladies, Henry, and myself, making the best of it; on the opposite side Fanny and Mr. Haden, in two chairs (I *believe*, at least, they had *two* chairs), talking together uninterruptedly. Fancy the scene! And what is to be fancied next? Why, that Mr. H. dines here again to-morrow. To-day we are to have Mr. Barlow. Mr. H. is reading *Mansfield Park* for the first time, and prefers it to *P. and P.*

Fanny has heard all that I have said to you about herself and Mr. H. Thank you very much for the sight of dearest Charles's letter to yourself. How pleasantly and how naturally he writes! and how perfect a picture of his disposition and feelings his style conveys! Poor dear fellow! Not a present! I have a great mind to send him all the twelve copies which were to have been dispersed among my near connections, beginning with the P. R. and ending with Countess Morley. Adieu.

Yours affectionately,
J. AUSTEN. Miss Austen.

Saturday [December 2, 1815].

MY DEAR CASSANDRA,—Henry came back yesterday, and might have returned the day before if he had known as much in time.

I had the comfort of a few lines on Wednesday morning from Henry himself, just after your letter was gone, giving so good an account of his feelings as made me perfectly easy. He met with the utmost care and attention at Hanwell, spent his two days there very quietly and pleasantly, and, being certainly in no respect the worse for going, we may believe that he must be better, as he is quite sure of being himself. To make his return a complete gala Mr. Haden was secured for dinner. I need not say that our evening was agreeable.

But you seem to be under a mistake as to Mr. H. You call him an apothecary. He is no apothecary; he has never been an apothecary; there is not an apothecary in this neighbourhood—the only inconvenience of the situation perhaps—but so it is; we have not a medical man within reach. He is a Haden, nothing but a Haden, a sort of wonderful nondescript creature on two legs, something between a man and an angel, but without the least spice of an apothecary. He is, perhaps, the only person *not* an apothecary hereabouts. He has never sung to us. He will not sing without a pianoforte accompaniment.

I am sorry my mother has been suffering, and am afraid this exquisite weather is too good to agree with her. *I* enjoy it all over me, from top to toe, from right to left, longitudinally, perpendicularly, diagonally; and I cannot but selfishly hope we are to have it last till Christmas—nice, unwholesome, unseasonable, relaxing, close, muggy weather.

Yours affectionately,
J. A.

It strikes me that I have no business to give the P. R. a binding, but we will take counsel upon the question.

Two more letters were written by the author to her publisher while the work was in his hands.

On December 11, she writes:—

As I find that *Emma* is advertised for publication as early as Saturday next, I think it best to lose no time in settling all that remains to be settled on the subject, and adopt this method as involving the smallest tax on your time. . . .

. . . The title-page must be '*Emma*, dedicated by permission to H.R.H. the Prince Regent.' And it is my particular wish that one set should be completed and sent to H.R.H. two or three days before the work is generally public. It should be sent under cover to the Rev. J. S. Clarke, Librarian, Carlton House. I shall subjoin a list of those persons to whom I must trouble you to forward also a set each, when the work is out; all unbound with 'From the Authoress' on the first page.

. . . I return also *Mansfield Park* as ready for a second edition, I believe, as I can make it. I am in Hans Place till the 16th; from that day inclusive, my direction will be Chawton, Alton, Hants.

On receipt of this, Mr. Murray seems to have sent round a note immediately, asking if it really was Miss Austen's wish that the dedication should be placed on the title-page, for we find Jane writing again the same day:—

DEAR SIR,—I am very much obliged by yours, and very happy to feel everything arranged to our mutual satisfaction. As to my direction about the title-page, it was arising from my ignorance only, and from my having never noticed the proper place for a dedication. I thank you for putting me right. Any deviation from what is usually done in such cases is the last thing I should wish for. I feel happy in having a friend to save me from the ill effect of my own blunder.

On December 11, Jane resumed her correspondence with Mr. Clarke:—

DEAR SIR,—My *Emma* is now so near publication that I feel it right to assure you of my not having forgotten your kind recommendation of an early copy for Carlton House, and that I have Mr. Murray's promise of its being sent to His Royal Highness, under cover to you, three days previous to the work being really out. I must make use of this opportunity to thank you, dear Sir, for the very high praise you bestow on my other novels. I am too vain to wish to convince you that you have praised them beyond their merit. My greatest anxiety at present is that this fourth work should not disgrace what was good in the others. But on this point I will do myself the justice to declare that, whatever may be my wishes for its success, I am very strongly haunted by the idea that to those readers who have preferred *Pride and Prejudice* it will appear inferior in wit; and to those who have preferred *Mansfield Park*, very inferior in good sense. Such as it is, however, I hope you will do me the favour of accepting a copy. Mr. Murray will have directions for sending one. I am quite honoured by your thinking me capable of drawing such a clergyman as you gave the sketch of in your note of November 16th. But I assure you I am *not*. The comic part of the character I might be equal to, but not the good, the enthusiastic, the literary. Such a man's conversation must at times be on subjects of science and philosophy, of which I know nothing; or at least occasionally abundant in quotations and allusions which a woman who, like me, knows only her own mother tongue, and has read little in that, would be totally without the power of giving. A classical education, or at any rate a very extensive acquaintance with

English literature, ancient and modern, appears to me quite indispensable for the person who would do any justice to your clergyman; and I think I may boast myself to be, with all possible vanity, the most unlearned and uninformed female who ever dared to be an authoress.

Believe me, dear Sir, Your obliged and faithful hum^{bl} Ser$^{t.,}$
JANE AUSTEN.

But Mr. Clarke had not finished with his suggestions, for he replied in a few days:—

Carlton House: Thursday [December 1815].

MY DEAR MADAM,—The letter you were so obliging as to do me the honour of sending, was forwarded to me in Kent, where, in a village, Chiddingstone, near Sevenoaks, I had been hiding myself from all bustle and turmoil and getting spirits for a winter campaign, and strength to stand the sharp knives which many a Shylock is wetting [*sic*] to cut more than a pound of flesh from my heart, on the appearance of *James the Second*.

On Monday I go to Lord Egremont's at Petworth—where your praises have long been sounded as they ought to be—I shall then look in on the party at the Pavilion for a couple of nights, and return to preach at Park Street Chapel, Green Street, on the Thanksgiving Day.

You were very good to send me *Emma*, which I have in no respect deserved. It is gone to the Prince Regent. I have read only a few pages, which I very much admired—there is so much nature and excellent description of character in everything you describe. Pray continue to write and make all your friends send sketches to help you—and *Mémoires pour servir*, as the French term it. Do let us have an English clergyman after your fancy—much novelty may be introduced—show, dear Madam, what good would be done if tythes were taken away entirely, and describe him burying his own mother, as I did, because the High Priest of the Parish in which she died did not pay her remains the respect he ought to do.

I have never recovered the shock. Carry your clergyman to sea as the friend of some distinguished naval character about a Court, you can then bring forward, like Le Sage, many interesting scenes of character and interest.

But forgive me, I cannot write to you without wishing to elicit your genius, and I fear I cannot do that without trespassing on your patience and good nature.

I have desired Mr. Murray to procure, if he can, two little works I ventured to publish from being at sea—sermons which I wrote and preached on the ocean, and the edition which I published of Falconer's *Shipwreck*.

Pray, dear Madam, remember that beside my cell at Carlton House, I have another which Dr. Barne procured for me at No. 37 Golden Square, where I often hide myself. There is a small library there much at your service, and if you can make the cell render you any service as a sort of halfway house when you come to Town, I shall be most happy. There is a maid servant of mine always there.

I hope to have the honour of sending you *James the Second* when it reaches a second edition, as some few notes may possibly be then added.

Yours, dear Madam, very sincerely,
J. S. Clarke.

It is evident that what the writer of the above letter chiefly desired, was that Jane Austen should depict a clergyman who should resemble no one so much as the Rev. J. S. Clarke. This is borne out again in a further letter in which Mr. Clarke expressed the somewhat tardy thanks of his Royal master.

Pavilion: March 27, 1816.

Dear Miss Austen,—I have to return you the thanks of His Royal Highness, the Prince Regent, for the handsome copy you sent him of your last excellent novel. Pray, dear Madam, soon write again and again. Lord St. Helens and many of the nobility, who have been staying here, paid you the just tribute of their praise.

The Prince Regent has just left us for London; and having been pleased to appoint me Chaplain and Private English Secretary to the Prince of Cobourg, I remain here with His Serene Highness and a select party until the marriage. Perhaps when you again appear in print you may chuse to dedicate your volumes to Prince Leopold: any historical romance, illustrative of the history of the august House of Cobourg, would just now be very interesting.

Believe me at all times,
Dear Miss Austen,
Your obliged friend,
J. S. CLARKE.

Jane's sensible reply put an end to any further suggestions:—

MY DEAR SIR,—I am honoured by the Prince's thanks and very much obliged to yourself for the kind manner in which you mention the work. I have also to acknowledge a former letter forwarded to me from Hans Place. I assure you I felt very grateful for the friendly tenor of it, and hope my silence will have been considered, as it was truly meant, to proceed only from an unwillingness to tax your time with idle thanks. Under every interesting circumstance which your own talent and literary labours have placed you in, or the favour of the Regent bestowed, you have my best wishes. Your recent appointments I hope are a step to something still better. In my opinion, the service of a court can hardly be too well paid, for immense must be the sacrifice of time and feeling required by it.

You are very, very kind in your hints as to the sort of composition which might recommend me at present, and I am fully sensible that an historical romance, founded on the House of Saxe Cobourg, might be much more to the purpose of profit or popularity than such pictures of domestic life in country villages as I deal in. But I could no more write a romance than an epic poem. I could not sit seriously down to write a serious romance under any other motive than to save my life; and if it were indispensable for me to keep it up and never relax into laughing at myself or at other people, I am sure I should be hung before I had finished the first chapter. No, I must keep to my own style and go on in my own way, and though I may never succeed again in that, I am convinced that I should totally fail in any other.

I remain, my dear Sir,
Your very much obliged, and sincere friend,
J. AUSTEN.

Chawton, near Alton, April 1, 1816.

CHAPTER XVIII.
PERSUASION 1815-1816

So far as we know, Jane went to London in 1815 perfectly sound in health. Her remark to Cassandra on her enjoyment of the muggy, unwholesome weather is written with the security of a person accustomed to be free from bodily ailments, and expecting that condition of things to continue. But, alas! we must look upon this visit, which seemed to mark the highest point in her modest fame, as marking also a downward stage in her career as regards both prosperity and health. Perhaps the excitement of the publication of *Emma*, and probably the close attention on the sick-bed of her brother which coincided with it—possibly even the muggy weather which she praised so highly—combined to diminish her vigour, and to sow the seeds of a disease, the exact nature of which no one seems ever to have been able to determine. These, however, were not the only disquieting circumstances which surrounded her. In the following March her favourite brother, Henry, was declared a bankrupt; and there are one or two indications of her being aware that all was not well with the firm in the autumn. The months which intervened while this catastrophe was impending must have been very trying to one already weakened by all that she had gone through. More agreeable associations, however, arose from the success of *Emma*. There was, for instance, a pleasant exchange of letters with the Countess of Morley, a lady of some literary capacity, to whom Jane had sent a copy of *Emma*, and who expressed her thanks and admiration in very warm terms. The author in her turn, speaking of Lady Morley's approval, says: 'It encourages me to depend on the same share of general good opinion which *Emma's* predecessors have experienced, and to believe that I have not yet, as almost every writer of fancy does sooner or later, overwritten myself.'

The end of March brought a still more flattering tribute to Jane's growing fame, in the shape of an article on *Emma* in the *Quarterly Review*. The *Review*, though dated October 1815, did not appear till March of the following year, and the writer of the article was none other than Sir Walter Scott.

The honour of an article in the *Quarterly* was no doubt mainly due to the fact that Jane had published her latest book with Mr. Murray, its owner. Though the praise contained in the article would scarcely satisfy an enthusiastic admirer of her works, Miss Austen felt she had no cause to complain. In thanking Mr. Murray for lending her a copy of the *Review*, she writes:—

The authoress of *Emma* has no reason, I think, to complain of her treatment in it, except in the total omission of *Mansfield Park*. I cannot but be sorry that so clever a man as the Reviewer of *Emma* should consider it as unworthy of being noticed. You will be pleased to hear that I have received the Prince's thanks for the *handsome* copy I sent him of *Emma*. Whatever he may think of *my* share of the work, yours seems to have been quite right.

The fact that she was honoured with a notice in the *Quarterly* did not prevent the author from collecting and leaving on record the more domestic criticisms of her family and friends.

OPINIONS OF *Emma*.

Captain F. Austen liked it extremely, observing that though there might be more wit in *P. and P.* and an higher morality in *M. P.*, yet altogether, on account of its peculiar air of Nature throughout, he preferred it to either.

Mrs. Frank Austen liked and admired it very much indeed, but must still prefer *P. and P.*

Mrs. J. Bridges preferred it to all the others.

Miss Sharp.—Better than *M. P.*, but not so well as *P. and P.* Pleased with the heroine for her originality, delighted with Mr. K., and called Mrs. Elton beyond praise—dissatisfied with Jane Fairfax.

Cassandra.—Better than *P. and P.* but not so well as *M. P.*

Fanny K.—Not so well as either *P. and P.* or *M. P.* Could not bear Emma herself. Mr. Knightley delightful. Should like J. F. if she knew more of her.

Mr. and Mrs. James Austen did not like it so well as either of the three others. Language different from the others; not so easily read.

Edward preferred it to *M. P.* only. Mr. K. liked by everybody.

Miss Bigg.—Not equal to either *P. and P.* or *M. P.* Objected to the sameness of the subject (Matchmaking) all through. Too much of Mrs. Elton and H. Smith. Language superior to the others.

My Mother thought it more entertaining than *M. P.*, but not so interesting as *P. and P.* No characters in it equal to Lady Catherine or Mr. Collins.

Miss Lloyd thought it as clever as either of the others, but did not receive so much pleasure from it as from *P. and P.* and *M. P.*

Fanny Cage liked it very much indeed, and classed it between *P. and P.* and *M. P.*

Mrs. and Miss Craven liked it very much, but not so much as the others.

Mr. Sherer did not think it equal to either *M. P.* (which he liked the best of all) or *P. and P.* Displeased with my pictures of clergymen.

Miss Bigg, on reading it a second time, liked Miss Bates much better than at first, and expressed herself as liking all the people of Highbury in general, except Harriet Smith, but could not help still thinking *her* too silly in her loves.

The Family at Upton Gray all very much amused with it. Miss Bates a great favourite with Mrs. Beaufoy.

Mr. and Mrs. Leigh Perrot saw many beauties in it, but could not think it equal to *P. and P.* Darcy and Elizabeth had spoilt them for anything else. Mr. K., however, an excellent character; Emma better luck than a matchmaker often has; pitied Jane Fairfax; thought Frank Churchill better treated than he deserved.

Countess Craven admired it very much, but did not think it equal to *P. and P.* which she ranked as the very first of its sort.

Mrs. Guiton thought it too natural to be interesting.

Mrs. Digweed did not like it so well as the others: in fact if she had not known the author would hardly have got through it.

Miss Terry admired it very much, particularly Mrs. Elton.

Henry Sanford—very much pleased with it—delighted with Miss Bates, but thought Mrs. Elton the best-drawn character in the book. *Mansfield Park*, however, still his favourite.

Mr. Haden—quite delighted with it. Admired the character of Emma.

Miss Isabella Herries did not like it. Objected to my exposing the sex in the character of the heroine. Convinced that I had meant Mrs. and Miss Bates for some acquaintance of theirs. People whom I never heard of before.

Mrs. Harriet Moore admired it very much, but *M. P.* still her favourite of all.

Countess of Morley delighted with it.

Mr. Cockerell liked it so little that Fanny would not send me his opinion.

Mrs. Dickson did not much like it—thought it very inferior to *P. and P.* Liked it the less from there being a Mr. and Mrs. Dixon in it.

Mrs. Brandreth thought the third volume superior to anything I had ever written—quite beautiful!

Mr. B. Lefroy thought that if there had been more incident it would be equal to any of the others. The characters quite as well-drawn and supported as in any, and from being more every-day ones, the more entertaining. Did not like the heroine so well as any of the others. Miss Bates excellent, but rather too much of her. Mr. and Mrs. Elton admirable and John Knightley a sensible man.

Mrs. B. Lefroy ranked *Emma* as a composition with *S. and S.* Not so *brilliant* as *P. and P.* nor so *equal* as *M. P.* Preferred Emma herself to all the heroines. The characters, like all the others, admirably well drawn and supported—perhaps rather less strongly marked than some, but only the more natural for that reason. Mr. Knightley, Mrs. Elton, and Miss Bates her favourites. Thought one or two of the conversations too long.

Mrs. Lefroy preferred it to *M. P.*, but liked *M. P.* the least of all.

Mr. Fowle read only the first and last chapters, because he had heard it was not interesting.

Mrs. Lutley Sclater liked it very much, better than *M. P.*, and thought I had 'brought it all about very cleverly in the last volume.'

Mrs. C. Cage wrote thus to Fanny: 'A great many thanks for the loan of *Emma*, which I am delighted with. I like it better than any. Every character is thoroughly kept up. I must enjoy reading it again with Charles. Miss Bates is incomparable, but I was nearly killed with those precious treasures. They are unique, and really with more fun than I can express. I am at Highbury all day, and I can't help feeling I have just got into a new set of acquaintance. No one writes such good sense, and so very comfortable.'

Mrs. Wroughton did not like it so well as *P. and P.* Thought the authoress wrong, in such times as these, to draw such clergymen as Mr. Collins and Mr. Elton.

Sir J. Langham thought it much inferior to the others.

Mr. Jeffrey (of the *Edinburgh Review*) was kept up by it three nights.

Miss Murden.—Certainly inferior to all the others.

Captain C. Austen wrote: '*Emma* arrived in time to a moment. I am delighted with her, more so I think than even with my favourite, *Pride and Prejudice*, and have read it three times in the passage.'

Mrs. D. Dundas thought it very clever, but did not like it so well as either of the others.

We do not know how Mr. Jeffrey's involuntary tribute of admiration was conveyed to the author, but we are sure she must have valued it very highly. It was not the first time she had collected a miscellaneous set of opinions on her work. The two following critiques on *Mansfield Park*—apparently from two ladies of the same family—will illustrate the sort of want of comprehension from which the author had to suffer when she got outside the limits of her own immediate circle.

Mrs. B.—Much pleased with it: particularly with the character of Fanny as being so very natural. Thought Lady Bertram like herself. Preferred it to either of the others; but imagined *that* might be want of taste, as she did not understand wit.

Mrs. Augusta B. owned that she thought *S. and S.* and *P. and P.* downright nonsense, but expected to like *M. P.* better, and having finished the first volume, flattered herself she had got through the worst.

Meanwhile, the banking-house of Austen, Maunde, and Tilson, had closed its doors; and on March 23, 1816, Henry Austen was declared a bankrupt: the immediate cause of the collapse being the failure of an Alton bank which the London firm had backed. No personal extravagance was charged against Henry; but he had the unpleasant sensation of starting life over again, and of having caused serious loss to several of his family, especially his brother Edward and Mr. Leigh Perrot, who had gone sureties for him on his appointment as Receiver-General for Oxfordshire. Jane herself was fortunate in losing no more than thirteen pounds—a portion of the profits of *Mansfield Park*.

Henry Austen possessed an extraordinary elasticity of nature which made a rebound from depression easy—indeed, almost inevitable—in his case. He returned at once to his original intention of taking Orders, as if the intervening military and banking career had been nothing more than an interruption of his normal course. Nor was it merely perfunctory performance of clerical duties to which he looked forward: he was in earnest, and began by making use of his former classical knowledge to take up a serious study of the New Testament in the original language. He seems to have been in advance of his age in this respect; for when he went to be examined by the Bishop, that dignitary, after asking him such questions as he thought desirable, put his hand on a book which lay near him on the table, and which happened to be a Greek Testament, and said: 'As for *this* book, Mr. Austen, I dare say it is some years since either you or I looked into it.'

Henry Austen became in time an earnest preacher of the evangelical school, and was for many years perpetual curate of Bentley, near Alton. He did not marry the 'Hanwell favourite,' but found a wife after some years in Miss Eleanor Jackson, who survived him.

It must have been somewhere about this time that Jane Austen succeeded in recovering the MS. of *Northanger Abbey*. An unsuccessful attempt to secure the publication of the novel in the year 1809 has already been noticed; but we learn from the *Memoir* that after four works of hers had been published, and somewhat widely circulated, one of her brothers (acting for her) negotiated with the publisher who had bought it, and found him very willing to receive back his money, and resign all claim to the copyright. When the bargain was concluded and the money paid, but not till then, the negotiator had the satisfaction of informing him that the work which had been so lightly esteemed was by the author of *Pride and Prejudice.*

Meanwhile, Jane had been for some months engaged on *Persuasion*. It was begun before she went to London in the autumn of 1815 for the publication of *Emma;* but that visit and all that happened to her during the winter must certainly have interrupted its composition, and possibly modified its tone. It is less high-spirited and more tender in its description of a stricken heart than anything she had attempted before.

In May, Cassandra and Jane left Chawton to spend three weeks at Cheltenham, stopping with their brother at Steventon, and with the Fowles at Kintbury on the way, and again at Steventon on their return. Jane must have been decidedly out of health, for the change in her did not escape the notice of her friends. But whatever was the exact state of her health during the first half of this year, it did not prevent her from being able, on July 18, to write 'Finis' at the end of the first draft of *Persuasion;* and thereby hangs an interesting tale, which we cannot do better than relate in the words of the *Memoir*.

The book had been brought to an end in July; and the re-engagement of the hero and heroine effected in a totally different manner in a scene laid at Admiral Croft's lodgings. But her performance did not satisfy her. She thought it tame and flat, and was desirous of producing something better. This weighed upon her mind—the more so, probably, on account of the weak state of her health; so that one night she retired to rest in very low spirits. But such depression was little in accordance with her nature, and was soon shaken off. The next morning she awoke to more cheerful views and brighter inspirations; the sense of power revived; and imagination resumed its course. She cancelled the condemned chapter, and wrote two others, entirely different, in its stead. The result is that we possess the visit of the Musgrove party to Bath; the crowded and animated scenes at the White Hart Hotel; and the charming conversation between Captain Harville and Anne Elliot, overheard by Captain Wentworth, by which the two faithful lovers were at last led to understand each other's feelings. The tenth and eleventh chapters of *Persuasion*, then, rather than the actual winding-up of the story, contain the latest of her printed compositions—her last contribution to the entertainment of the public. Perhaps it may be thought that she has seldom written anything more brilliant; and that, independent of the original manner in which the *dénouement* is brought about, the pictures of Charles Musgrove's good-natured boyishness and of his wife's jealous selfishness would have been incomplete without these finishing strokes. The cancelled chapter exists in manuscript. It is certainly inferior to the two which were substituted for it; but it was such as some writers and some readers might have been contented with; and it contained touches which scarcely any other hand could have given, the suppression of which may be almost a matter of regret.

For the cancelled chapter in *Persuasion*, and for other posthumous writings of the author, we will refer our readers to the second edition of the *Memoir*. They will not fail to note the delicate touches put to the characters of the Crofts by the Admiral's triumph over the servant who was 'denying' Mrs. Croft, and by the frequent excursions of husband and wife together 'upstairs to hear a noise, or downstairs to settle their accounts, or upon the landing to trim the lamp.' But the added chapters take one altogether into a higher province of fiction, where the deepest emotion and the most delicate humour are blended in one scene: a scene that makes one think that, had its author lived, we might have had later masterpieces of a different type from that of their predecessors.

Persuasion is of about the same length as *Northanger Abbey*, and it seems natural to suppose that there was some purpose in this similarity, and that the two works were intended to be published together—as in the end they were—each as a two-volume novel. She certainly contemplated the publication of *Northanger Abbey* (which at that stage bore the name of *Catherine*) after she had recovered it in 1816, and when she wrote the 'advertisement' which appears in the first edition of the book. Yet afterwards she seems rather to have gone back from this intention. Writing to Fanny Knight, March 13, 1817, she says:—

I *will* answer your kind questions more than you expect. *Miss Catherine* is put upon the shelf for the present, and I do not know that she will ever come out; but I have a something ready for publication, which may perhaps appear about a twelvemonth hence. It is short—about the length of *Catherine*. This is for yourself alone.

Catherine is of course *Northanger Abbey*, and the 'something' is *Persuasion*. She returns to the latter in writing again to Fanny, March 23, telling her she will not like it, and adding 'You may perhaps like the heroine, as she is almost too good for me.'

Two remarkable points in these extracts are: the statement that *Persuasion* was 'ready for publication,' but was not to appear for a twelvemonth, and the idea that the character of the heroine was, as it were, imposed upon the author by an external force which she was powerless to resist. The intended delay in publishing *Persuasion* shows how unwilling she was to let anything go till she was quite sure she had polished it to the utmost: and we may imagine that, had health returned, the one comparatively dull and lifeless part of the book—the long story of Mrs. Smith—would have been somehow or other brought to life by touches which she knew so well how to impart.

As for the doubt about publishing *Catherine* at all, it was not unnatural. She might reasonably hesitate to put an immature work by the side of her most mature: she might (and we know that she *did*) feel that the social usages of sixteen years ago, which she was describing in this tale, were no longer those of the day; and it was possible that a satire on Mrs. Radcliffe was not what the public now wanted. The members of the Austen family, who managed the publication of her novels after her death, thought differently; and we are grateful to them for having done so.

Had she followed all the advice given her by her friends, she would have produced something very different from either *Northanger Abbey* or *Persuasion*. It must have been in the course of the year 1816 that she drew up the following 'plan of a novel, according to hints from various quarters,' adding below the names of the friends who gave the hints.

Scene to be in the country. Heroine, the daughter of a clergyman: one who, after having lived much in the world, had retired from it, and settled on a curacy with a very small fortune of his own. He, the most excellent man that can be imagined, perfect in character, temper, and manners, without the smallest drawback or peculiarity to prevent his being the most delightful companion to his daughter from one year's end to the other. Heroine, a faultless character herself, perfectly good, with much tenderness and sentiment and not the least wit, very highly accomplished, understanding modern languages, and (generally speaking) everything that the most accomplished young women learn, but particularly excelling in music—her favourite pursuit—and playing equally well on the pianoforte and harp, and singing in the first style. Her person quite beautiful, dark eyes and plump cheeks. Book to open with the description of father and daughter, who are to converse in long speeches, elegant language, and a tone of high serious sentiment. The father to be induced, at his daughter's earnest request, to relate to her the past events of his life. This narrative will reach through the greater part of the first volume; as besides all the circumstances of his attachment to her mother, and their marriage, it will comprehend his going to sea as chaplain to a distinguished naval character about the Court; his going afterwards to Court himself, which introduced him to a great variety of characters and involved him in many interesting situations, concluding with his opinion of the benefits of tithes being done away, and his having buried his own mother (heroine's lamented grandmother) in consequence of the High Priest of the parish in which she died refusing to pay her remains the respect due to them. The father to be of a very literary turn, an enthusiast in literature, nobody's enemy but his own; at the same time most zealous in the discharge of his pastoral duties, the model of an exemplary parish priest. The heroine's friendship to be sought after by a young woman in the same neighbourhood, of talents and shrewdness, with light eyes and a fair skin, but having a considerable degree of wit; heroine shall shrink from the acquaintance. From this outset the story will proceed and contain a striking variety of adventures. Heroine and her father never above a fortnight together in one place: he being driven from his curacy by the vile arts of some totally unprincipled and heartless young man, desperately in love with the heroine, and pursuing her with unrelenting passion. No sooner settled in one country of Europe than they are necessitated to quit it and retire to another, always making new acquaintance, and always obliged to leave them. This will, of course, exhibit a wide variety of characters, but there will be no mixture. The scene will be for ever shifting from one set of people to another; but all the good will be unexceptionable in every respect, and there will be no foibles or weaknesses but with the wicked, who will be completely depraved and infamous, hardly a resemblance of humanity left in them. Early in her career, in the progress of her first removal, heroine must meet with the hero—all perfection, of course, and only prevented from paying his addresses to her by some excess of refinement. Wherever she goes somebody falls in love with her, and she receives repeated offers of marriage, which she always refers wholly to her father, exceedingly angry that *he* should not be first applied to. Often carried away by the anti-hero, but rescued either by her father or the hero. Often reduced to support herself and her father by her talents, and work for her bread; continually cheated and defrauded of her hire; worn down to a skeleton, and now and then starved to death. At last, hunted out of civilised society, denied the poor shelter of the humblest cottage, they are compelled to retreat into Kamschatka, where the poor father, quite worn down, finding his end approaching, throws himself on the ground, and, after four or five hours of tender advice and parental admonition to his miserable child, expires in a fine burst of literary enthusiasm, intermingled with invectives against holders of tithes. Heroine inconsolable for some time, but afterwards crawls back towards her former country, having at least twenty narrow escapes of falling into the hands of anti-hero; and at last, in the very nick of time, turning a corner to avoid him, runs into the arms of the hero himself, who, having just shaken off the scruples which fettered him before, was at the very moment setting off in pursuit of her. The tenderest and completest *éclaircissement* takes place, and they are happily united. Throughout the whole work heroine to be in the most elegant society, and living in high style. The name of the work not to be *Emma*, but of same sort as *Sense and Sensibility* and *Pride and Prejudice*.

CHAPTER XIX.
AUNT JANE 1814-1817

ANY attempt at depicting the charm and attractiveness of Jane Austen's character must be quite incomplete if it fails to take into account the special manner in which she showed these qualities as an aunt. She herself says in joke to a young niece that she had always maintained the importance of aunts; and she evidently felt, in all seriousness, the responsibility of that relationship, though she would have been one of the last to display her sense of it by any didactic or authoritative utterance. The author of the *Memoir* tells us that her two nieces who were grown up in her lifetime could say how valuable to them had been her advice in 'the little difficulties and doubts of early womanhood'; and Lord Brabourne quotes here and there extracts from his mother's diary, such as these: 'Aunt Jane and I had a very interesting conversation'; 'Aunt Jane and I had a delicious morning together'; 'Aunt Jane and I very snug'; and so on, until the sad ending: 'I had the misery of losing my dear Aunt Jane after a lingering illness.'

Some letters of hers to three of her nieces give a good idea of her value and importance to them, whether as grown women or as children.

Fanny Knight, sensible as she was, and early accustomed to responsibility, felt at a loss how to distinguish in her own mind between inclination and love when seriously courted in 1814 by a man of unexceptionable position and character. A reference to her aunt brought her two delightful letters. No definite opinion was expressed or formal advice given in these letters, but they must have helped her by their sympathy, and cleared her mind by the steadiness with which they contemplated the case in all its bearings.

Chawton: Friday [November 18, 1814].

I feel quite as doubtful as you could be, my dearest Fanny, as to *when* my letter may be finished, for I can command very little quiet time at present; but yet I must begin, for I know you will be glad to hear as soon as possible, and I really am impatient myself to be writing something on so very interesting a subject, though I have no hope of writing anything to the purpose. I shall do very little more, I dare say, than say over again what you have said before.

I was certainly a good deal surprised *at first*, as I had no suspicion of any change in your feelings, and I have no scruple in saying that you cannot be in love. My dear Fanny, I am ready to laugh at the idea, and yet it is no laughing matter to have had you so mistaken as to your own feelings. And with all my heart I wish I had cautioned you on that point when first you spoke to me; but, though I did not think you then *much* in love, I did consider you as being attached in a degree quite sufficiently for happiness, as I had no doubt it would increase with opportunity, and from the time of our being in London together I thought you really very much in love. But you certainly are not at all—there is no concealing it.

What strange creatures we are! It seems as if your being secure of him had made you indifferent.

He is just what he ever was, only more evidently and uniformly devoted to *you*. This is all the difference. How shall we account for it?

My dearest Fanny, I am writing what will not be of the smallest use to you. I am feeling differently every moment, and shall not be able to suggest a single thing that can assist your mind. I could lament in one sentence and laugh in the next, but as to opinion or counsel I am sure that none will be extracted worth having from this letter.

Poor dear Mr. A.! Oh, dear Fanny! your mistake has been one that thousands of women fall into. He was the *first* young man who attached himself to you. That was the charm, and most powerful it is. Among the multitudes, however, that make the same mistake with yourself, there can be few indeed who have so little reason to regret it; *his* character and *his* attachment leave you nothing to be ashamed of.

Upon the whole, what is to be done? You have no inclination for any other person. His situation in life, family, friends, and, above all, his character, his uncommonly amiable mind, strict principles, just notions, good habits, *all* that *you* know so well how to value, *all* that is really of the first importance—everything of this nature pleads his cause most strongly. You have no doubt of his having superior abilities, he has proved it at the University; he is, I dare say, such a scholar as your agreeable, idle brothers would ill bear a comparison with.

Oh, my dear Fanny! the more I write about him the warmer my feelings become—the more strongly I feel the sterling worth of such a young man and the desirableness of your growing in love with him again. I recommend this most thoroughly. There *are* such beings in the world, perhaps one in a thousand, as the creature you and I should think perfection, where grace and spirit are united to worth, where the manners are equal to the heart and understanding; but such a person may not come in your way, or, if he does, he may not be the eldest son of a man of fortune, the near relation of your particular friend, and belonging to your own county.

Think of all this, Fanny. Mr. A. has advantages which we do not often meet in one person. His only fault, indeed, seems modesty. If he were less modest he would be more agreeable, speak louder, and look impudenter; and is not it a fine character of which modesty is the only defect? I have no doubt he will get more lively and more like yourselves as he is more with you; he will catch your ways if he belongs to you. And, as to there being any objection from his *goodness*, from the danger of his becoming even evangelical, I cannot admit *that*. I am by no means convinced that we ought not all to be evangelicals, and am at least persuaded that they who are so from reason and feeling must be happiest and safest.

And now, my dear Fanny, having written so much on one side of the question, I shall turn round and entreat you not to commit yourself farther, and not to think of accepting him unless you really do like him. Anything is to be preferred or endured rather than marrying without affection; and if his deficiencies of manner, &c. &c., strike you more than all his good qualities, if you continue to think strongly of them, give him up at once. Things are now in such a state that you must resolve upon one or the other—either to allow him to go on as he has done, or whenever you are together behave with a coldness which may convince him that he has been deceiving himself. I have no doubt of his suffering a good deal for a time—a great deal when he feels that he must give you up; but it is no creed of mine, as you must be well aware, that such sort of disappointments kill anybody.

Yours very affectionately,
JANE AUSTEN.

23 Hans Place: Wednesday [November 30, 1814].

Now, my dearest Fanny, I will begin a subject which comes in very naturally. You frighten me out of my wits by your reference. Your affection gives me the highest pleasure, but indeed you must not let anything depend on my opinion; your own feelings, and none but your own, should determine such an important point. So far, however, as answering your question, I have no scruple. I am perfectly convinced that your present feelings, supposing you were to marry *now*, would be sufficient for his happiness; but when I think how very, very far it is from a '*now*,' and take everything that *may be* into consideration, I dare not say 'Determine to accept him'; the risk is too great for *you*, unless your own sentiments prompt it.

You will think me perverse perhaps; in my last letter I was urging everything in his favour, and now I am inclining the other way, but I cannot help it; I am at present more impressed with the possible evil that may arise to *you* from engaging yourself to him—in word or mind—than with anything else. When I consider how few young men you have yet seen much of; how capable you are (yes, I do still think you *very* capable) of being really in love; and how full of temptation the next six or seven years of your life will probably be (it is the very period of life for the *strongest* attachments to be formed)—I cannot wish you, with your present very cool feelings, to devote yourself in honour to him. It is very true that you never may attach another man his equal altogether; but if that other man has the power of attaching you *more*, he will be in your eyes the most perfect.

I shall be glad if you *can* revive past feelings, and from your unbiassed self resolve to go on as you have done, but this I do not expect; and without it I cannot wish you to be fettered. I should not be afraid of your *marrying* him; with all his worth you would soon love him enough for the happiness of both; but I should dread the continuance of this sort of tacit engagement, with such an uncertainty as there is of *when* it may be completed. Years may pass before he is independent; you like him well enough to marry, but not well enough to wait; the unpleasantness of appearing fickle is certainly great; but if you think you want punishment for past illusions, there it is, and nothing can be compared to the misery of being bound *without* love—bound to one, and preferring another; *that* is a punishment which you do *not* deserve.

I shall be most glad to hear from you again, my dearest Fanny, but it must not be later than Saturday, as we shall be off on Monday long before the letters are delivered; and write *something* that may do to be read or told.

I cannot suppose we differ in our ideas of the Christian religion. You have given an excellent description of it. We only affix a different meaning to the word *evangelical*.

Yours most affectionately,
J. AUSTEN.

Miss Knight, Godmersham Park, Faversham, Kent.

Two remarks in these letters seem to betray the close observer of human nature from the novelist's point of view. Her optimistic opinion as to recovery from disappointments in love may perhaps be adduced by some critics as an argument to show that her feelings were not very deep; we should rather quote them as an instance of her candour—of her saying what other writers cannot help thinking, though they may not like to express the thought. Readers of *Persuasion* are well aware that the author made room for cases (at all events, in the lives of women) where such disappointments, though they may not kill, yet give a sombre tone to the life and spirits of the sufferer through a long series of years.

There is close observation also in the distinction drawn between the amount of love sufficient for a speedy marriage, and that necessary for a long engagement, if unhappiness and possible discredit are to be avoided. On this occasion, neither marriage nor engagement happened to Fanny Knight. Her son tells us that differences in religious ideas tended by degrees to separate the lovers—if lovers they could be called. Her doubt as to caring enough for 'Mr. A.' became a certainty in the course of the year 1815. When her aunt, in November of that year, joked with her about an imaginary tenderness for Mr. Haden, 'the apothecary,' it was no doubt pure 'chaff'; but we may be sure she would not have indulged in it if any serious attachment had then occupied her niece's mind.

The remaining letters of this series which we possess were written, after an interval of more than two years, in February and March 1817, only a few months before Jane's death. All idea of Fanny's engaging herself to 'Mr. A.' has now passed away; yet, with natural inconsistency, she lives in dread of his marrying some one else. By this time there is a 'Mr. B.' on the stage, but his courtship, though apparently demonstrative, is not really serious; and the last letter keeps away from love affairs altogether. As to 'Mr. A.,' we are told that he found his happiness elsewhere within a couple of years; while Fanny became engaged to Sir Edward Knatchbull in 1820.

Chawton: [February 20, 1817].

MY DEAREST FANNY,—You are inimitable, irresistible. You are the delight of my life. Such letters, such entertaining letters, as you have lately sent! such a description of your queer little heart! such a lovely display of what imagination does! You are worth your weight in gold, or even in the new silver coinage. I cannot express to you what I have felt in reading your history of yourself—how full of pity and concern, and admiration and amusement, I have been! You are the paragon of all that is silly and sensible, common-place and eccentric, sad and lively, provoking and interesting. Who can keep pace with the fluctuations of your fancy, the capprizios of your taste, the contradictions of your feelings? You are so odd, and all the time so perfectly natural!—so peculiar in yourself, and yet so like everybody else!

It is very, very gratifying to me to know you so intimately. You can hardly think what a pleasure it is to me to have such thorough pictures of your heart. Oh, what a loss it will be when you are married! You are too agreeable in your single state—too agreeable as a niece. I shall hate you when your delicious play of mind is all settled down into conjugal and maternal affections.

Mr. B—— frightens me. He will have you. I see you at the altar. I have *some* faith in Mrs. C. Cage's observation, and still more in Lizzy's; and, besides, I know it *must* be so. He must be wishing to attach you. It would be too stupid and too shameful in him to be otherwise; and all the family are seeking your acquaintance.

Do not imagine that I have any real objection; I have rather taken a fancy to him than not, and I like the house for you. I only do not like you should marry anybody. And yet I do wish you to marry very much, because I know you will never be happy till you are; but the loss of a Fanny Knight will be never made up to me. My 'affec. niece F. C. B——' will be but a poor substitute. I do not like your being nervous, and so apt to cry—it is a sign you are not quite well.

I enjoy your visit to Goodnestone, it must be a great pleasure to you; you have not seen Fanny Cage in comfort so long. I hope she represents and remonstrates and reasons with you properly. Why should you be living in dread of his marrying somebody else? (Yet, how natural!) You did not choose to have him yourself, why not allow him to take comfort where he can? In your conscience you *know* that he could not bear a companion with a more animated character. You cannot forget how you felt under the idea of its having been possible that he might have dined in Hans Place.

My dearest Fanny, I cannot bear you should be unhappy about him. Think of his principles; think of his father's objection, of want of money, &c., &c. But I am doing no good; no, all that I urge against him will rather make you take his part more, sweet, perverse Fanny.

And now I will tell you that we like your Henry to the utmost, to the very top of the glass, quite brimful. He is a very pleasing young man. I do not see how he could be mended. He does really bid fair to be everything his father and sister could wish; and William I love very much indeed, and so we do all; he is quite our own William. In short, we are very comfortable together; that is, we can answer for *ourselves*.

Friday.—I had no idea when I began this yesterday of sending it before your brother went back, but I have written away my foolish thoughts at such a rate that I will not keep them many hours longer to stare me in the face.

Ben and Anna walked here last Sunday to hear Uncle Henry, and she looked so pretty, it was quite a pleasure to see her, so young and so blooming, and so innocent.

Your objection to the quadrilles delighted me exceedingly. Pretty well, for a lady irrecoverably attached to *one* person! Sweet Fanny, believe no such thing of yourself, spread no such malicious slander upon your understanding, within the precincts of your imagination. Do not speak ill of your sense merely for the gratification of your fancy; yours is sense which deserves more honourable treatment. You are *not* in love with him; you never *have* been really in love with him.

Yours very affectionately,
J. AUSTEN.

Chawton: Thursday [March 13, 1817].

As to making any adequate return for such a letter as yours, my dearest Fanny, it is absolutely impossible. If I were to labour at it all the rest of my life, and live to the age of Methuselah, I could never accomplish anything so long and so perfect; but I cannot let William go without a few lines of acknowledgment and reply.

I have pretty well done with Mr. ———. By your description, he *cannot* be in love with you, however he may try at it; and I could not wish the match unless there were a great deal of love on his side.

Poor Mrs. C. Milles, that she should die on the wrong day at last, after being about it so long! It was unlucky that the Goodnestone party could not meet you, and I hope her friendly, obliging, social spirit, which delighted in drawing people together, was not conscious of the division and disappointment she was occasioning. I am sorry and surprised that you speak of her as having little to leave, and must feel for Miss Milles, though she *is* Molly, if a material loss of income is to attend her other loss. Single women have a dreadful propensity for being poor, which is one very strong argument in favour of matrimony, but I need not dwell on such arguments with *you*, pretty dear.

To you I shall say, as I have often said before, do not be in a hurry, the right man will come at last; you will in the course of the next two or three years meet with somebody more generally unexceptionable than anyone you have yet known, who will love you as warmly as possible, and who will so completely attract you that you will feel you never really loved before.

Aunt Cassandra walked to Wyards yesterday with Mrs. Digweed. Anna has had a bad cold, and looks pale. She has just weaned Julia.

Chawton: Sunday [March 23, 1817].

I am very much obliged to you, my dearest Fanny, for sending me Mr. W.'s conversation; I had great amusement in reading it, and I hope I am not affronted, and do not think the worse of him for having a brain so very different from mine; but my strongest sensation of all is *astonishment* at your being able to press him on the subject so perseveringly; and I agree with your papa, that it was not fair. When he knows the truth he will be uncomfortable.

You are the oddest creature! Nervous enough in some respects, but in others perfectly without nerves! Quite unrepulsable, hardened, and impudent. Do not oblige him to read any more. Have mercy on him, tell him the truth, and make him an apology. He and I should not in the least agree, of course, in our ideas of novels and heroines. Pictures of perfection, as you know, make me sick and wicked; but there is some very good sense in what he says, and I particularly respect him for wishing to think well of all young ladies; it shows an amiable and a delicate mind. And he deserves better treatment than to be obliged to read any more of my works.

Do not be surprised at finding Uncle Henry acquainted with my having another ready for publication. I could not say No when he asked me, but he knows nothing more of it. You will not like it, so you need not be impatient. You may *perhaps* like the heroine, as she is almost too good for me.

Thank you for everything you tell me. I do not feel worthy of it by anything that I can say in return, but I assure you my pleasure in your letters is quite as great as ever, and I am interested and amused just as you could wish me.

The Papillons came back on Friday night, but I have not seen them yet, as I do not venture to church. I cannot hear, however, but that they are the same Mr. P. and his sister they used to be.

Very affectionately yours,
J. AUSTEN.

Miss Knight, Godmersham Park, Canterbury.

Very different in tone and subject were the letters, addressed about the same time as the two earlier of this series, to her other niece, Anna. Not that Anna was without her own love story: on the contrary, it came to a straightforward and satisfactory climax in her marriage to Ben Lefroy, which took place in November 1814; and no doubt, she, like her cousin, had received letters of sympathy and advice on the realities of life from her aunt. Her own romance, however, did not prevent her from interesting herself in the creations of her brain: indeed, all the three children of James Austen—Anna, Edward, and little Caroline—had indulged freely in the delights of authorship from a very youthful age. It was a novel of Anna's which caused the present correspondence; and we can see from the delicate hints of her aunt that *Pride and Prejudice* and *Mansfield Park* had not been without their influence over its matter and style. Readers of these letters will note the kindness with which Jane, now deep in the composition of *Emma*, turns aside from her own work to criticise and encourage, associating her views all the time with those of Cassandra—who was to her like a Court of Appeal—and allowing ample freedom of judgment also to Anna herself. They will see also that her vote is for 'nature and spirit,' above everything; while yet she insists on the necessity of accuracy of detail for producing the illusion of truth in fiction.

[May or June, 1814.]

MY DEAR ANNA,—I am very much obliged to you for sending your MS. It has entertained me extremely; all of us, indeed. I read it aloud to your Grandmama and Aunt Cass, and we were all very much pleased. The spirit does not droop at all. Sir Thos., Lady Helena and St. Julian are very well done, and Cecilia continues to be interesting in spite of her being so amiable. It was very fit you should advance her age. I like the beginning of Devereux Forester very much, a great deal better than if he had been very good or very bad. A few verbal corrections are all that I felt tempted to make.

I do not like a lover speaking in the 3rd person; it is too much like the formal part of Lord Orville, and, I think, is not natural. If *you* think differently, however, you need not mind me. I am impatient for more, and only wait for a safe conveyance to return this book.

[August 10, 1814.]

I like the name *Which is the Heroine* very well, and I dare say shall grow to like it very much in time; but *Enthusiasm* was something so very superior that every common title must appear to disadvantage. I am not sensible of any blunders about Dawlish; the library was particularly pitiful and wretched twelve years ago and not likely to have anybody's publications. There is no such title as Desborough either among dukes, marquises, earls, viscounts, or barons. These were your inquiries. I will now thank you for your envelope received this morning.

Your Aunt Cass is as well pleased with St. Julian as ever, and I am delighted with the idea of seeing Progillian again.

Wednesday 17.—We have now just finished the first of the three books I had the pleasure of receiving yesterday. I read it aloud and we are all very much amused, and like the work quite as well as ever. I depend on getting through another book before dinner, but there is really a good deal of respectable reading in your forty-eight pages. I have no doubt six will make a very good-sized volume. You must be quite pleased to have accomplished so much. I like Lord Portman and his brother very much. I am only afraid that Lord P.'s good nature will make most people like him better than he deserves. The whole Portman family are very good, and Lady Anne, who was your great dread, you have succeeded particularly well with. Bell Griffin is just what she should be. My corrections have not been more important than before; here and there we have thought the sense could be expressed in fewer words, and I have scratched out Sir Thos. from walking with the other men to the stables, &c., the very day after his breaking his arm; for, though I find your papa did walk out immediately after *his* arm was set, I think it can be so little usual as to appear unnatural in a book.

Lyme will not do. Lyme is towards forty miles' distance from Dawlish and would not be talked of there. I have put Starcross instead. If you prefer Exeter that must be always safe.

I have also scratched out the introduction between Lord Portman and his brother and Mr. Griffin. A country surgeon (don't tell Mr. C. Lyford) would not be introduced to men of their rank.

I *do* think you had better omit Lady Helena's postscript. To those that are acquainted with *Pride and Prejudice* it will seem an imitation.

We are reading the last book. They must be two days going from Dawlish to Bath. They are nearly 100 miles apart.

Thursday.—We finished it last night after our return from drinking tea at the Great House. The last chapter does not please us quite so well; we do not thoroughly like the play, perhaps from having had too much of plays in that way lately, and we think you had better not leave England. Let the Portmans go to Ireland; but as you know nothing of the manners there, you had better not go with them. You will be in danger of giving false representations. Stick to Bath and the Foresters. There you will be quite at home.

Your Aunt C. does not like desultory novels, and is rather afraid yours will be too much so, that there will be too frequently a change from one set of people to another, and that circumstances will be sometimes introduced of apparent consequence which will lead to nothing. It will not be so great an objection to *me* if it does. I allow much more latitude than she does, and think nature and spirit cover many sins of a wandering story, and people in general do not care so much about it for your comfort.

I should like to have had more of Devereux. I do not feel enough acquainted with him. You were afraid of meddling with him, I dare say. I like your sketch of Lord Clanmurray, and your picture of the two poor young girls' enjoyment is very good. I have not yet noticed St. Julian's serious conversation with Cecilia, but I like it exceedingly. What he says about the madness of otherwise sensible women on the subject of their daughters coming out is worth its weight in gold.

I do not see that the language sinks. Pray go on.

[September 9, 1814.]

We have been very much amused by your three books, but I have a good many criticisms to make, more than you will like. We are not satisfied with Mrs. Forester's settling herself as tenant and near neighbour to such a man as Sir T. H., without having some other inducement to go there. She ought to have some friend living thereabouts to tempt her. A woman going with two girls just growing up into a neighbourhood where she knows nobody but one man of not very good character, is an awkwardness which so prudent a woman as Mrs. F. would not be likely to fall into. Remember she is very prudent. You must not let her act inconsistently. Give her a friend, and let that friend be invited to meet her at the Priory, and we shall have no objection to her dining there as she does; but otherwise a woman in her situation would hardly go there before she had been visited by other families. I like the scene itself, the Miss Lesleys, Lady Anne, and the music very much. . . . Sir Thomas H. you always do very well. I have only taken the liberty of expunging one phrase of his which would not be allowed—'Bless my heart!' It is too familiar and inelegant. Your grandmother is more disturbed at Mrs. Forester's not returning the Egertons' visit sooner than by anything else. They ought to have called at the Parsonage before Sunday. You describe a sweet place, but your descriptions are often more minute than will be liked. You give too many particulars of right hand and left. Mrs. Forester is not careful enough of Susan's health. Susan ought not to be walking out so soon after heavy rains, taking long walks in the dirt. An anxious mother would not suffer it. I like your Susan very much indeed, she is a sweet creature, her playfulness of fancy is very delightful. I like her as she is now exceedingly, but I am not quite so well satisfied with her behaviour to George R. At first she seems all over attachment and feeling, and afterwards to have none at all; she is so extremely composed at the ball and so well satisfied apparently with Mr. Morgan. She seems to have changed her character.

You are now collecting your people delightfully, getting them exactly into such a spot as is the delight of my life. Three or four families in a country village is the very thing to work on, and I hope you will write a great deal more, and make full use of them while they are so very favourably arranged.

You are but *now* coming to the heart and beauty of your book. Till the heroine grows up the fun must be imperfect, but I expect a great deal of entertainment from the next three or four books, and I hope you will not resent these remarks by sending me no more.

They are not so much like the Papillons as I expected. Your last chapter is very entertaining, the conversation on genius, &c.; Mr. St. Julian and Susan both talk in character, and very well. In some former parts Cecilia is perhaps a little too solemn and good, but upon the whole her disposition is very well opposed to Susan's, her want of imagination is very natural. I wish you could make Mrs. Forester talk more; but she must be difficult to manage and make entertaining, because there is so much good common sense and propriety about her that nothing can be made very *broad*. Her economy and her ambition must not be staring. The papers left by Mrs. Fisher are very good. Of course one guesses something. I hope when you have written a great deal more, you will be equal to scratching out some of the past. The scene with Mrs. Mellish I should condemn; it is prosy and nothing to the purpose; and indeed the more you can find in your heart to curtail between Dawlish and Newton Priors, the better I think it will be—one does not care for girls till they are grown up. Your Aunt C. quite enters into the exquisiteness of that name—Newton Priors is really a nonpareil. Milton would have given his eyes to have thought of it. Is not the cottage taken from Tollard Royal?

[September 28, 1814.]

I hope you do not depend on having your book again immediately. I kept it that your grandmama may hear it, for it has not been possible yet to have any public reading. I have read it to your Aunt Cassandra, however, in our own room at night, while we undressed, and with a great deal of pleasure. We like the first chapter extremely, with only a little doubt whether Lady Helena is not almost too foolish. The matrimonial dialogue is very good certainly. I like Susan as well as ever, and begin now not to care at all about Cecilia; she may stay at Easton Court as long as she likes. Henry Mellish, I am afraid, will be too much in the common novel style—a handsome, amiable, unexceptionable young man (such as do not much abound in real life), desperately in love and all in vain. But I have no business to judge him so early.

We feel really obliged to you for introducing a Lady Kenrick; it will remove the greatest fault in the work, and I give you credit for considerable forbearance as an author in adopting so much of our opinion. I expect high fun about Mrs. Fisher and Sir Thomas.

Devereux Forester's being ruined by his vanity is extremely good, but I wish you would not let him plunge into a 'vortex of dissipation.' I do not object to the thing, but I cannot bear the expression; it is such thorough novel slang, and so old that I dare say Adam met with it in the first novel he opened.

Walter Scott has no business to write novels, especially good ones. It is not fair. He has fame and profit enough as a poet, and should not be taking the bread out of other people's mouths.

I do not like him, and do not mean to like *Waverley* if I can help it, but fear I must.

I am quite determined, however, not to be pleased with Mrs. West's *Alicia De Lacy*, should I ever meet with it, which I hope I shall not. I think I *can* be stout against anything written by Mrs. West. I have made up my mind to like no novels really but Miss Edgeworth's, yours, and my own.

What can you do with Egerton to increase the interest for him? I wish you could contrive something, some family occurrence to bring out his good qualities more. Some distress among brothers and sisters to relieve by the sale of his curacy! Something to carry him mysteriously away, and then be heard of at York or Edinburgh in an old great coat. I would not seriously recommend anything improbable, but if you could invent something spirited for him it would have a good effect. He might lend all his money to Captain Morris, but then he would be a great fool if he did. Cannot the

Morrises quarrel and he reconcile them? Excuse the liberty I take in these suggestions.

The Webbs are really gone! When I saw the wagons at the door, and thought of all the trouble they must have in moving, I began to reproach myself for not having liked them better, but since the wagons have disappeared my conscience has been closed again, and I am excessively glad they are gone.

I am very fond of Sherlock's sermons and prefer them to almost any.

Anna's marriage took place on November 8. Her husband was afterwards a clergyman, but he did not take Orders until about three years after the marriage; and the first home of the young couple was at Hendon, to which place the following letter was addressed, Jane being at that time with her brother Henry, in Hans Place:—

Hans Place: [November 28, 1814].

MY DEAR ANNA,—I assure you we all came away very much pleased with our visit. We talked of you for about a mile and a half with great satisfaction; and I have been just sending a very good report of you to Miss Benn, with a full account of your dress for Susan and Maria.

We were all at the play last night to see Miss O'Neill in *Isabella*. I do not think she was quite equal to my expectations. I fancy I want something more than can be. I took two pocket-handkerchiefs, but had very little occasion for either. She is an elegant creature, however, and hugs Mr. Young delightfully. I am going this morning to see the little girls in Keppel Street. Cassy was excessively interested about your marriage when she heard of it, which was not until she was to drink your health on the wedding day.

She asked a thousand questions in her usual manner, what he said to you and what you said to him. If your uncle were at home he would send his best love, but I will not impose any base fictitious remembrances on you. Mine I can honestly give, and remain

> Your affectionate Aunt,
> J. AUSTEN.

Early in December, Anna sent her aunt another packet, which elicited the following letter:—

> Hans Place: Wednesday.

MY DEAR ANNA,—I have been very far from finding your book an evil, I assure you. I read it immediately, and with great pleasure. I think you are going on very well. The description of Dr. Griffin and Lady Helena's unhappiness is very good, just what was likely to be. I am curious to know what the end of *them* will be. The name of Newton Priors is really invaluable; I never met with anything superior to it. It is delightful; one could live upon the name of Newton Priors for a twelvemonth. Indeed, I do think you get on very fast. I only wish other people of my acquaintance could compose as rapidly. I am pleased with the dog scene and with the whole of George and Susan's love, but am more particularly struck with your *serious* conversations, etc. They are very good throughout. St. Julian's history was quite a surprise to me. You had not very long known it yourself, I suspect; but I have no objection to make to the circumstance, and it is very well told. His having been in love with the aunt gives Cecilia an additional interest with him. I like the idea—a very proper compliment to an aunt! I rather imagine indeed that nieces are seldom chosen but out of compliment to some aunt or another. I dare say Ben was in love with me once, and would never have thought of you if he had not supposed me dead of a scarlet fever.

[Mrs. Heathcote] writes me word that Miss Blachford is married, but I have never seen it in the papers, and one may as well be single if the wedding is not to be in print.

> Your affectionate Aunt,
> J. A.

In August 1815 the Lefroys moved from Hendon, and took a small house called Wyards, near Alton, and within a walk of Chawton. Wyards is more than once mentioned in our letters.

This is the last letter we possess dealing with Anna's story; and we can understand that the attention of either writer was soon diverted from it by more serious considerations: that of Anna by family cares, that of her aunt by Henry's illness and bankruptcy, and by her own publication of *Emma* and subsequent failure of health. The last history of the MS. was sad enough. After the death of her kind critic, Anna could not induce herself to go on with the tale; the associations were too melancholy. Long afterwards, she took it out of its drawer, and, in a fit of despondency, threw it into the fire. Her daughter, who tells us this, adds that she herself—a little girl—was sitting on the rug, and remembers that she watched the destruction, amused with the flame.

A similar fate befell a tragedy written at a very early age by Anna's little sister Caroline, who was her junior by about twelve years. Caroline believed it to be a necessary part of a tragedy that all the *dramatis personae* should somehow meet their end, by violence or otherwise, in the last act; and this belief produced such a scene of carnage and woe as to cause fits of laughter among unsympathetic elders, and tears to the author, who threw the unfortunate tragedy into the fire on the spot.

Caroline, however, continued to write stories; and some of them are alluded to in a series of little childish letters written to her by her Aunt Jane, which survive, carefully pieced together with silver paper and gum, and which are worth preserving for the presence in them of love and playfulness, and the entire absence of condescension.

> December 6.

MY DEAR CAROLINE,—I wish I could finish stories as fast as you can. I am much obliged to you for the sight of Olivia, and think you have done for her very well; but the good-for-nothing father, who was the real author of all her faults and sufferings, should not escape unpunished. I hope *he* hung himself, or took the sur-name of *Bone* or underwent some direful penance or other.

Yours affectionately,
J. AUSTEN.

Chawton: Monday, July 15.

MY DEAR CAROLINE,—I have followed your directions and find your handwriting admirable. If you continue to improve as much as you have done, perhaps I may not be obliged to shut my eyes at all half a year hence. I have been very much entertained by your story of Carolina and her aged father; it made me laugh heartily, and I am particularly glad to find you so much alive upon any topic of such absurdity, as the usual description of a heroine's father. You have done it full justice, or, if anything be wanting, it is the information of the venerable old man's having married when only twenty-one, and being a father at twenty-two.

I had an early opportunity of conveying your letter to Mary Jane, having only to throw it out of window at her as she was romping with your brother in the Back Court. She thanks you for it, and answers your questions through me. I am to tell you that she has passed her time at Chawton very pleasantly indeed, that she does not miss Cassy so much as she expected, and that as to *Diana Temple*, she is ashamed to say it has never been worked at since you went away....

Edward's visit has been a great pleasure to us. He has not lost one good quality or good look, and is only altered in being improved by being some months older than when we saw him last. He is getting very near our own age, for *we* do not grow older of course.

Yours affectionately,
J. AUSTEN.

Chawton: Wednesday, March. 13 [1815].

MY DEAR CAROLINE,—I am very glad to have an opportunity of answering your agreeable little letter. You seem to be quite my own niece in your feelings towards Mme. de Genlis. I do not think I could even now, at my sedate time of life, read *Olympe et Théophile* without being in a rage. It really is too bad! Not allowing them to be happy together when they *are* married. Don't talk of it, pray. I have just lent your Aunt Frank the first volume of *Les Veillées du Château*, for Mary Jane to read. It will be some time before she comes to the horror of Olympe. . . .

I had a very nice letter from your brother not long ago, and I am quite happy to see how much his hand is improving. I am convinced that it will end in a very gentlemanlike hand, much above par.

We have had a great deal of fun lately with post-chaises stopping at the door; three times within a few days we had a couple of agreeable visitors turn in unexpectedly—your Uncle Henry and Mr. Tilson, Mrs. Heathcote and Miss Bigg, your Uncle Henry and Mr. Seymour. Take notice it was the same Uncle Henry each time.

I remain, my dear Caroline,
Your affectionate Aunt,
J. AUSTEN.

Hans Place: Monday night [October 30, 1815].

MY DEAR CAROLINE,—I have not felt quite equal to taking up your Manuscript, but think I shall soon, and I hope my detaining it so long will be no inconvenience. It gives us great pleasure that you should be at Chawton. I am sure Cassy must be delighted to have you. You will practise your music of course, and I trust to you for taking care of my instrument and not letting it be ill-used in any respect. Do not allow anything to be put on it but what is very light. I hope you will try to make out some other tune besides the Hermit. . . .

I am sorry you got wet in your ride; now that you are become an Aunt you are a person of some consequence and must excite great interest whatever you do. I have always maintained the importance of Aunts as much as possible, and I am sure of your doing the same now.

        Believe me, my dear Sister-Aunt,
           Yours affectionately,
              J. AUSTEN.

[January 23, 1817.]

MY DEAR CAROLINE,—I am always very much obliged to you for writing to me, and have now I believe two or three notes to thank you for; but whatever may be their number, I mean to have this letter accepted as a handsome return for all, for you see I have taken a complete, whole sheet of paper, which is to entitle me to consider it as a very long letter whether I write much or little.

We were quite happy to see Edward, it was an unexpected pleasure, and he makes himself as agreeable as ever, sitting in such a quiet comfortable way making his delightful little sketches. He is generally thought grown since he was here last, and rather thinner, but in very good looks. . . . He read his two chapters to us the first evening—both good, but especially the last in our opinion. We think it has more of the spirit and entertainment of the early part of his work.. . .

I feel myself getting stronger than I was half a year ago, and can so perfectly well walk to Alton, *or* back again, without the slightest fatigue that I hope to be able to do both when summer comes. I spent two or three days with your Uncle and Aunt lately, and though the children are sometimes very noisy and not under such order as they ought and easily might, I cannot help liking them and even loving them, which I hope may be not wholly inexcusable in their and your affectionate Aunt,

J. AUSTEN.

The Pianoforte often talks of you; in various keys, tunes, and expressions, I allow—but be it Lesson or Country Dance, Sonata or Waltz, *you* are really its constant theme. I wish you could come and see us, as easily as Edward can.

J. A.

Wednesday night. [1817.]

You send me great news indeed, my dear Caroline, about Mr. Digweed, Mr. Trimmer, and a Grand Pianoforte. I wish it had been a small one, as then you might have pretended that Mr. D.'s rooms were too damp to be fit for it, and offered to take charge of it at the Parsonage. . . .

I look forward to the four new chapters with pleasure.—But how can you like Frederick better than Edgar? You have some eccentric tastes however, I know, as to Heroes and Heroines. Goodbye.

Yours affectionately,
J. AUSTEN.

Chawton: Wednesday, March 26 [1817].

MY DEAR CAROLINE,—Pray make no apologies for writing to me often, I am always very happy to hear from you. . . .

I think you very much improved in your writing, and in the way to write a very pretty hand. I wish you could practise your fingering oftener. Would not it be a good plan for you to go and live entirely at Mr. Wm. Digweed's? He could not desire any other remuneration than the pleasure of hearing you practise.

I like Frederick and Caroline better than I did, but must still prefer Edgar and Julia. Julia is a warm-hearted, ingenuous, natural girl, which I like her for; but I know the word *natural* is no recommendation to you. . . .

How very well Edward is looking! You can have nobody in your neighbourhood to vie with him at all, except Mr. Portal. I have taken one ride on the donkey and like it very much—and you must try to get me quiet, mild days, that I may be able to go out pretty constantly. A great deal of wind does not suit me, as I have still a tendency to rheumatism. In short I am a poor honey at present. I will be better when you can come and see us.

Yours affectionately,
J. AUSTEN.

Caroline Austen contributed to the *Memoir* written by her brother many of the personal reminiscences of their aunt. She was the niece to whom Jane in her last illness sent a recommendation to read more and write less during the years of girlhood. Caroline obeyed the injunction; she became a very well-read woman, and never wrote stories for publication. She was, however, an admirable talker: able to invest common things with a point and spirit peculiarly her own. She was also an ideal aunt, both to nieces and nephews, who all owe a great deal to her companionship and devotion.

CHAPTER XX.

FAILING HEALTH 1816-1817

DURING the last year of Jane Austen's life, when her health was gradually failing, and she was obliged to depend—ever more and more exclusively—on her immediate family for society, she had at least the satisfaction of having her two sailor brothers nearer at hand than had often been the case.

After Frank's return from the Baltic, early in 1814, nothing occurred of a more serious nature than the Great Naval Review in June—which only indirectly affected him, as he was not then in command of a ship—to prevent his attending to his family. He settled down to a domestic life with wife and children, first of all occupying the Great House at Chawton, but soon moving to Alton.

Charles, who for ten years had had active but unexciting work outside the theatre of war, now came more to the front. Commanding the *Phœnix* frigate, he operated against Murat, when that eccentric sovereign took part with Napoleon on the escape of the latter from Elba. Charles was sent in pursuit of a Neapolitan squadron cruising in the Adriatic; and subsequently he blockaded Brindisi, and waited for the garrison to hoist the white flag of the Bourbons. Later on, he was kept busy with Greek pirates in the Archipelago, until the *Phœnix* was lost off Smyrna in 1816, when he returned home. The *Phœnix* had been a lucky ship, Admiral Halsted having made his fortune in her; but her luck was worn out. When she went down, the pilot was on board; no lives were lost, and no blame fell on the captain. It must have been, however, a disappointing end to an exciting time; and, as the war was over, it might be long before he got another ship.

A letter from Charles to Jane, during this command, written from Palermo, May 6, 1815, furnishes us with one of the few indications that exist of fame achieved by her during her lifetime:—

Books became the subject of conversation, and I praised *Waverley* highly, when a young man present observed that nothing had come out for years to be compared with *Pride and Prejudice*, *Sense and Sensibility*, &c. As I am sure you must be anxious to know the name of a person of so much taste, I shall tell you it is Fox, a nephew of the late Charles James Fox. That you may not be too much elated at this morsel of praise, I shall add that he did not appear to like *Mansfield Park* so well as the two first, in which, however, I believe he is singular.

We may compare this account with the quotation given in the *Memoir* from Sir Henry Holland's *Recollections:*—

I have the picture before me still of Lord Holland lying on his bed, when attacked with gout; his admirable sister, Miss Fox, reading aloud—as she always did on these occasions—some one of Miss Austen's novels, of which he was never wearied.

It is as difficult to follow the various stages of Jane's illness as it is to understand the exact nature of her complaint. She must have begun to feel her malady early in the year 1816; for some friends at a distance, whom she visited in the spring, 'thought that her health was somewhat impaired, and observed that she went about her old haunts and recalled the old recollections connected with them in a particular manner—as if she did not expect ever to see them again.' This is, however, almost the only indication that we have of any diminution of vigour at that time; for the three letters to Fanny Knight, given by Lord Brabourne as written in 1816, must be transferred to 1817; and so must the two short extracts on pp. 150, 151 of the *Memoir*, as they evidently refer to a family event which occurred in the March of the later year. The tone of her letters through the remainder of 1816, and at the beginning of the next year, was almost invariably cheerful, and she showed by the completion of *Persuasion* that she was capable of first-rate literary work during the summer of 1816. The fact is that, as to health, she was an incurable optimist; her natural good spirits made her see the best side, and her unselfishness prompted the suppression of anything that might distress those around her. Nothing, for instance, could be more lively than the following letter to Edward Austen, written while he was still at Winchester School, but had come home for his last summer holidays.

Chawton: July 9, 1816.

MY DEAR EDWARD,—Many thanks. A thank for every line, and as many to Mr. W. Digweed for coming. We have been wanting very much to hear of your mother, and are happy to find she continues to mend, but her illness must have been a very serious one indeed. When she is really recovered, she ought to try change of air, and come over to us. Tell your father I am very much obliged to him for his share of your letter, and most sincerely join in the hope of her being eventually much the better for her present discipline. She has the comfort moreover of being confined in such weather as gives one little temptation to be out. It is really too bad, and has been too bad for a long time, much worse than anybody *can* bear, and I begin to think it will never be fine again. This is a *finesse* of mine, for I have often observed that if one writes about the weather, it is generally completely changed before the letter is read. I wish it may prove so now, and that when Mr. W. Digweed reaches Steventon to-morrow, he may find you have had a long series of hot dry weather. We are a small party at present, only grandmamma, Mary Jane, and myself. Yalden's coach cleared off the rest yesterday. . . .

I am glad you recollected to mention your being come home. My heart began to sink within me when I had got so far through your letter without its being mentioned. I was dreadfully afraid that you might be detained at Winchester by severe illness, confined to your bed perhaps, and quite unable to hold a pen, and only dating from Steventon in order, with a mistaken sort of tenderness, to deceive me. But now I have no doubt of your being at home, I am sure you would not say it so seriously unless it actually were so. We saw a countless number of post-chaises full of boys pass by yesterday morning—full of future heroes, legislators, fools, and villains. You have never thanked me for my last letter, which went by the cheese. I cannot bear not to be thanked. You will not pay us a visit yet of course; we must not think of it. Your mother must get well first, and you must go to Oxford and *not* be elected; after that a little change of scene may be good for you, and your physicians I hope will order you to the sea, or to a house by the side of a very considerable pond. Oh! it rains again. It beats against the window. Mary Jane and I have been wet through once already to-day; we set off in the donkey-carriage for Farringdon, as I wanted to see the improvements Mr. Woolls is making, but we were obliged to turn back before we got there, but not soon enough to avoid a pelter all the way home. We met Mr. Woolls. I talked of its being bad weather for the hay, and he returned me the comfort of its being much worse for the wheat. We hear that Mrs. S. does not quit Tangier: why and wherefore? Do you know that our Browning is gone? You must prepare for a William when you come, a good-looking lad, civil and quiet, and seeming likely to do. Good bye. I am sure Mr. W. D. will be astonished at my writing so much, for the paper is so thin that he will be able to count the lines if not to read them.

Yours affec^{ly},
J. AUSTEN.

Mr. J. E. Austen.

There was a second family visit this year to Cheltenham, where Cassandra and Jane had already been in the spring. Probably their connexion with this watering-place was through Mrs. James Austen, and *hers* was through her sister, Mrs. Fowle of Kintbury. Mr. Fowle had lived at Elkstone near Cheltenham, and continued to hold that benefice, which was in the gift of the Craven family. The Fowles would naturally renew their intercourse with their old friends in the neighbourhood, and *he* would go to see his curate and acquaint himself with the circumstances of his parish. The visits to Gloucestershire were therefore for pleasure and business as well as health.

In August 1816 it was a recent serious illness of Mrs. James Austen which took the party there; Mrs. Austen being accompanied by her daughter Caroline, and her sister-in-law Cassandra. Meanwhile, Jane remained with her mother at Chawton, where she had Edward Austen as a visitor.

During Cassandra's absence Jane wrote to her as follows:—

Chawton: September 4, 1816.

We go on very well here, Edward is a great pleasure to me; he drove me to Alton yesterday. I went principally to carry news of you and Henry, and made a regular handsome visit, staying there while Edward went on to Wyards with an invitation to dinner: it was declined, and will be so again to-day probably, for I really believe Anna is not equal to the fatigue. The Alton four drank tea with us last night, and we were very pleasant:—Jeu de Violon, &c.—all new to Mr. Sweney—and he entered into it very well. It was a renewal of former agreeable evenings.

We all (except my mother) dine at Alton tomorrow, and perhaps may have some of the same sports again, but I do not think Mr. and Mrs. D. will add much to our wit. Edward is writing a novel— we have all heard what he has written—it is extremely clever, written with great ease and spirit; if he can carry it on in the same way it will be a first-rate work, and in a style, I think, to be popular. Pray tell Mary how much I admire it—and tell Caroline that I think it is hardly fair upon her and myself to have him take up the novel line.

Sunday [September 8].

MY DEAREST CASSANDRA,—I have borne the arrival of your letter to-day extremely well; anybody might have thought it was giving me pleasure. I am very glad you find so much to be satisfied with at Cheltenham. While the waters agree, everything else is trifling.

Our day at Alton was very pleasant, venison quite right, children well-behaved, and Mr. and Mrs. Digweed taking kindly to our charades and other games. I must also observe, for his mother's satisfaction, that Edward at my suggestion devoted himself very properly to the entertainment of Miss S. Gibson. Nothing was wanting except Mr. Sweney, but he, alas! had been ordered away to London the day before. We had a beautiful walk home by moonlight.

Thank you, my back has given me scarcely any pain for many days. I have an idea that agitation does it as much harm as fatigue, and that I was ill at the time of your going from the very circumstance of your going. I am nursing myself up now into as beautiful a state as I can, because I hear that Dr. White means to call on me before he leaves the country.

I have not seen Anna since the day you left us; her father and brother visited her most days. Edward and Ben called here on Thursday. Edward was in his way to Selborne. We found him very agreeable. He is come back from France, thinking of the French as one could wish—disappointed in everything. He did not go beyond Paris.

I have a letter from Mrs. Perigord; she and her mother are in London again. She speaks of France as a scene of general poverty and misery: no money, no trade, nothing to be got but by the innkeepers, and as to her own present prospects she is not much less melancholy than before.

I enjoyed Edward's company very much, as I said before, and yet I was not sorry when Friday came. It had been a busy week, and I wanted a few days' quiet and exemption from the thought and contrivancy which any sort of company gives. I often wonder how *you* can find time for what you do, in addition to the care of the house; and how good Mrs. West could have written such books and collected so many hard words, with all her family cares, is still more a matter of astonishment. Composition seems to me impossible with a head full of joints of mutton and doses of rhubarb.

We do not much like Mr. Cooper's new sermons. They are fuller of regeneration and conversion than ever, with the addition of his zeal in the cause of the Bible Society.

This is the last letter which we have from Jane to Cassandra. Probably the sisters were not parted again, except when Cassandra went for a few days to Scarlets, on the death of their uncle, Mr. Leigh Perrot, at the end of the following March; and if Jane wrote then, it must have been in such depression of mind and weakness of body, that her sister would not have preserved the writing for others to see.

In the meanwhile, the autumn of 1816 was probably occupied with the preparation of *Persuasion* for the press; and, on the whole, we should gather from the evidence before us that the earlier part of the winter saw one of those fallacious instances of temporary improvement which so often deceive nurses and patients alike, in cases of internal complaints. 'I have certainly gained strength through the winter,' she says, on January 24, 1817. On the 23rd: 'I feel myself stronger than I was half a year ago'; and it was in this spirit of hopefulness that she had written the following lively letter to Edward Austen, when he had left Winchester and was about to enter on the career of an Oxford undergraduate.

Chawton: Monday [December 16, 1816].

MY DEAR EDWARD,—One reason for my writing to you now is, that I may have the pleasure of directing to you $Esq^{re.}$ I give you joy of having left Winchester. Now you may own how miserable you were there; now it will gradually all come out, your crimes and your miseries—how often you went up by the Mail to London and threw away fifty guineas at a tavern, and how often you were on the point of hanging yourself, restrained only, as some ill-natured aspersion upon poor old Winton has it, by the want of a tree within some miles of the city. Charles Knight and his companions passed through Chawton about 9 this morning; later than it used to be. Uncle Henry and I had a glimpse of his handsome face, looking all health and good humour. I wonder when you will come and see us. I know what I rather speculate upon, but shall say nothing. We think uncle Henry in excellent looks. Look at him this moment, and think so too, if you have not done it before; and we have the great comfort of seeing decided improvement in uncle Charles, both as to health, spirits, and appearance. And they are each of them so agreeable in their different way, and harmonise so well, that their visit is thorough enjoyment. Uncle Henry writes very superior sermons. You and I must try to get hold of one or two, and put them into our novels: it would be a fine help to a volume; and we could make our heroine read it aloud of a Sunday evening, just as well as Isabella Wardour, in *The Antiquary*, is made to read the *History of the Hartz Demon*, in the ruins of St. Ruth; though I believe, upon recollection, Lovell is the reader. By the bye, my dear Edward, I am quite concerned for the loss your mother mentions in her letter. Two chapters and a half to be missing is monstrous! It is well that *I* have not been at Steventon lately, and therefore cannot be suspected of purloining them: two strong twigs and a half towards a nest of my own would have been something. I do not think, however, that any theft of that sort would be really very useful to me. What should I do with your strong, manly, spirited sketches, full of variety and glow? How could I possibly join them on to the little bit (two inches wide) of ivory on which I work with so fine a brush, as produces little effect after much labour?

You will hear from uncle Henry how well Anna is. She seems perfectly recovered. Ben was here on Saturday, to ask uncle Charles and me to dine with them, as to-morrow, but I was forced to decline it, the walk is beyond my strength (though I am otherwise very well), and this is not a season for donkey-carriages; and as we do not like to spare uncle Charles, he has declined it too.

Tuesday. Ah, ha! Mr. Edward. I doubt your seeing uncle Henry at Steventon to-day. The weather will prevent your expecting him, I think. Tell your father, with aunt Cass's love and mine, that the pickled cucumbers are extremely good, and tell him also—'tell him what you will.' No, don't tell him what you will, but tell him that grandmamma begs him to make Joseph Hall pay his rent, if he can.

You must not be tired of reading the word *uncle*, for I have not done with it. Uncle Charles thanks your mother for her letter; it was a great pleasure to him to know the parcel was received and gave so much satisfaction, and he begs her to be so good as to give three shillings for him to Dame Staples, which shall be allowed for in the payment of her debt here.

I am happy to tell you that Mr. Papillon will soon make his offer, probably next Monday, as he returns on Saturday. His *intention* can no longer be doubtful in the smallest degree, as he has secured the refusal of the house which Mr. Baverstock at present occupies in Chawton, and is to vacate soon, which is of course intended for Mrs. Elizabeth Papillon.

Adieu, Amiable! I hope Caroline behaves well to you.

Yours affec^{ly},
J. AUSTEN.

J. E. Austen, Esq.

The same bright tone pervades the following letter to Alethea Bigg, from which one of the remarks quoted above, as to the improvement of her health, is taken.

Chawton: January 24, 1817.

MY DEAR ALETHEA,—I think it time there should be a little writing between us, though I believe the epistolary debt is on *your* side, and I hope this will find all the Streatham party well, neither carried away by the flood, nor rheumatic through the damps. Such mild weather is, you know, delightful to *us*, and though we have a great many ponds, and a fine running stream through the meadows on the other side of the road, it is nothing but what beautifies us and does to talk of. . . . *I have certainly gained strength through the winter and am not far from being well*; and I think I understand my own case now so much better than I did, as to be able by care to keep off any serious return of illness. I am more and more convinced that *bile* is at the bottom of all I have suffered, which makes it easy to know how to treat myself. You . . . will be glad to hear thus much of me, I am sure. . . . We have just had a few days' visit from Edward, who brought us a good account of his father, and the very circumstance of his coming at all, of his father's being able to spare him, is itself a good account. . . . He grows still, and still improves in appearance, at least in the estimation of his aunts, who love him better and better, as they see the sweet temper and warm affections of the boy confirmed in the young man: I tried hard to persuade him that he must have some message for William, but in vain. . . . This is not a time of year for donkey-carriages, and our donkeys are necessarily having so long a run of luxurious idleness that I suppose we shall find they have forgotten much of their education when we use them again. We do not use two at once, however; don't imagine such excesses. . . . Our own new clergyman is expected here very soon, perhaps in time to assist Mr. Papillon on Sunday. I shall be very glad when the first hearing is over. It will be a nervous hour for our pew, though we hear that he acquits himself with as much ease and collectedness, as if he had been used to it all his life. We have no chance we know of seeing you between Streatham and Winchester: you go the other road and are engaged to two or three houses; if there should be any change, however, you know how welcome you would be. . . .

We have been reading the *Poet's Pilgrimage to Waterloo*, and generally with much approbation. Nothing will please all the world, you know; but parts of it suit me better than much that he has written before. The opening—*the proem* I believe he calls it— is very beautiful. Poor man! one cannot but grieve for the loss of the son so fondly described. Has he at all recovered it? What do Mr. and Mrs. Hill know about his present state?

Yours aff^{ly}, J. AUSTEN.

The real object of this letter is to ask you for a receipt, but I thought it genteel not to let it appear early. We remember some excellent orange wine at Manydown, made from Seville oranges, entirely or chiefly. I should be very much obliged to you for the receipt, if you can command it within a few weeks.

Three days later, Jane felt well enough to set to work on a fresh novel: thoroughly fresh, for it bore no resemblance to any of her previous stories. A short *résumé* of this beginning is given in the *Memoir*, and from it the reader will see that the scene is laid at a new watering-place, which is being exploited by two of the leading characters. In the twelve chapters which she wrote, the *dramatis personae* are sketched in with vigour and decision; but there is little of the subtle refinement which we are accustomed to associate with her work, and certainly nothing of the tender sentiment of *Persuasion*. It is unfair, however, to judge from the first draft of a few introductory chapters, written as they no doubt were to relieve the tedium of long hours of confinement, and written perhaps also to comfort her friends by letting them see that she was still able to work. It is probable, too, that a long step in the downward progress of her condition was taken in the course of the seven weeks during which she was writing for the last time. It began 'in her usual firm and neat hand, but some of the latter pages were first traced in pencil—probably, when she was too ill to sit long at a desk—and afterwards written over in ink." The last date on the MS. is March 17. She was, no doubt, by this time making frequent use of the temporary couch, which, as we are told, she had contrived out of two or three chairs, so as to leave the one real sofa free for her mother. She professed to like her own couch best; but the importunity of a young niece obliged her to confess that she used it always, because she thought that her mother would not use the sofa enough unless it were absolutely reserved for her service.

In February and March followed the three letters written to Fanny Knight—portions of which are given in the last chapter. They chiefly concern Fanny's own affairs, and show how lively Jane's mind still was, and with what unselfish care she could divert it from her own sufferings to the concerns which interested those nearest to her.

We now append the sentences in those letters which refer to her own state of health, and which certainly read as if some serious accession of illness had intervened while the correspondence was in progress.

February 20, 1817.—I am almost entirely cured of my rheumatism—just a little pain in my knee, now and then, to make me remember what it was and keep on flannel. Aunt Cassandra nursed me so beautifully.

March 13.—I am got tolerably well again, quite equal to walking about and enjoying the air, and by sitting down and resting a good while between my walks I get exercise enough. I have a scheme however for accomplishing more, as the weather grows spring-like. I mean to take to riding the donkey; it will be more independent and less troublesome than the use of the carriage, and I shall be able to go about with Aunt Cassandra in her walks to Alton and Wyards.

March 23.—Many thanks for your kind care of my health; I certainly have not been well for many weeks, and about a week ago I was very poorly. I have had a good deal of fever at times, and indifferent nights; but I am considerably better now and am recovering my looks a little, which have been bad enough—black and white and every wrong colour. I must not depend upon being ever very blooming again. Sickness is a dangerous indulgence at my time of life.

Evening.—I was languid and dull and very bad company when I wrote the above; I am better now, to my own feelings at least, and wish I may be more agreeable. We are going to have rain, and after that very pleasant genial weather, which will exactly do for me, as my saddle will then be completed, and air and exercise is what I want.

Tuesday.—I took my first ride yesterday, and liked it very much. I went up Mounter's Lane and round by where the new cottages are to be, and found the exercise and everything very pleasant; and I had the advantage of agreeable companions, as Aunt Cass and Edward walked by my side. Aunt Cass is such an excellent nurse, so assiduous and unwearied! But you know all that already.

At the end of March she made her will—a brief and simple document of which the operative part was in these words: 'To my dearest sister Cassandra Elizabeth, everything of which I may die possessed, or which may hereafter be due to me, subject to the payment of my funeral expenses and to a legacy of £50 to my brother Henry and £50 to Madame Bigeon.'

About the same time another will was causing great disappointment to the Austen family; and as Jane was affected by anything that affected her nearest relations, we must probably attribute to it some share in the rapid decay of her bodily strength.

Her uncle, Mr. Leigh Perrot, died at Scarlets on March 28. He was childless, and left a considerable fortune. As he was also a kind-hearted man and had always shown particular favour to the Austens, it was reasonably expected that they would reap some immediate benefit under his will. Most of the family were in narrow circumstances, and they had lately been crippled by the failure of Henry's business and the lawsuit about Edward's Hampshire property; a legacy, therefore, would have been very acceptable. Mr. Leigh Perrot, however, was actuated in making his will by a stronger motive than love to sister and nephews. He was devoted to his wife, and was perhaps anxious to show that his devotion was increased in consequence of the false accusation with which she had been assailed at Bath in 1799-1800. He showed it by leaving everything to her for her life, and placing Scarlets and a considerable sum at her free disposal. At the same time he left a large sum (subject to her life interest) to James Austen and his heirs, and £1000 apiece to *each* of Mrs. Austen's children who should survive his wife. Mrs. Leigh Perrot, also, at a later date, gave allowances to some members of the family, and eventually made Edward Austen her heir. None of these advantages, however, fell to them immediately; and the disappointment caused by their uncle's disposition of his property is reflected in the following letter from Jane to her brother Charles.

[April 6, 1817.]

MY DEAREST CHARLES,—Many thanks for your affectionate letter. I was in your debt before, but I have really been too unwell the last fortnight to write anything that was not absolutely necessary. I have been suffering from a bilious attack attended with a good deal of fever. A few days ago my complaint appeared removed, but I am ashamed to say that the shock of my uncle's will brought on a relapse, and I was so ill on Friday and thought myself so likely to be worse that I could not but press for Cassandra's returning with Frank after the funeral last night, which she of course did; and either her return, or my having seen Mr. Curtis, or my disorder's chusing to go away, have made me better this morning. I live upstairs however for the present, and am coddled. I am the only one of the legatees who has been so silly, but a weak body must excuse weak nerves.

My mother has borne the forgetfulness of *her* extremely well— her expectations for herself were never beyond the extreme of moderation, and she thinks with you that my Uncle always looked forward to surviving her. She desires her best love, and many thanks for your kind feelings; and heartily wishes that her younger children had more, and all her children something immediately....

Nothing can be kinder than Mrs. Cooke's enquiries after you [and Harriet] in all her letters, and there was no standing her affectionate way of speaking of *your* countenance, after her seeing you. God bless you all.

Conclude me to be going on well if you hear nothing to the contrary.

Yours ever truly, J. A.

Tell dear Harriet that whenever she wants me in her service again she must send a hackney chariot all the way for me—for I am not strong enough to travel any other way, and I hope Cassy will take care that it is a green one....

We will end this chapter with Caroline Austen's account of her last visit to her Aunt Jane, which occurred about this time.

It had been settled that about the end of March, or the beginning of April, I should spend a few days at Chawton, in the absence of my father and mother, who were just then engaged with Mrs. Leigh Perrot in arranging her late husband's affairs; but Aunt Jane became too ill to have me in the house, and so I went instead to my sister Mrs. Lefroy at Wyards. The next day we walked over to Chawton to make enquiries after our aunt. She was then keeping her room, but said she would see us, and we went up to her. She was in her dressing-gown, and was sitting quite like an invalid in an arm-chair, but she got up and kindly greeted us, and then, pointing to seats which had been arranged for us by the fire, she said 'There is a chair for the married lady, and a little stool for you, Caroline.' It is strange, but those trifling words were the last of hers that I can remember, for I retain no recollection of what was said by anyone in the conversation that ensued. I was struck by the alteration in herself. She was very pale, her voice was weak and low, and there was about her a general appearance of debility and suffering; but I have been told that she never had much acute pain. She was not equal to the exertion of talking to us, and our visit to the sick room was a very short one, Aunt Cassandra soon taking us away. I do not suppose we stayed a quarter of an hour; and I never saw Aunt Jane again.

CHAPTER XXI.

WINCHESTER 1817

EVEN after the beginning of April, Jane's hopefulness did not desert her. 'I am happy,' says James Austen, writing to his daughter Anna, 'to give you a good account, written by herself in a letter from your Aunt Jane; but all who love—and that is all who know her—must be anxious on her account.'

When May came, she consented to the proposal of those around her that she should move to Winchester, in order to get the best medical advice that the neighbourhood afforded. The Lyford family had maintained for some time a high character for skill in the profession of medicine at that place; and the Mr. Lyford of the day was a man of more than provincial reputation, in whom great London consultants expressed confidence. Accordingly, on Saturday, May 24, she bade farewell to her mother and her home, and her brother James's carriage conveyed Cassandra and herself to Winchester. The little cavalcade—for they were attended by two riders—started in sadness and in rain; and all must have doubted whether she would ever come back to Chawton.

She was going, however, to a place for which she felt the veneration which all good Hampshire people owe to their county town: a veneration shared by a good many Englishmen outside the limits of the county.

The sisters took lodgings in College Street, in the house next to what was then called 'Commoners,' and is now the head master's house. On the front wall of the little house where they lived there is now a plaque commemorating the stay of Jane Austen. Near to them, in the Close, were living their old friends Mrs. Heathcote and Miss Bigg, who did all they could to add to their comforts; while at the school were their nephew, Charles Knight, and young William Heathcote—either of whom they might hope to see from time to time.

The course of the illness, and its fatal termination, are shown pretty clearly in the letters which follow; the most informing and the most pathetic of which (next to her own) are the two written by Cassandra to Fanny Knight after all was ended.

Some of the letters are undated, and we cannot therefore be certain of the order in which they were written; we must also allow for the probable fact that Cassandra did not say more than was necessary to her mother of Jane's increasing weakness and discomfort.

Mr. Lyford spoke encouragingly, though it is believed that he had, from the first, very little expectation of a permanent cure. Some temporary rally there seems to have been; and, soon after settling in her lodgings, Jane was able to write as follows to Edward Austen:—

Mrs. David's, College Street, Winton:
Tuesday [May 27, 1817].

I know no better way, my dearest Edward, of thanking you for your most affectionate concern for me during my illness than by telling you myself, as soon as possible, that I continue to get better. I will not boast of my handwriting; neither that nor my face have yet recovered their proper beauty, but in other respects I am gaining strength very fast. I am now out of bed from 9 in the morning to 10 at night: upon the sopha, 'tis true, but I eat my meals with aunt Cass in a rational way, and can employ myself, and walk from one room to another. Mr. Lyford says he will cure me, and if he fails, I shall draw up a memorial and lay it before the Dean and Chapter, and have no doubt of redress from that pious, learned, and disinterested body. Our lodgings are very comfortable. We have a neat little drawing-room with a bow window overlooking Dr. Gabell's garden. Thanks to the kindness of your father and mother in sending me their carriage, my journey hither on Saturday was performed with very little fatigue, and had it been a fine day, I think I should have felt none; but it distressed me to see uncle Henry and Wm. Knight, who kindly attended us on horseback, riding in the rain almost all the way. We expect a visit from them to-morrow, and hope they will stay the night; and on Thursday, which is Confirmation and a holiday, we are to get Charles out to breakfast. We have had but one visit yet from *him*, poor fellow, as he is in sick-room, but he hopes to be out to-night. We see Mrs. Heathcote every day, and William is to call upon us soon. God bless you, my dear Edward. If ever you are ill, may you be as tenderly nursed as I have been. May the same blessed alleviations of anxious, sympathising friends be yours: and may you possess, as I dare say you will, the greatest blessing of all in the consciousness of not being unworthy of their love. *I* could not feel this.

Your very affec^{te} Aunt,
J. A.

Had I not engaged to write to you, you would have heard again from your Aunt Martha, as she charged me to tell you with her best love.

J. E. Austen, Esq.,
Exeter College, Oxford.

The original of this letter, which is preserved, bears sad testimony to the truth of her remark about her handwriting. Some few days after this, she must have written her last extant letter, quoted in the short Memoir prefixed to the original edition of *Northanger Abbey:*—

My attendant is encouraging, and talks of making me quite well. I live chiefly on the sofa, but am allowed to walk from one room to the other. I have been out once in a Sedan-chair, and am to repeat it, and be promoted to a wheel-chair as the weather serves. On this subject I will only say further that my dearest sister, my tender, watchful, indefatigable nurse, has not been made ill by her exertions. As to what I owe to her, and to the anxious affection of all my beloved family on this occasion, I can only cry over it, and pray to God to bless them more and more.

Some allusion to the family disappointment about the will probably followed, and she added: 'But I am getting too near complaint. It has been the appointment of God, however secondary causes may have operated.'

Jane's mother could still indulge in the hope of her amendment. In a note to Anna, she says:—

You will be happy to hear that our accounts from Winchester are very good. Our letter this morning, which was written yesterday evening, says 'Jane has had a better night than she has had for many weeks and has been comfortable all day. Mr. Lyford says he thinks better of her than he has ever done, though he must still consider her in a precarious state.'

And, in another letter—

I had a very comfortable account of your Aunt Jane this morning; she now sits up a little. Charles Knight came this morning: he saw her yesterday, and says she looks better and seem'd very cheerful. She hoped to be well enough to see Mrs. Portal to-day; your Mamma is there (went yesterday by the coach), which I am very glad of. Cassandra did not quite like the nurse they had got, so wish'd Mrs. J. A. to come in her stead, as she promised she would whenever she was wanted.

Mrs. James Austen went to Winchester on a Friday; perhaps Friday, June 6. Two or three days afterwards, her husband wrote to their son Edward, who no doubt was following at Oxford with painful interest the varying news. James, at any rate, cherished no illusions as to the possibility of a cure.

Steventon: Thursday.

MY DEAR EDWARD,—I grieve to write what you will grieve to read; but I must tell you that we can no longer flatter ourselves with the least hope of having your dear valuable Aunt Jane restored to us. The symptoms which returned after the first four or five days at Winchester, have never subsided, and Mr. Lyford has candidly told us that her case is desperate. I need not say what a melancholy gloom this has cast over us all. Your Grandmamma has suffered much, but her affliction can be nothing to Cassandra's. She will indeed be to be pitied. It is some consolation to know that our poor invalid has hitherto felt no very severe pain—which is rather an extraordinary circumstance in her complaint. I saw her on Tuesday and found her much altered, but composed and cheerful. She is well aware of her situation. Your Mother has been there ever since Friday and returns not till all is over—how soon that may be we cannot say—Lyford said he saw no signs of immediate dissolution, but added that with such a pulse it was impossible for any person to last long, and indeed no one can wish it—an easy departure from this to a better world is all that we can pray for. I am going to Winchester again to-morrow; you may depend upon early information, when any change takes place, and should then prepare yourself for what the next letter *may* announce.

Mrs. Heathcote is the greatest possible comfort to them all. . . .

We all join in love.

> Your affectionate Father,
> J. AUSTEN.

Edward's young sister Caroline (aged twelve) adds a few unhappy lines about her aunt, saying: 'I now feel as if I had never loved and valued her enough.'

Jane Austen 'retained her faculties, her memory, her fancy, her temper, and her affections—warm, clear, and unimpaired to the last. Neither her love of God, nor of her fellow-creatures flagged for a moment.' Her two clergyman brothers were near at hand to administer the consolations of religion, and she made a point of receiving the Holy Communion while she was still strong enough to follow the Service with full attention.

'While she used the language of hope to her correspondents, she was fully aware of her danger, though not appalled by it. It is true that there was much to attach her to life. She was happy in her family; she was just beginning to feel confidence in her own success; and, no doubt, the exercise of her great talents was an enjoyment in itself. We may well believe that she would gladly have lived longer; but she was enabled without dismay or complaint to prepare for death. She was a humble, believing Christian. Her life had been passed in the performance of home duties, and the cultivation of domestic affections, without any self-seeking or craving after applause. She had always sought, as it were by instinct, to promote the happiness of all who came within her influence, and doubtless she had her reward in the peace of mind which was granted her in her last days. Her sweetness of temper never failed. She was ever considerate and grateful to those who attended on her. At times, when she felt rather better, her playfulness of spirit revived, and she amused them even in their sadness. Once, when she thought herself near her end, she said what she imagined might be her last words to those around her, and particularly thanked her sister-in-law for being with her, saying: "You have always been a kind sister to me, Mary."'

She wrote whilst she could hold a pen, and with a pencil when a pen had become too laborious. Even a day or two before her death she was able to compose some light verses on St. Swithin, Winchester Races, and the weather. But the record of the last sad hours and of her death in the early morning of Friday, July 18, will be best read in the letter of Cassandra to Fanny Knight.

Winchester: Sunday [July 20, 1817].

MY DEAREST FANNY,—Doubly dear to me now for her dear sake whom we have lost. She did love you most sincerely, and never shall I forget the proofs of love you gave her during her illness in writing those kind, amusing letters at a time when I know your feelings would have dictated so different a style. Take the only reward I can give you in the assurance that your benevolent purpose *was* answered; you *did* contribute to her enjoyment.

Even your last letter afforded pleasure. I merely cut the seal and gave it to her; she opened it and read it herself, afterwards she gave it me to read, and then talked to me a little and not uncheerfully of its contents, but there was then a languor about her which prevented her taking the same interest in anything she had been used to do.

Since Tuesday evening, when her complaint returned, there was a visible change, she slept more and much more comfortably; indeed, during the last eight-and-forty hours she was more asleep than awake. Her looks altered and she fell away, but I perceived no material diminution of strength, and, though I was then hopeless of a recovery, I had no suspicion how rapidly my loss was approaching.

I *have* lost a treasure, such a sister, such a friend as never can have been surpassed. She was the sun of my life, the gilder of every pleasure, the soother of every sorrow; I had not a thought concealed from her, and it is as if I had lost a part of myself. I loved her only too well—not better than she deserved, but I am conscious that my affection for her made me sometimes unjust to and negligent of others; and I can acknowledge, more than as a general principle, the justice of the Hand which has struck this blow.

You know me too well to be at all afraid that I should suffer materially from my feelings; I am perfectly conscious of the extent of my irreparable loss, but I am not at all overpowered and very little indisposed, nothing but what a short time, with rest and change of air, will remove. I thank God that I was enabled to attend her to the last, and amongst my many causes of self-reproach I have not to add any wilful neglect of her comfort.

She felt herself to be dying about half an hour before she became tranquil and apparently unconscious. During that half-hour was her struggle, poor soul! She said she could not tell us what she suffered, though she complained of little fixed pain. When I asked her if there was anything she wanted, her answer was she wanted nothing but death, and some of her words were: 'God grant me patience, pray for me, oh, pray for me!' Her voice was affected, but as long as she spoke she was intelligible.

I hope I do not break your heart, my dearest Fanny, by these particulars; I mean to afford you gratification whilst I am relieving my own feelings. I could not write so to anybody else; indeed you are the only person I have written to at all, excepting your grandmamma—it was to her, not your Uncle Charles, I wrote on Friday.

Immediately after dinner on Thursday I went into the town to do an errand which your dear aunt was anxious about. I returned about a quarter before six and found her recovering from faintness and oppression; she got so well as to be able to give me a minute account of her seizure, and when the clock struck six she was talking quietly to me.

I cannot say how soon afterwards she was seized again with the same faintness, which was followed by the sufferings she could not describe; but Mr. Lyford had been sent for, had applied something to give her ease, and she was in a state of quiet insensibility by seven o'clock at the latest. From that time till half-past four, when she ceased to breathe, she scarcely moved a limb, so that we have every reason to think, with gratitude to the Almighty, that her sufferings were over. A slight motion of the head with every breath remained till almost the last. I sat close to her with a pillow in my lap to assist in supporting her head, which was almost off the bed, for six hours; fatigue made me then resign my place to Mrs. J. A. for two hours and a half, when I took it again, and in about an hour more she breathed her last.

I was able to close her eyes myself, and it was a great gratification to me to render her those last services. There was nothing convulsed which gave the idea of pain in her look; on the contrary, but for the continual motion of the head, she gave one the idea of a beautiful statue, and even now, in her coffin, there is such a sweet, serene air over her countenance as is quite pleasant to contemplate.

This day, my dearest Fanny, you have had the melancholy intelligence, and I know you suffer severely, but I likewise know that you will apply to the fountain-head for consolation, and that our merciful God is never deaf to such prayers as you will offer.

The last sad ceremony is to take place on Thursday morning; her dear remains are to be deposited in the Cathedral. It is a satisfaction to me to think that they are to lie in a building she admired so much; her precious soul, I presume to hope, reposes in a far superior mansion. May mine one day be re-united to it!

Your dear papa, your Uncle Henry, and Frank, and Edwd. Austen instead of his father, will attend. I hope they will none of them suffer lastingly from their pious exertions. The ceremony must be over before ten o'clock, as the Cathedral service begins at that hour, so that we shall be at home early in the day, for there will be nothing to keep us here afterwards.

Your Uncle James came to us yesterday, and is gone home to-day. Uncle H. goes to Chawton to-morrow morning; he has given every necessary direction here, and I think his company there will do good. He returns to us again on Tuesday evening.

I did not think to have written a long letter when I began, but I have found the employment draw me on, and I hope I shall have been giving you more pleasure than pain. Remember me kindly to

Mrs. J. Bridges (I am so glad she is with you now), and give my best love to Lizzie and all the others.

I am, my dearest Fanny, Most affectionately yours, CASS. ELIZ. AUSTEN.

I have said nothing about those at Chawton, because I am sure you hear from your papa.

During these sad days, Anna Lefroy had written to her grandmother at Chawton, offering to go to her. Mrs. Austen answered:—

I thank you sincerely for all your kind expressions, and your offer. I am certainly in a good deal of affliction, but trust God will support me. I was not prepared for the blow, though it in a manner hung over us; I had reason to think it at a distance, and was not quite without hope that she might in part recover. After a few months' illness she may be said to have died suddenly. Mr. Lyford supposed a large blood-vessel had given way. I hope her sufferings were not severe—they were not long. I had a letter from Cassandra this morning. She is in great affliction, but bears it like a Christian. Dear Jane is to be buried in the Cathedral, I believe on Thursday—in which case Cassandra will come home as soon as it is over.

Cassandra did go home, and a few days later wrote again to Fanny Knight as follows:—

Chawton: Tuesday [July 29, 1817].

MY DEAREST FANNY,—I have just read your letter for the third time, and thank you most sincerely for every kind expression to myself, and still more warmly for your praises of her who I believe was better known to you than to any human being besides myself. Nothing of the sort could have been more gratifying to me than the manner in which you write of her, and if the dear angel is conscious of what passes here, and is not above all earthly feelings, she may perhaps receive pleasure in being so mourned. Had *she* been the survivor I can fancy her speaking of *you* in almost the same terms. There are certainly many points of strong resemblance in your characters; in your intimate acquaintance with each other, and your mutual strong affection, you were counterparts.

Thursday was not so dreadful a day to me as you imagined. There was so much necessary to be done that there was no time for additional misery. Everything was conducted with the greatest tranquillity, and but that I was determined I would see the last, and therefore was upon the listen, I should not have known when they left the house. I watched the little mournful procession the length of the street; and when it turned from my sight, and I had lost her for ever, even then I was not overpowered, nor so much agitated as I am now in writing of it. Never was human being more sincerely mourned by those who attended her remains than was this dear creature. May the sorrow with which she is parted with on earth be a prognostic of the joy with which she is hailed in heaven!

I continue very tolerably well—much better than any one could have supposed possible, because I certainly have had considerable fatigue of body as well as anguish of mind for months back; but I really am well, and I hope I am properly grateful to the Almighty for having been so supported. Your grandmamma, too, is much better than when I came home.

I did not think your dear papa appeared unwell, and I understand that he seemed much more comfortable after his return from Winchester than he had done before. I need not tell you that he was a great comfort to me; indeed, I can never say enough of the kindness I have received from him and from every other friend.

I get out of doors a good deal and am able to employ myself. Of course those employments suit me best which leave me most at leisure to think of her I have lost, and I do think of her in every variety of circumstance. In our happy hours of confidential intercourse, in the cheerful family party which she so ornamented, in her sick room, on her death-bed, and as (I hope) an inhabitant of heaven. Oh, if I may one day be re-united to her there! I know the time must come when my mind will be less engrossed by her idea, but I do not like to think of it. If I think of her less as on earth, God grant that I may never cease to reflect on her as inhabiting heaven, and never cease my humble endeavours (when it shall please God) to join her there.

In looking at a few of the precious papers which are now my property I have found some memorandums, amongst which she desires that one of her gold chains may be given to her goddaughter Louisa, and a lock of her hair be set for you. You can need no assurance, my dearest Fanny, that every request of your beloved aunt will be sacred with me. Be so good as to say whether you prefer a brooch or ring. God bless you, my dearest Fanny.

Believe me, most affectionately yours,

CASS. ELIZTH. AUSTEN.

So ends the story of Jane Austen's life. We can only hope that we have succeeded in conveying to the reader even a small part of the feeling which we ourselves entertain of the charm of her personality—a charm almost as remarkable in its way as the brightness of her genius. In one respect it is easy to write about her—there is nothing to conceal. Some readers may perhaps add 'There is little to tell'; and it is true that, though the want of incident in her life has often been exaggerated, her occupations were largely those of helpfulness and sympathy towards others whose lot was more variable than hers, and the development of her own powers to be the delight of generations of readers.

But this position gave her quite sufficient opportunity of showing her character—and it is a character which it is a continual pleasure to contemplate. Her perfect balance and good sense did not diminish her liveliness. Her intellectual qualities did not prevent the enjoyment of a dance, or attention to the most domestic duties. Her consciousness of genius left room for a belief that Cassandra was wiser and better than herself. Her keen and humorous observation of the frailties of mankind was compatible with indulgence towards the faults of her neighbours. Her growing fame did not make her the less accessible and delightful to her nieces, who could consult their aunt and obtain a willing listener in any difficulty whatever, from a doubtful love affair to the working of a sampler. Indeed, she is a standing witness to the truth that eccentricity and self-consciousness are not essential parts of genius.

When her body had been laid in Winchester Cathedral, the small band of mourners went back in sadness to their different homes. They were very fond and very proud of her; and each, we are told, loved afterwards to fancy a resemblance in some niece or daughter of their own to the dear sister Jane, whose perfect equal they yet never expected to see.

Cassandra returned to Chawton and devoted a further ten years to the care of her aged mother. Till old Mrs. Austen's death in 1827, Martha Lloyd remained an inmate, and everything went on, nominally, as before; but the 'chief light was quenched and the loss of it had cast a shade over the spirits of the survivors.' So, when the young Austens went to stay there, expecting to be particularly happy, they could not help feeling something of the chill of disappointment. Later, Martha became the second wife of Francis Austen, while Cassandra lived on at Chawton. One of her great-nieces remembers seeing her towards the end of her life at a christening, 'a pale, dark-eyed old lady, with a high arched nose and a kind smile, dressed in a long cloak and a large drawn bonnet, both made of black satin.' She died of a sudden illness in 1845, at the house of her brother Francis, near Portsmouth—at his house, but in his absence; for he and his family had to leave for the West Indies (where he was to take up a command) while she lay dying. She was tended by her brothers Henry and Charles and her niece Caroline. She was buried beside her mother at Chawton.

All her brothers survived her, except James, who was in bad health when his sister Jane died, and followed her in 1819.

Edward (Knight) saw his children and his children's children grow up around him, and died at Godmersham as peacefully as he had lived, in 1852.

Henry held the living of Steventon for three years after the death of his brother James, till his nephew, William Knight, was ready to take it. He was afterwards Perpetual Curate of Bentley, near

Farnham. Later on, he lived for some time in France, and he died at Tunbridge Wells in 1850.

Both the sailor brothers rose to be Admirals. Charles was employed in the suppression of the Slave Trade and against Mehemet Ali, and became Rear-Admiral in 1846. In 1850 he commanded in the East Indian and Chinese waters, and died of cholera on the Irawaddy River in 1852, having 'won the hearts of all by his gentleness and kindness whilst he was struggling with disease.'

Francis had thirty years on shore after the end of the long war; and his only subsequent foreign service was the command of the West Indian and North American Station, 1845-48. He, however, constantly rose in his profession, and enjoyed the esteem and respect of the Admiralty. He ended by being G.C.B. and Admiral of the Fleet, and did not die until 1865, aged ninety-one.

Shortly before the end of her life, Jane Austen wrote on a slip of paper:—

Profits of my novels, over and above the £600 in the Navy Fives.

	£ s.
Residue from the 1st edit. of *Mansfield Park* remaining in Henrietta St., March 1816	13 7
Received from Egerton, on 2nd edit. of *Sense and S.*, March 1816	12 15
February 21, 1817, First Profits of *Emma*	38 18
March 7, 1817. From Egerton—2nd edit. of *S. and S.*	19 13

Northanger Abbey and *Persuasion* were published in four volumes by John Murray in 1818, and to the former was prefixed a short biographical notice of the author from the pen of Henry

Austen. In 1832 Mr. Bentley bought the copyright of all the novels, except *Pride and Prejudice* (which Jane Austen had sold outright to Mr. Egerton), from Henry and Cassandra Austen, the joint proprietors, for the sum of two hundred and fifty pounds. Mr. Bentley must also have bought from Mr. Egerton's executors the copyright of *Pride and Prejudice*, for he proceeded to issue a complete edition of the novels with a biographical notice (also by Henry) containing a few extra facts not mentioned in the original edition of *Northanger Abbey*.

(James) Edward Austen, who added 'Leigh' to his name on succeeding to the property of Scarlets in 1836, wrote (in 1869-70) the *Memoir* of his aunt which has been so often used in these pages, and which, as the work of three eyewitnesses, enjoys an authority greater than that of any other account of her. Its publication coincided with the beginning of a great advance in her fame, and we think it may be claimed that it was an important contributory cause of that advance. Before that date, an appreciation of her genius was rather the special possession of small literary circles and individual families; since that date it has been widely spread both in England and in America. From her death to 1870, there was only one complete edition of her works, and nothing, except a few articles and reviews, was written about her. Since 1870, editions, lives, memoirs, &c., have been almost too numerous to count. We, who are adding to this stream of writings, cannot induce ourselves to believe that the interest of the public is yet exhausted.

CHRONOLOGY OF JANE AUSTEN'S LIFE

1775,	Dec. 16	Birth, at Steventon.
1779,	June	Charles John Austen born.
1780,	July	James Austen matriculated at Oxford (St. John's).
1782		Jane and Cassandra at Oxford under care of Mrs. Cawley (sister of Dr. Cooper).
1783		Mrs. Cawley having moved to Southampton, Jane nearly died there of a fever. Mrs. Cooper (her aunt) took the infection and died (October).
1784		*The Rivals* acted at Steventon.
1784	or 1785	Jane and Cassandra left Mrs. Latournelle's school at Reading, and returned home.
1786		Eliza Comtesse de Feuillide came to England.
		Birth of her son.
1787		James Austen in France.
1788,	July	Henry Austen matriculated at Oxford (St. John's).
		Francis Austen went to sea.

1791		Edward Austen married Elizabeth Bridges.
1792, March		James Austen married Anne Mathew.
1794, Feb.		Comte de Feuillide guillotined.
1795 (?)		Cassandra engaged to Thomas Fowle.
	May	Mrs. James Austen died.
1795-6		Mr. Tom Lefroy at Ashe.
1796		*First Impressions* (*Pride and Prejudice*) begun.
		Jane subscribed to *Camilla*.
1797, Jan.		James Austen married Mary Lloyd.
	Feb.	Thomas Fowle died of fever in the W. Indies.
	Nov.	Jane, with mother and sister, went to Bath.
		First Impressions refused by Cadell.
		Sense and Sensibility (already sketched in *Elinor and Marianne*) begun.
	Dec.	Henry Austen married Eliza de Feuillide.
1798, Aug.		Lady Williams (Jane Cooper) killed in a carriage accident.
		Mrs. Knight gave up Godmersham to the Edward Austens.

Jane's first visit there.

1798,	Aug.	First draft of *Northanger Abbey* begun.
1799,	May	Jane at Bath with the Edward Austens.
	Aug.	Mrs. Leigh Perrot's trouble at Bath.
1801,	May	Family move from Steventon to Bath. Visit to Sidmouth.
		Possible date of Jane's romance in the west of England.
1802		Austens at Dawlish and Teignmouth.
		Visit of sisters to Steventon and Manydown.
		Jane received an offer of marriage from an old friend.
1803		*Northanger Abbey* (called *Susan*) revised, and sold to Crosby of London.
1804		Probable date of *The Watsons*.
	Sept.	Austens at Lyme.
	Dec.	Mrs. Lefroy of Ashe killed by a fall from her horse.
1805,	Jan.	Death of Jane's father at Bath.
1806,	July	Austens left Bath for Clifton, Adlestrop, and Stoneleigh.

1806	-7	Austens settled at Southampton.
1807,	March	Took possession of house in Castle Square.
1808,	Sept.	Cassandra at Godmersham.
	Oct.	Mrs. Edward Austen died there after the birth of her eleventh child (John).
1809,	April	Jane attempted to secure publication of *Susan* (*Northanger Abbey*).
		Austens left Southampton.
	July	Austens took possession of Chawton (having been at Godmersham). Jane's authorship resumed.
1811,	April	Jane with Henry in London (Sloane Street) bringing out *Sense and Sensibility*.
	Oct.	*Sense and Sensibility* published.
1812		Death of Mrs. T. Knight. Edward Austen took the name of 'Knight.'
1813,	Jan.	Publication of *Pride and Prejudice*.
	April	Death of Mrs. Henry Austen (Eliza).
	Sept.	Jane's last visit to Godmersham.
		Second edition of *Sense and Sensibility*.
1814,	Jan.	*Emma* begun.
	March	Jane went to London with Henry (reading *Mansfield Park* by the way).

	May	*Mansfield Park* published.
		Threat of lawsuit for Chawton.
	Nov.	Marriage of Anna Austen to Ben Lefroy.
1815, March		*Emma* finished.
	Oct.	Illness of Henry.
	Nov.	Jane shown over Carlton House by Dr. Clarke.
	Dec.	Publication of *Emma*.
1816, March		Bankruptcy of Henry Austen (Jane's health began to break about this time).
	May	Jane and Cassandra at Kintbury and Cheltenham.
	July	*Persuasion* finished.
	Aug.	End of *Persuasion* re-written.
		Henry took Orders.
1817, Jan.		Jane began new work.
	March	Ceased to write.
		Death of Mr. Leigh Perrot.
		Jane made her will.
	May 24	Jane moved to Winchester, and revived somewhat.
	June 16	Cassandra sent a hopeless account to Fanny Knight.

July 18	Death.
July 24	Burial in Winchester Cathedral.

LITERARY ANALYSIS

Introduction: Hearing the Real Jane Austen

We all have a picture of Jane Austen in our minds. For many, she is the demure figure from a silhouette, a proper Regency-era spinster writing elegant novels in a quiet country parsonage. We know her characters—the witty Elizabeth Bennet, the sensible Elinor Dashwood, the quietly resilient Anne Elliot—so well that they feel like friends. But what about the woman who created them? Who was she, really? What did she sound like?

For anyone who has ever longed to pull back the curtain and meet the author herself, Jane Austen, Her Life and Letters: A Family Record is an absolute treasure. Written by her grandnephew William Austen-Leigh and her great-grandnephew Richard Arthur Austen-Leigh, this is no ordinary biography. It is a unique and intimate account that combines family history with the most valuable source of all: Jane's own voice, captured in the lively, witty, and deeply personal letters she wrote to her family. It's our best chance to sit down with the real Miss Austen and listen to her talk.

Plot: Weaving a Life from Letters

Because this is a biography, its "plot" is the narrative of a real life. The book traces Jane Austen's journey chronologically, from her birth and happy childhood in the Steventon rectory, through the family's move to Bath, her productive writing years at Chawton Cottage, and her final illness and death in Winchester. The authors provide a steady, respectful narrative that guides us through the key events and relationships of her life.

What makes this structure so uniquely engaging is its dual nature. The biographers' formal narrative acts as the thread, but the vibrant, colorful beads strung upon it are Jane's own letters. One moment, the authors are describing the social scene in Bath; the next, we are reading Jane's own hilarious, sharp-tongued commentary on a terrible ball she attended or the ridiculous hat worn by an acquaintance. This constant shift between the formal historical account and the immediate, informal voice of Jane herself creates a dynamic and deeply personal reading experience. The plot is not just what happened to her; it's how she felt about it, in her own words.

Characters: A Portrait of the Real Miss Austen and Her Circle

The book offers a rich portrait not just of Jane, but of the entire Austen clan, the close-knit world that was her everything.

Jane Austen: The version of Jane we meet here is far more complex and spirited than the "quiet aunt" stereotype. Through her letters, she reveals herself to be incredibly observant, deeply affectionate, and possessed of a wickedly dry sense of humor. She is a devoted sister and aunt, but also a sharp social critic who misses nothing. When she writes to her sister Cassandra, "What shall I do with your 'Betsey's' ugly Pictures? I will not have them put up, for they are too frightful," we hear the authentic, unsanitized voice of a real person, not a literary saint.

Cassandra Austen: As the recipient of most of the letters, Jane's older sister is the book's silent, central pillar. She was Jane's closest confidante, and their deep bond is the emotional core of the narrative. Though we rarely hear her voice directly (as she destroyed most of Jane's most intimate letters), her presence is felt on every page as the trusted soulmate to whom Jane could reveal her true thoughts.

The Austen Family: Jane's parents, her many brothers (two of whom became admirals!), and her beloved nieces and nephews form the backdrop of her life. They were her support system, her first readers, and the living source material for her unparalleled insights into family dynamics. The biography paints a vivid picture of a loyal, intelligent, and loving family that provided the stable sanctuary from which Jane could observe the wider world.

Themes: More Than Just a Biography

This book is a rich tapestry of historical and personal themes that resonate deeply with our understanding of Austen and her work.

The Domestic Sphere as a Creative Wellspring: The biography brilliantly illustrates how Austen's seemingly limited, domestic world was, in fact, the perfect laboratory for her genius. The letters are filled with the minutiae of daily life—sewing, shopping, visiting neighbors, gossiping about engagements. It was in observing these small human dramas that she found the universal truths that make her novels so enduring.

The Indispensable Role of Family: More than anything, this is a book about family. It highlights how crucial the Austen clan was to Jane's life and career. They provided financial support, emotional stability, and intellectual encouragement. In an era when a woman writing for publication was an anomaly, her family's pride and belief in her work were essential.

A Woman's Life in Regency England: Through Jane's own candid observations, we get a firsthand account of the realities facing a woman of her class. We see the constant preoccupation with money, the social pressure to marry, and the constraints on women's freedom. Yet, we also see the rich world of female friendship, sisterly devotion, and the profound intellectual life she carved out for herself despite these limitations.

Style and Technique

The book's style is a fascinating blend of two distinct voices.

The Biographers' Style: The Austen-Leighs write in a formal, measured, and respectful prose characteristic of the early 20th century. Their narrative is clear and well-researched, providing a solid framework and contextualizing the letters for the reader. They are the calm, knowledgeable curators of the family legacy.

Jane Austen's Epistolary Style: This is where the book truly comes alive. Jane's letter-writing voice is a marvel—it's immediate, energetic, and sparkles with the same wit found in her novels. She can be both deeply sincere and hilariously catty in the same paragraph. Consider her description of a neighbor: "Mrs.

Hall, of Sherborne, was brought to bed yesterday of a dead child, some weeks before she expected, owing to a fright. I suppose she happened unawares to look at her husband." This kind of sharp, dry humor is pure Austen, and the letters are full of it.

The primary technique is the seamless integration of these two styles, creating a dialogue between the historical record and the living, breathing voice of the past.

Historical Context and Modern Relevance

Published in 1913, Jane Austen, Her Life and Letters is itself a historical artifact. It reflects the Victorian and Edwardian desire to present a respectable, sanitized version of their famous ancestor, cementing the image of a gentle "Aunt Jane" that later biographers would seek to complicate. The authors were protective of the family name and undoubtedly curated the letters to present her in the best possible light.

For the modern reader, this context is fascinating. The book gives us a dual window: one into the Regency era in which Jane lived, and another into the early 20th-century mindset that shaped how she was remembered. Its modern relevance is immense. It provides a trove of primary source material that allows us to get closer to the real Austen. It enriches our reading of her novels by showing us the raw material of her life—the people, places, and social situations that she transformed into timeless art.

The Modern Reader's Experience

Reading this book today is a deeply rewarding experience. It can feel like you're Browse a fascinating museum exhibit. The Austen-Leighs' narrative is like the informative placards on the wall—helpful, clear, and a bit formal. But the letters are the main exhibit: the actual artifacts, buzzing with the personality of their creator. You get to see the stitches on the fabric of her life. For any fan of her novels, moments of recognition will spark constantly. You'll read about a pompous clergyman and think of Mr. Collins, or see a description of a naval brother and think of Captain Wentworth.

Why It Still Matters

This biography remains an essential text for anyone serious about Jane Austen. It preserves family anecdotes and portions of letters that provide an invaluable foundation for all subsequent Austen scholarship. Its great contribution is that it doesn't just tell us about Jane Austen; it lets her speak for herself. By placing her letters at the forefront, it allows us to connect with her intellect, her humor, and her heart directly. It is the essential companion piece to her fictional work, grounding her universally beloved stories in the specific reality of her life.

Reading Tips (for Contemporary Audiences)

Savor the Letters: Don't rush through the narrative to get to the next letter. The real magic is in Jane's own words. Read them slowly and listen for her distinctive voice.

Embrace the Details: The book is filled with names of neighbors, cousins, and acquaintances. Don't worry about keeping them all straight. Instead, enjoy the rich tapestry of her social world.

Read Alongside the Novels: If you're re-reading Pride and Prejudice or Persuasion, have this book on hand. Dipping into her life and letters while reading her fiction will illuminate her work in surprising and delightful ways.

Conclusion

Jane Austen, Her Life and Letters: A Family Record is more than a biography; it's a conversation with the past. It's a lovingly assembled monument from a family to its most brilliant member, but its greatest gift is that it allows the monument to speak. It closes the distance of two centuries, inviting us into the drawing-rooms and garden paths of Regency England to meet the woman behind the legend. For anyone who believes Jane Austen to be one of the finest observers of the human heart, this book is an unmissable opportunity to observe hers.

ABOUT THE AUTHOR

Austen-Leigh and Austen-Leigh

William and Richard Austen-Leigh: Guardians of a Literary Legacy

William Austen-Leigh (1845-1921) and his nephew, Richard Arthur Austen-Leigh (1872-1961), represent a unique authorial collaboration, united by their familial connection to one of England's most celebrated novelists. Their joint work, "Jane Austen, Her Life and Letters: A Family Record," published in 1913, stands as a pivotal biography of Jane Austen. More than just a factual account, it was a meticulous, loving preservation of family memory, offering insights into Austen's life and context that only those within her direct lineage could truly provide.  Their combined efforts solidified their place as indispensable contributors to Austen scholarship, ensuring that the nuances of her private world were not lost to history.

The Austen-Leigh family were direct descendants of Jane Austen's brother, James Austen, through his son, James Edward Austen-Leigh. This lineage granted them unparalleled access to family papers, letters, and oral traditions that were unavailable to other biographers. Their work was, in essence, a continuation and expansion of the foundational biographical efforts begun by their forebear, James Edward Austen-Leigh, who published A Memoir of Jane Austen in 1870. The 1913 work by William and Richard built upon this initial memoir, enriching it with newly discovered correspondence and a more detailed chronological narrative.

William Austen-Leigh: The Elder Statesman of Austen Scholarship

William Austen-Leigh, born in 1845, was a grandson of James Edward Austen-Leigh, making him a great-nephew of Jane Austen. Educated at Eton College and King's College, Cambridge, William followed a path that combined scholarship with a life of quiet academic and clerical pursuits. He was ordained as a priest in the Church of England, and his life reflected the intellectual and genteel sensibilities often associated with the Austen family.

William was deeply devoted to his famous great-aunt's memory and to the family's role as custodians of her story. He spent years meticulously collecting, transcribing, and organizing family documents, letters, and anecdotes related to Jane Austen. His scholarly approach ensured accuracy and thoroughness, even as he worked from a position of affectionate bias. He understood the profound importance of primary sources and the unique perspective that a family record could offer, particularly given Jane Austen's relatively private life and her family's initial reluctance to disclose too many personal details. William's efforts laid the groundwork for the 1913 biography, assembling much of the raw material and establishing the narrative framework. He brought a patient, scholarly rigor to the task, ensuring that the collected information was presented coherently and chronologically.

Richard Arthur Austen-Leigh: The Younger Partner and Architectural Mind

Richard Arthur Austen-Leigh, born in 1872, was William's nephew and thus a great-great-nephew of Jane Austen. Like his uncle, Richard was educated at Eton College and then at King's College, Cambridge. He later pursued a career that diverged somewhat from traditional scholarship; he became a successful architect and surveyor, a profession that might seem far removed from literary biography. However, his meticulous nature, attention to detail, and ability to organize complex information, all hallmarks of his architectural training, proved invaluable to their collaborative project.

Richard's role in the "Life and Letters" was crucial, particularly as the project progressed and William's health or age may have limited his full involvement. Richard took on the considerable task of shaping the vast amount of material gathered by William into a cohesive and readable narrative. His architectural eye may have even contributed to the structural integrity of the biography, ensuring a well-ordered and clear presentation of Jane Austen's life story. He brought a fresh perspective while maintaining the family's respectful and protective approach to Austen's image.

The Collaborative Masterpiece: "Jane Austen, Her Life and Letters"

The 1913 publication was a culmination of decades of familial dedication to Jane Austen's memory. It expanded significantly upon James Edward Austen-Leigh's earlier Memoir by incorporating newly discovered letters and details. Crucially, it presented a more detailed chronological account of Austen's life, weaving together excerpts from her letters with biographical narration. This was an era before extensive literary criticism and academic analysis of Austen's works had fully developed; thus, providing a robust factual foundation of her life was of paramount importance.

The book aimed to present Jane Austen not just as a literary genius but as a beloved family member – a witty, intelligent, and deeply observant woman who was an integral part of her domestic and social sphere. While it occasionally shied away from potentially revealing personal details, reflecting the Victorian sensibilities of the time and the family's desire to protect her privacy, it nevertheless offered the most comprehensive and intimate portrait available for decades. It provided scholars and enthusiasts with essential dates, locations, and personal anecdotes that became the bedrock for all subsequent Austen biographies.

The collaboration between William and Richard Austen-Leigh was a testament to their shared reverence for their literary ancestor. William provided the deep historical knowledge and archival diligence, while Richard brought a more structured, perhaps even editorial, hand to shape the narrative into its final form. Their combined efforts ensured that the family's unique access to primary sources was utilized to create a definitive record.

Both William Austen-Leigh and Richard Arthur Austen-Leigh lived long lives, dedicated to their respective professions and their shared familial legacy. William passed away in 1921, and Richard in 1961. Their "Jane Austen, Her Life and Letters" remains an essential resource for anyone studying Jane Austen. It serves as a reminder of the enduring power of family history and the invaluable role played by dedicated descendants in preserving the memory and context of literary giants. Without their meticulous work, our understanding of Jane Austen's private world would be far less complete.

Printed in Dunstable, United Kingdom